Guidebook to Direct Democracy
IN SWITZERLAND AND BEYOND

THE INITIATIVE & REFERENDUM INSTITUTE EUROPE
Guidebook to Direct Democracy
IN SWITZERLAND AND BEYOND

Bruno Kaufmann, Rolf Büchi, Nadja Braun

2007 EDITION

THE IRI GUIDEBOOK TO DIRECT DEMOCRACY – 2007 EDITION

DEVELOPED, WRITTEN, EDITED BY
Bruno Kaufmann, Rolf Büchi, Nadja Braun

ENGLISH EDITOR
Paul Carline

CO-EDITORS
Brian Beedham, Virgina Beramendi-Heine, Stephen Boucher,
Frank Remeth, Stephan Lausch, Wilfried Marxer

IN COOPERATION WITH
Peter Fankhauser, Presence Switzerland (PRS). PRS is an official body of the Swiss Confederation and promotes the dissemination of information about Switzerland worldwide [www.presence.ch].

CONCEPT, DESIGN AND LAYOUT
swissinfo/Swiss Radio International Webfactory, Bern

PHOTOGRAPHY
Simon Opladen, Bern
Cover picture: After the vote, slips are counted in a schoolroom used as a polling station.

PRINTED IN SWITZERLAND BY
Rub Graf-Lehmann AG, Bern [www.rubmedia.ch]

This publication has been sponsored by Presence Switzerland PRS [www.presence.ch] and the Swiss Agency for Development and Cooperation [www.deza.ch]

To order, contact
The Initiative & Referendum Institute Europe
Box 200540, DE-35017 Marburg
Phone +49 6421 28 24 748 / Fax +49 6421 28 28 991
guidebook@iri-europe.org
www.iri-europe.org

Second edition (English): 3,000 copies
Information valid as of June 1st 2006
available in French, Spanish, German and Italian

ISBN-10: 3-00-019057-0
ISBN-13: 978-3-00-019057-5

© 2006 Initiative & Referendum Institute Europe
All rights reserved. No parts of this publication may be reproduced or transmitted in any form or by any means, including information storage and retrieval systems, without prior permission in writing from the Initiative & Referendum Institute Europe.

Contents

PREFACE	Direct Democracy – a multifaceted learning process By Federal Councillor Micheline Calmy-Rey, Head of the Swiss Federal Department of Foreign Affairs	6
INTRODUCTION	Initiatives & Referendums Making democracy more truly representative	9
ESSAYS 1	The year of decisions How a citizen deals with six elections and 30 referendums within ten months	17
2	Citizens centre stage in politics When the people put their collective foot on the accelerator	25
3	Back to the future The story of a democratic revolution at the heart of Europe	33
4	As centralised as necessary, as decentralised as possible On modern federalism	41
5	The land of the contented losers Direct democracy reveals where in society the shoe pinches	49
6	Jura: democracy, not nationalism How the Jura was able to make itself independent without violence	57
7	The myth of the incompetent citizen Direct-democratic rights have an effect on those who use these rights	65
8	Out loud Why complete strangers suddenly start talking to each other in public	73
9	Added-value voting A system which promotes growth strengthens society – and makes people happier	79
10	Design determines the quality Instructions for a citizen-friendly democracy	87
11	The democratisation of democracy Switzerland's direct democracy, sophisticated as it is, is still far from perfect	97
12	Utopia becomes reality From Norway to Taiwan and from New Zealand to Ecuador – and now the EU!	105
RESOURCES	Overview	113
FACTSHEETS	Factsheets 1-29	114
SURVEYS 1	All popular votes in Switzerland since 1848	189
2	Direct-democratic procedures and plebiscites in the constitutions of 32 European states	232
3	Global Overview of Direct Democracy in selected regions of the world	265
4	Glossary of direct-democracy terms	308
INFORMATION	Towards the 1st World Conference on Direct Democracy in 2008	321
	The Initiative & Referendum Institute Europe	322
	About / Acknowledgements	324
	Index	326

Direct Democracy – a multifaceted learning process

Preface by Swiss Federal Councillor Micheline Calmy-Rey

The popular rights of initiative and referendum are striking and distinctive features of the Swiss political system. While it is true that direct-democratic institutions are not unique to Switzerland, there is no other country in which citizens are so regularly summoned to the ballot-box. Critics maintain that Swiss direct democracy has become a "holy cow" and that it slows down economic development and institutional reform. They argue that it is too slow and too expensive, and that the complexity of the issues demands too much of the voters. I do not share this view.

It is true that by international comparison voter turnout in Switzerland is low. But the level of turnout for referendum votes depends on the issue being voted on. The referendum on Switzerland's accession to the EEC in 1992 brought out 79 percent of the registered electorate. It is also worthy of note that opinion polls show that an overwhelming majority of the Swiss want to maintain the compass and frequency of referendum voting at its traditional level and do not wish our system of direct democracy to be changed in any way.

The charge is sometimes made that in a direct democracy no-one takes responsibility for political decisions: that politicians "hide" behind the electorate, whereas in indirect democracies political responsibility is clearly defined. It is certainly true that in Switzerland "the people" – or as we say "the sovereign" – bears the final political responsibility. This in no way absolves the government from adopting its own position, making its policies public and engaging in an intensive dialogue with the citizens. This is also an exercise of political responsibility.

The Federal Council, the cantonal governments and the local authorities constantly defend business interests in public talks and citizens' meetings, and also in the media. We do this much more often and intensively than leading politicians in purely representative democracies. Winning or losing in a referendum vote often depends on the powers of persuasion of members of the government and on the quality of the official referendum material. We therefore bear a considerable responsibility. Swiss direct democracy has been shaped in the course of many decades (more than a century and half, in fact) through a multifaceted learning process. The legislative referendum was introduced in 1874, the popular initiative in 1891. In the years after its founding in 1848, the major challenge for the new federal state was to hold together a Swiss society which was politically and socially fragmented. Popular rights made it possible for minority groups to be integrated into the socio-political system and gave them a tool for articulating their particular interests. Thus, for example, the Catholic section of the population, the workers, and members of the minority language groups were all able to have their voices heard.

Another important value of direct democracy is that it helps to give legitimacy to the political system and to the political decisions of the government and parliament. It should be clear that I am not speaking here of a plebiscitary democracy, in which the political leadership uses national ballots to secure the blessing of a compliant populace for its decisions. I am speaking of direct democracy, in which there is a perpetual dialogue between the government and the people. In Switzerland we can never pursue policies against the will of the people; we can only make politics together with the people.

And that is how it should be. For if we succeed in convincing people of the rightness of our policies, then these policies will be sustainable and viable in the long term. Direct democracy is a mechanism for ensuring that there is never too great a gap between the interests of the people and the policies of the government. Mass protests against government policy – such as we have seen in France in 2006 against the planned introduction of a new employment law which would make it easier to hire and fire young people – are scarcely imaginable in direct-democratic Switzerland, precisely because the public is involved from the start in the debate and in the decision-making. To that extent I am pleased that cautious steps are also being taken in the EU towards direct decision-making by the citizens.

Critics also maintain that direct democracy stifles innovation. Where a government is more reformist or innovative than the general population, citizens can use referendums to "apply the handbrake". However, it would be a mistake to think that governments are always more reform-minded and innovative than the people. The popular initiative is frequently referred to as the "accelerator".

Initiatives often introduce new, innovative and sometimes quite radical ideas into the political debate. That is something very positive, for democracy thrives on dialogue and diversity of opinion.

Direct democracy politicises citizens and helps to create a lively civil society, for democracy needs debate about the right way forward. Public debate about political issues is generally much wider and more exhaustive in Switzerland than in other democratic systems, precisely because citizens are asked to vote several times a year on popular initiatives and mandatory or optional referendums, and not merely once every four years in general elections. As a result, Swiss people tend to demonstrate a much greater understanding of politics and political contexts.

It is a positive thing that there is a debate on the future of our country and its institutions. But direct democracy should not be a taboo subject. There is no doubt that the fear of having to sacrifice direct democracy, or even parts of it, is one reason for the sceptical attitude in our country towards the EU. It seems clear that reform of direct democracy would be inevitable in the context of a possible Swiss accession to the EU. But it would not at all be a case of doing away with direct democracy; rather it would be about ensuring our effectiveness as a member of the EU by adapting our institutions, whilst at the same time retaining what is of proven value and what, indeed, is part and parcel of our national identity.

It is quite clear to me that the value of our direct democracy cannot be calculated primarily in terms of Swiss francs. Direct democracy has made a major contribution towards the shaping and preservation of our multilingual, multicultural state. That alone is an expression of supreme efficiency. So there is no question that direct democracy has a future, in Switzerland and across the globe. However, we have to constantly adapt and reform this institution. Only then will it retain its dynamism and its effectiveness.

Micheline Calmy-Rey
Federal Councillor
Head of the Swiss Federal Department of Foreign Affairs

Initiatives & Referendums
Making democracy more truly representative

Dear reader,

Never before have so many people been able to vote on so many substantive issues as in 2006. Voters in Bolivia went to the polls to decide on decentralization; several US states held referendums on permitting same-sex marriages; Catalans had the last word on the new statute of autonomy; citizens voted on the new constitution in Mauritania and on the powers of the Prime Minister in Italy. And Europe got a new sovereign state, Montenegro – by referendum.

There were also vast numbers of popular decisions at regional and local levels – such as the referendum in the Swedish capital Stockholm on the introduction of a congestion charge – and equally large numbers of popular initiatives in many countries throughout the world. For the first time ever, citizens began to collect signatures for cross-border initiatives. Within the European Union, campaigns were begun to collect a milion signatures for a citizen-friendly EU initiative right and for abolishing the use of Strasbourg as a second venue for the European Parliament.

The developments in direct democracy of 2006 do not represent a new trend, but they do strongly reinforce an existing one. Since the millennium, more and more countries around the world have begun to use referendums in addition to elections, and more and more people now have the possibility of exerting an influence on the political agenda by means of a right of initiative. Throughout the world, representative democracy is being reformed and modernised. Existing indirect decision-making structures are being revitalised and given greater legitimacy by the addition of direct-democratic procedures and practice. Things looked very different not so many years ago.

As recently as 1980, it was still a minority of the world's population (46% in 54 countries) which was living in societies which enjoyed the minimum democratic standard of the rule of law, basic human rights, a choice of political parties and free elections. A quarter of a century later, more than 130 states now satisfy these requirements. This means that more than 70% of the people in the world now live under conditions which are to a greater or lesser extent "democratic". This significant progress has created the foundation for the next major step: the democratisation of democracy.

A MUCH FINER DISTRIBUTION OF POWER

Direct democracy – the right of citizens to be directly involved in political decision-making – is a core element of this next step. Direct democracy implies a much finer distribution of power, making it not surprisingly just as controversial as the introduction of universal suffrage (voting rights for all men and women) once was. Those who oppose the extension of democracy often use arguments – such as that the citizens are not competent to make important political decisions, for example – which are in fundamental opposition to the democratic principle of popular sovereignty. After all, modern direct democracy is a way in which representative democracy can become truly representative.

It is the goal of the Initiative and Referendum Institute Europe, which was founded in 2001, to make a significant contribution to improving the knowledge of the history and practice of direct democracy – in the world in general, and especially in Europe.

That is why the IRI "Guidebook to Direct Democracy" focuses on the place where the tools which allow citizens to take part in political decision-making are the most extensive and have been used for the longest period of time – Switzerland. Over the past 150 years, citizens' rights have been continually extended and now cover all the levels of political life (national, cantonal and local) and all areas of politics (including foreign policy).

The IRI Europe "Guidebook to Direct Democracy" does not restrict itself to Switzerland, however, but places that country's rich experience within the European and global contexts, where the rights of political co-decision making are being extended to more and more people in more and more countries, going far beyond simply electing political parties and their representatives to include the possibility of influencing the political agenda by means of initiatives, and deciding important substantive issues through referendums.

The 2007 IRI Guidebook to Direct Democracy in Switzerland and beyond offers a variety of entry-points into the subject: the twelve introductory essays present the major contexts and challenges; the many factsheets serve to deepen the factual and analytical basis on a selection of specific themes; and the concluding surveys contains further materials, facts and links on the institutions and the practice of direct democracy around the world.

A COMPLEMENT TO INDIRECT DEMOCRACY

Direct democracy, as a complement to indirect democracy, became established in Switzerland as early as in the 19th century and has been developed further since then. In hundreds of referendums over more than one hundred years, Swiss citizens have learned to make decisions on substantive political issues, whether at the national (federal) level, in the cantons or in the local communities. What does this mean in practice? What political tools are there for the citizens to use? How do they function? What are their direct and indirect effects? These and many other questions are answered in this book.

In Switzerland, direct democracy means that a referendum process takes place either because a group of voters demands it, or because it is stipulated in the constitution. The government cannot call a referendum: direct democracy implies the existence and use of tools for the sharing of political power which are in the hands of the citizens and serve their interests; direct democracy cannot be controlled for party-political or other vested interests by the government or parliament. There is no plebiscite in Switzerland i.e. there is no popular vote procedure which is initiated and executed at the exclusive discretion of the authorities, whether government, president or parliament.

There are three main procedures in Swiss direct democracy. Firstly there is the obligatory referendum: if parliament wishes to add something to the constitution, or amend it, the constitution itself lays down that the draft amendment or supplement has to be approved (or rejected) in a national referendum vote. Secondly there is the facultative, or optional, referendum: new laws or changes to laws, which have been passed by parliament, are subject to the facultative referendum, which means that they also have to receive final approval or rejection in a referendum vote – if 50,000 voters support a demand for this. Thirdly there is the citizens' initiative: citizens have the right to make legislative proposals which must be decided in a referendum vote if the proposal gains the support of 100,000 voters.

This allows a part of the electorate to place before the whole electorate issues which parliament does not wish to deal with, or which have not even occurred to parliament. Officially validated citizens' initiatives (i.e. ones which satisfy all the statutory requirements) will proceed to the referendum vote if that is what the initiative sponsors want, regardless of the wishes of either government or parliament.

Thus direct democracy and popular votes are not the same thing: not all popular vote procedures are direct-democratic. A plebiscite has a quite different effect than a real referendum. Direct democracy empowers the citizens; plebiscites are tools for the exercise of power by those in power. Much misunderstanding and confusion could be avoided if direct-democratic and plebiscitary procedures were clearly distinguished from one another, and even had different names.

Modern, efficient and peaceful

In our first essay we accompany a Swiss woman through a normal year of elections and referendums. This typical citizen has six elections and thirty referendums on her calendar. We gain an insight into the political life of a Swiss citizen and how she deals with direct democracy. The second essay portrays the course of a popular initiative (the "Disabled Initiative"), and a referendum (the "Army Reform Referendum"), the political processes connected with these, and their effects. Even though most citizens' initiative proposals are rejected in the referendum vote, they nonetheless have important effects. They can result in changes in society in line with the sponsors' aims, or they can block certain proposals, either temporarily or even permanently. It is a fundamental aspect of the principle of direct democracy in Switzerland that the most important political decisions are made – or can be subsequently controlled – by the voters themselves.

The third essay deals with how direct democracy came into being in Switzerland, its sources, and the differences between modern and pre-modern democracy. There are continuities in the development of Swiss democracy, but modern direct democracy did not emerge seamlessly and painlessly from the form of indirect democracy which came into being with the creation of the Swiss federal state after the French Revolution. The same difficulties presented themselves in the liberal Switzerland of 1848 as can be observed today in many states which claim the title of "democracy": the elected representatives fought – as they continue to fight today – against the introduction of a direct democracy which serves the interests of the citizens.

The Switzerland of 1848, formed from 25 small and tiny independent states, faced a very similar challenge as is faced today by the European Union, now also consisting of 25 states. The 25 cantons of Switzerland did not become a unitary state, but a federation in which the federal authorities have only as much power as is ceded to them by the citizens and the cantons. Switzerland had to find a way of taking proper account of both the democratic rights of the citizens and the interests and independent status of the cantons, especially of the smaller ones against the larger ones. The fourth essay describes the interplay of direct democracy and federalism and the attempt to find a solution to that challenge: where possible, decisions ought to be taken locally and by those who will be affected by them; only if absolutely necessary should they be taken at a "trans-local" level (canton or federation). In other words, decision-making should be as decentralised as possible, and as centralised as necessary.

Popular initiatives and referendums have a multitude of direct and indirect effects and serve a variety of purposes. They function as supplementary means of contact between civil society and the political system, through which both fears and hopes, resistance to change and the bringing forward of new ideas, interests and needs can be transmitted from civil society to the political system. One of the most important functions of citizens' initiatives is to place those needs, interests and problems on the political agenda which the authorities and political parties have either neglected or deliberately ignored. Direct democracy measures the pulse of society, acts as an early warning system and a mirror for society and ties politicians more closely to civil society. How that happens, what issues are dealt with, who are the players, with what success and what consequences – these are the themes of the fifth essay.

Improving self-esteem and the political competence

The sixth essay considers the effects of direct democracy on politics and the form of the state. The referendum has made a decisive contribution to the transformation of Swiss majority democracy into a consensus democracy. The right to force a referendum (by collecting signatures) on a law passed by parliament puts constant pressure on those in power to take into account the interests of as wide a spectrum of political forces as possible when they are making their decisions. At the same time, groups which are insufficiently integrated into society can use the tools of initiative and referendum to counter the lack of representation – provided that those groups have the necessary communication, organisational and campaigning skills. The fact that the tools can be used at any time has an integrative effect, countering the danger that relationship conflicts between more and less powerful groups in society can degenerate into violence. The resolution of the conflict over the Jura region is an object lesson in how such conflicts can be resolved in modern societies through the tools of direct democracy.

In the seventh essay we move to the effects of direct democracy on the development of personality. The dominance of power by politicians in purely parliamentary democracies shapes the relationship between rulers and ruled, even to the very way they conceive of democracy. Direct democracy shatters that imbalance of power, with the result that the quality of the relationship between rulers and ruled is fundamentally altered. There is a corresponding alteration in the way both elected representatives and citizens see themselves – the image they have of their respective roles in political life. All in all, citizens' rights reinforce both self-esteem and political competence of the voters and counter feelings of alienation and powerlessness. That this kind of added-value can also accrue to the media is shown in our eighth essay. In a direct democracy, both media and authorities have to make a special effort to provide accurate and full information to the citizens and to enter into a continuing dialogue with them.

Recent research findings on the economic benefits of direct democracy have aroused considerable interest – and not a little astonishment. Conventional wisdom maintained that extensive rights of co-determination acted as a brake on innovation and economic growth. Empirical, comparative studies proved the exact opposite. Our ninth essay shows how the widespread use of direct-democratic procedures actually strengthens the economy, reduces tax avoidance and lowers the level of public debt.

The Globalisation of Direct Democracy

In the three final essays, we show that the positive effects of direct democracy which have been described earlier do not appear automatically, but are conditioned by numerous factors. One crucial factor – the design of direct democracy – is dealt with in essay ten. In order to function properly and fulfil its potential, including living up to public expectations, direct democracy has to be well-designed and carefully implemented. Any attempt to make direct democracy toothless and ineffective, or a failure to make it as user-friendly as possible, is merely a continuation of the age-old battle against civil rights. The Swiss procedures – at all political levels – do especially well in international comparisons precisely because of their user- and citizen-friendliness. However, when a comparison is made of all those Swiss cantons with well-developed procedures of citizen involvement in decision-making, it is apparent that the frequency of use of those procedures depends on a host of other factors. While good design is a sine qua non of a properly functioning direct democracy, by itself it is not enough. Our eleventh essay shows that if the fundamental conditions for democracy – the rule of law; respect for the constitution, basic human rights and international law; the renunciation of the use of force; a democratic press and media; transparency of decision-making; openness to self-criticism; the commitment of all those involved to observe the principles of democracy – are not met, if the public and the political parties are not prepared to hold to the principle of democracy, then direct-democratic procedures will not be able to function, no matter how well-designed they are.

The final essay looks beyond the borders of Switzerland to the wider Europe, where the next few years present the prospect of the most extensive use of direct-democratic tools to date – in the context of european integration and the global trend towards more participatory decision-making processes. In addition to the proposed paneuropean referendum on the next EU constitutional treaty (which the EU leader would like to sign by 2008) there is also the proposed introduction of the very first trans-national citizens' right – the European Citizens' Initiative. This new democratic tool should in future give to a minimum of one million European citizens the right to propose a new law or a new article of the constitution to the European Commission – thus giving to 0.2% of the EU electorate the same right which the directly-elected European Parliament has enjoyed since 1979.

The IRI Guidebook 2007 Edition is available in several languages. The contents represent the results of years of painstaking work on the part of the editorial team. Many individuals and institutions have been involved, both directly and indirectly, in this work.

Dear reader, we hope that what we have brought together here will both inspire, assist and encourage you in your work and activities and to think critically about the issues raised. We welcome your feedback and suggestions for forthcoming editions of our IRI Europe "Guidebook to Direct Democracy".

Bruno Kaufmann, Rolf Büchi, Nadja Braun & Paul Carline

Marburg/Brussels, Summer 2006

It is a real challenge and one which requires some preparation. On referendum day a citizen may decide on a variety of issues such as fair rents, affordable health insurance, four car-free days per year, equal rights for the disabled and non-nuclear electric power.

1
The year of decisions

Astrid R. lives in Zurich. As a resident and voter of this city, Astrid took part in six elections and 30 referendums in a single year. For her, this is not too demanding. She is happy to shoulder the responsibility that direct democracy needs. Follow the annual political life of one woman in Switzerland's biggest city.

"We get two daily papers, I watch the news and political programmes on TV and I like listening to the car radio on my way to work. But what I find especially important are the discussions I have with my female friends and with Spyros, my husband. At home we talk about politics a lot and our political discussions have become much more intense since our daughter reached voting age."

On 18th May 2003, Astrid was able to vote on nine federal, one cantonal and two local issues. There were also elections for office holders in the church authorities. This was a particularly intense day of decisions, even for the election- and referendum-hardened Swiss.

In the press and from a number of commentators there was talk of too much being asked of the voters. It wasn't realistic, they said, to expect that the voters would be able to judge for themselves and decide on nine complex issues. Putting so many issues to a popular vote on the same day was only over-burdening an already demanding direct democracy.

Astrid doesn't share at all this scepticism about the voters' capabilities. "It's not a burden, she states emphatically, it's living politics." There was just as little panic in evidence in the voting offices of the Swiss towns and communities in May 2003; rather the mood was relaxed, with a confidence born of long experience that the vote counting would not cause any particular problems.

The results of the popular votes confirmed an established trend: all seven citizens' initiatives were rejected by a clear majority, both of the total voters and of the cantons. "A defeat for the political Left," agreed the papers the next day.

A NATION OF IDIOTS?

"Seven intelligent initiatives, seven resounding 'Noes': why do the Swiss vote against their own interests?," asked Constantin Seibt from the left-wing "Wochenzeitung", clearly puzzled at the way citizens had voted. "The question is why a majority of people obstinately vote against proposals which would benefit them socially, and even against their down-to-earth selfish interests. Are Swiss voters simply idiots?"

If we were to follow Seibt's way of thinking, we would have to conclude that the Swiss are 1) politically incompetent, 2) bribable or easily manipulated by propaganda from financially powerful interests, 3) easily led, like sheep and, 4) they have always been like that: Out of the total of 160 popular initiatives only 15 (up to 21.05.2006), and mainly symbolic and toothless ones, have been approved.

That brings us to one of the big challenges of Swiss direct democracy: isn't it annoying that the majority of voters repeatedly vote differently from the way they ought to vote – at least in the opinion of those who believe that they know better? Isn't it annoying that people want to and are able to decide for themselves what they are concerned about and what not? Fair rents, affordable health insurance, four car-free days per year, equal rights for the disabled, non-nuclear electric power, a renewal of the moratorium on building new nuclear power stations, a better choice of professional training for young people: the "Wochenzeitung" had recommended a "Yes" vote on all seven issues – and both the people and the cantons gave a resounding "No" to all seven.

Most Swiss voters support the "bourgeois" parties. They are cautious about change, especially if it costs money – and nearly everything costs money, as everyone knows. Not all the losers quarrelled with the verdicts on May 18th: "To put it simply, we on the Left ought to accept the defeats of last Sunday like a football team: we just weren't good enough in the second half," is how one Zurich city politician from the "alternative list" expressed it.

Astrid R. is very familiar with the sense of frustration which comes when the majority has once again voted against what she considered to be right. All Swiss citizens have experienced political defeat, everyone has been part of a minority many times: there is no majority position which can be predicted in advance. "People voted 'No' to the popular initiative 'equal rights for the disabled' because they didn't feel concerned, or because they thought it was going to cost too much money. That doesn't mean that the initiative was a waste of time. There has been a lot of debate, which made people more aware of the issue, something has been achieved."

Highly valued citizens

The 18th May was not the first test which politicians had had to face in the year 2003. The first elections and popular votes were on 9th February. As always, three to four weeks before the vote every citizen had received the appropriate official documents in the post. At the federal (national) level, the votes were about an extension of direct democracy and one other issue.

Astrid R.: "I think it's good in principle that we can vote. The government always makes its own recommendations, it talks to the people and tells them how they should vote – but what happens is, of course, what is decided in the popular vote. The government has to bow to the people's decisions. So no-one can say that we citizens do not have a say in political decision-making. I don't feel overloaded by the fact that there are more and more popular votes; I don't think that there are too many. I can very well decide for myself whether I want to vote on a particular issue or not; no-one is standing with a gun to my head and telling me what to do. We can vote if we want to, if we feel that we ought to. That's why I think that here in Switzerland we are more down-to-earth about politics. Your opinion is really valued, you get the ballot paper and referendum booklet in an envelope with your name on it and you can decide what you think."

Her husband Spyros finds big differences between the political systems in Greece and Switzerland, even at the structural level: "Greece has only had a more or less functioning parliamentary system since 1974. So despite their ancient inheritance, the Greeks cannot look back on a long tradition of democracy. The political parties still play far too great a role in the political process. The state is still far too centralised and there are hardly any direct-democratic rights."

The referendum debate on the proposed reform of civil rights had not made waves. The very low turnout (29%) showed that citizens put a relatively low value on the importance of this reform. On the other hand, the clear "Yes" to the increase in citizens' rights – the introduction of a "general initiative" and an extension to the optional referendum on international treaties – showed how well-rooted direct democracy is in Switzerland. On this occasion, only the most conscientious voters took part – such as Astrid R. and particularly Spyros, who always votes on principle ("If I believe in the democratic system, then I must exercise my democratic rights"). But the strong support for the increase in citizens' rights came from all social strata, and was especially marked in women voters and in voters from the rural areas.

In addition to the two federal proposals which went to referendum vote on 9th February, voters also had to decide on a number of other substantive issues at the local (City of Zurich) and cantonal (canton Zurich) levels. As so often, it was about the spending of public money. As a voter of the city of Zurich, Astrid was able to vote on a proposal to borrow money to upgrade the city's power station; as a voter of the canton Zurich, she was being asked to vote on a cantonal subsidy to the Glattal railway. There were also Justices of the Peace to be elected.

"I only vote when I'm happy that I know enough about the issue and have made up my own mind on it. I listen to others, but I form my own opinion. I don't follow any particular party line, but I am, of course, influenced by what the parties say. If I haven't come to any clear view, then I don't go to vote – as with the Justices of the Peace, for example. I don't know the people, don't know if they're good or not, so I didn't vote," explains Astrid.

ELECTIONS IN THE CANTON...

April 6th was the day for the elections to the cantonal parliament ("Kantonsrat") and the cantonal government ("Regierungsrat"). They took place in a society and a party-political landscape which had changed a great deal since the end of the Cold War. On the centre-right of the political spectrum, the FDP (Radical Democratic Party) – which had traditionally been the dominant party – had been losing ground steadily since 1990, and the SVP (Swiss People's Party) – further to the right than the FDP – had previously been a rather small party, but had increased in strength to become what is today the largest party. On the left, the SP (Social Democratic Party), with particularly strong roots in Winterthur and Zurich, had succeeded in consolidating its position. While the SVP had been able to increase its number of seats in Zurich's city parliament (community council) and the cantonal parliament in successive elections, it had not been able to make a corresponding increase in its share of power in the city and cantonal governments. In the cantonal government, two of the seven members are from the SVP. In the city government ("Stadtrat"), the SVP is not represented at all. It had managed to gain extra seats on the city parliament the previous year, but in the elections for city government it had once again come away empty-handed. In the city of Zurich, the social-democratic SP, which regularly gets 35% of the votes, had effectively become the party of government. Since 1990, the direction of politics has been determined by a Left/Green majority in government and the FDP.

The "mega-vote" on 18th May 2003 was followed by what was, for Switzerland, an exceptionally hot summer. There was a break from politics and people enjoyed their holidays: a refreshing swim in a lake or a cold beer in the shade. But soon the political caravan resumed its progress: the election campaigns for the federal parliamentary elections (set for 19th October) started up. As the canton with the largest population, Zurich sends 34 members to the 200-member National Council. In the Council of States, by contrast, all 20 full cantons – big and small alike – are represented by two deputies each. The former six "half cantons" (Basel City, Basel Country, Obwalden, Nidwalden, Appenzell Outer-Rhodes and Appenzell Inner-Rhodes), have one representative each. The National Council (the "Big Chamber") and the Council of States (the "Small Chamber") have the same status and rights and together form the federal parliament – the Federal Assembly.

...AND IN THE CONFEDERATION

The most recent parliamentary elections continued the developments which became visible already in the elections in 1995 and 1999. Voter turnout at these elections had risen steadily over the preceding ten years. The results show that changes of society are transforming the party system in Switzerland too – national developments corresponded to developments in the canton Zurich. The most significant changes in the distribution of power between the parties were not between Right and Left, but between the parties of the "bourgeois" majority, which, under the influence of the European question and the reawakened struggle for national identity, split into the centre-right FDP and CVP (Christian Democratic Party) and the nationalistically oriented right-wing SVP. The SVP became the most powerful party in the national parliament, which had a knock-on effect on the composition of the federal government's college of seven, elected on 10th December 2003. For the first time in 131 years, one of the federal councillors (Ruth Metzler) was not confirmed, and the "magic formula" for deciding the distribution of seats in the federal government (2 FDP, 2 CVP, 2 SP, 1 SVP) which had stood since 1959 had to be changed. Christoph Blocher joined the government on 1st January 2004 as the second SVP representative. The CVP now has only one member in the executive.

Astrid R. followed these developments – the consequences of the October elections – with interest. She also had the opportunity to vote on nine more cantonal issues on 30th November: some of them non-controversial (such as the division of responsibilities between the canton and the local authorities) and others contested (such as a change in the relationship between church and state). Astrid R. is happy with her right to be involved in political decision-making – even if many issues are hard nuts to crack. But it's the same for almost everyone in this country at the heart of Europe, in which every year is a year of decisions.

RELATED INFORMATION [F=FACTSHEET, S=SURVEY]
F1   Election and referendum diary canton Zurich: 2003
F2   Cantonal popular (referendum) votes: 1970–2003
F11 Voting behaviour in initiatives & referendums
F19 The result of the parliamentary elections in 2003
S1   All popular votes in Switzerland since 1848
S4   Glossary of direct-democracy terms

Popular initiatives cannot be put to the vote from one day to the next. They are part of a longer-term process which it may take up to a decade to complete. At the beginning is usually an idea for radical change.

Citizens centre stage in politics

When the people put their collective foot on the accelerator — or on the brake — important decisions are made. Read about how initiatives and referendums are used in Switzerland, and understand what happens when citizens no longer play the bit parts, but take the lead role in the political drama.

The two main pillars of direct democracy are the initiative and the referendum. The initiative is the more dynamic instrument. It allows a minority of the voters to place an issue of their own choosing on the political agenda and to have it decided by referendum. Eligible voters thus have the right to participate directly in legislation, regardless of whether the government or parliament likes it or not. At the federal level in Switzerland there is the constitutional initiative, and at the cantonal level the legislative initiative. 100,000 eligible voters can demand an amendment to or revision of the federal constitution. If the Federal Parliament rejects the initiative, the proposal is submitted to popular vote, unless the proposers withdraw their initiative. By around 2007, the initiative rights at the federal (national) level are due to be supplemented by a "General Popular Initiative," which will oblige the parliament to draft a new law or an amendment to the constitution if this has been requested by 100,000 registered voters (by signing an initiative).

Popular initiative "Equal Rights for the Disabled"
On 18th May 2003, the Swiss electorate of just over 4.76 million was able to vote in the federal referendum on the popular initiative "Equal Rights for the Disabled," which was proposing the addition of a new article to the federal constitution.

"The law guarantees equal rights for disabled people. It provides for measures for removing and compensating for existing disadvantages. Access to buildings and other facilities and the use of institutions and services intended for the general public will be guaranteed, as long as the costs are within reasonable limits." (Art. 8 § 4)

Between August 1998 and June 1999, more than 120,000 signatures had been collected by no fewer than 35 organisations for the disabled. In the four years between the official submission of the initiative and the deciding referendum, the proposal had been debated by the Swiss government (the Federal Council) and by both chambers of the federal parliament (the Federal Assembly) – but had been rejected by both of these, primarily on economic grounds.

In its recommendation that the voters also reject the initiative proposal – included in the referendum booklet sent to all registered voters before the vote – the government argued that: "A right of direct access to buildings would have significant financial consequences for both the public and private spheres." The government also pointed out that the new law on the disabled, which was adopted almost unanimously by the parliament in December 2003, and which came into force on 1st January 2004, would remove the existing disadvantages.

The popular initiative "Equal Rights for the Disabled" didn't have the slightest chance of success in the referendum vote on 18th May 2003. On a turnout of exactly 50%, 62.3% of the voters (1,439,893) voted against the proposal, 37.7% (870,249) in favour. The free access for the disabled to all areas of public life, for which the initiative had campaigned, was approved by only 3 of the 26 cantons – Geneva (59%), Jura (54.9%) and Ticino (54%). For the initiative to have been accepted, a majority of the cantons would also have had to vote in favour and not merely a simple majority of the total electorate, as is prescribed in Switzerland for all constitutional amendments: the result was thus even further away from the goal the initiative had to reach.

As the example of the "Disabled Initiative" shows, popular initiatives cannot be put to the vote from one day to the next. They are part of a long-term process which may take up to a decade to complete. At the beginning is usually an idea for radical change – for example, redressing the inequality of opportunity of people with disabilities. At the provisional end of a long initiative process such as this, the usual result is a referendum defeat for the proposal (fewer than one out of ten initiatives is accepted). Yet in many cases, the parliament goes some way to meeting the initiative's aims with either a direct (where both proposals are voted on at the same time) or indirect (as in the case of the initiative on the disabled) counter-proposal.

"It's true – we lost today," admitted Mark Zumbühl, spokesman for the Pro Infirmis charity for the disabled, on Sunday evening, "but at the same time, we have also made progress through the political battle which we fought over months and years: the unsatisfactory state of affairs which currently faces disabled people in Switzerland has been brought to the attention of the wider public."

Popular referendum "Army XXI"

At the same time as the vote on the "Disabled Initiative" on 18th May, Swiss voters were also able to vote on a reform package relating to national defence. In October 2002, a large majority in parliament had approved an amendment to the law on the military, creating the foundations for the so-called "Army XXI" (21st-century army). Opposing the proposed reduction of the armed forces by a third, former professional soldiers used the optional referendum option to demand a referendum on the amendment.

the difference in the number of communes within a canton – canton Bern has 400, canton Fribourg 246. For historical reasons, many decisions in canton Fribourg are taken in communal assemblies.

Despite the extraordinary degree of commonality in its forms – such as the universally practised popular initiative, popular referendum and obligatory referendum – the overall system of direct democracy in Switzerland reflects the enormous cultural, linguistic and institutional variety of the country. With a few exceptions, citizens' rights are more fully developed in the German-speaking cantons than in the French-speaking ones or the single Italian-speaking canton Ticino. This has to do not least with the historical circumstance that the German-speaking cantons confer much greater autonomy on their communes than is the case in the other language areas.

Accessibility and openness of the instruments are decisive for the extent of their use. For example: if in canton A 1,000 signatures are required to validate an optional referendum, while in the similarly-sized canton B the requirement is for 10,000 signatures, then it is fair to assume that there will be more referendum votes in canton A than in canton B. Besides the signature quorums, the amount of time allowed for the collection of signatures also plays a significant role in the ease of use and frequency of initiatives and referendums. Overall, the trend in recent years in Switzerland is for an opening up of the rules of direct democracy i.e. for hurdles to be lowered.

The citizens as the main actors

In the past, a favourite spot for collecting signatures was outside the polling stations on voting days, because one could be sure of catching most of the politically active voters there within a few hours. Since the introduction of unrestricted postal voting in 1996, the number of those who still go to the polling station in person has steadily decreased: in some communes it is as low as 10%.

The example of postal voting shows how the conditions for the exercise of direct democracy in Switzerland are subject to change, a process which will undoubtedly continue – for example, if electronic voting were ever introduced. On the one hand, such reforms can make public participation in referendum votes easier – as can be seen in the slightly higher average turnout figures since postal voting was introduced. On the other hand, however, voting from home creates new problems for a system in which direct personal contact and political dialogue between citizens continue to play a key role.

For regardless of whether citizens are pressing the reform accelerator by means of the popular initiative – or alternatively using the referendum to activate the emergency brake – by virtue of the tools of direct democracy, they take their place on the political stage alongside the organs of the state, such as the government and parliament. In contrast to almost every other country in the world, alterations to the constitution are decided upon by the people as the sovereign power: in these questions, the function of both government and parliament is to advise the citizens.

So when the Swiss voters said "No" to the "Disabled Initiative" and "Yes" to the reform of the army, they were not playing the bit parts, but the lead roles in the national political drama.

RELATED INFORMATION [F=FACTSHEET, S=SURVEY]
F6   Postal voting
F7   Electronic voting – the first real practice
F12 Popular initiatives, accepted by people and cantons
F16 The Army XXI referendum on 18 May, 2003
F17 The popular initiative "Equal rights for the disabled"
F18 Citizens' rights at the federal level in Switzerland
S1   All popular votes in Switzerland since 1848
S4   Glossary of direct-democracy terms

The constitutional referendum found its way from France to Switzerland and later spread across Europe, and at present there is a struggle to implement it at the European level in the context of the approval of the new constitution for the European Union.

3

Back to the future

Modern direct democracy has had a profound impact on the character and history of the Swiss and of Switzerland. Nothing unites people more than knowing the fundamental value of their direct-democratic rights. Together, they can preserve the freedom of every citizen and foster peaceful coexistence in a multicultural state. Here is the story of a democratic revolution in Europe's heart.

"The people are no longer willing to be governed from above; they demand their share in the making of laws and the exercise of power (…) they demand that self-government finally means what it says," wrote Florian Gengel, editor of the Bern newspaper "Der Bund," in August 1862.

In Switzerland, the liberal movement succeeded in achieving what it failed to achieve elsewhere: the creation of a nation-state and modern democracy. The half-century between 1798 and 1848 – full of conflict and occasionally descending into chaos – can be seen as a period of foundation. It began with the "Helvetic Republic," the shortlived attempt to transform the loose federation of states of the old confederation into a unitary state on the French model. Subsequently, the old order was partially restored in two stages (1803 Acts of Mediation; 1815 new federal treaty) and Switzerland was converted back into a conservative league of states.

However, economic and social development proceeded in a contrary direction to that of the Restoration. In 1830/31, there were democratic revolutions in twelve cantons; the old ruling order was replaced by modern, democratic institutions – though for the time being citizens still had no direct participation in law-making. All cantons, with the sole exception of the canton Fribourg, approved their new constitutions in popular votes. These changes laid the foundations for the Swiss political and constitutional system which still exists today. The Swiss federal state of 1848 was born out of bitter struggles and civil war.

The 1848 federal constitution institutionalised a new state order on the model of the liberal-democratic cantons. It was designed from the start to be open to revision and already included the right of popular initiative for total revision of the constitution, in addition to the obligatory constitutional referendum. It created a framework for the bourgeois-liberal government and its modernising policies. At the same time, it can be seen as a declaration of intent: national democracy, the nation and the Swiss people, the nation-state and the federal state were at that time imagined goals rather than present reality.

There was dissatisfaction with the new democracy almost from the beginning, but opposition demands for greater participatory rights were at first resisted. It required a second democratic revolution before direct democracy could be added to representative democracy against the resistance of the ruling liberal elite and a new quality of democracy brought to the relationship between the rulers and the ruled. This second revolution was carried out by the Democratic Movement of the 1860s. It defeated the ruling liberal elite and in the canton Zurich made the decisive breakthrough to modern direct democracy. The new constitution of 1869 in the canton Zurich brought together a series of participatory rights (the constitutional and legislative initiatives, the obligatory legislative and constitutional referendums, the finance referendum), institutionalizing a degree of modern direct (though exclusively male) democracy which had never existed anywhere else before that time. It served as a model for the change in the political system from indirect to direct democracy in other cantons and in the federation.

The introduction of direct democracy – as with other changes, both before and after – took place first in the cantons and only later (and in a weaker form) in the federation. The history of the emergence of direct democracy in Switzerland ended with the introduction of the optional referendum (1874) and the popular initiative (1891) at the federal level. The referendum meant that constitutional development was placed on a different footing – with considerable consequences for the entire political system. From representative government and majoritarian democracy arose Swiss "referendum democracy" – a consociational democracy whose basic features continue to this day and which is accepted as legitimate by the citizens.

After 1891 direct democracy was further extended. The introduction (in 1918) of a proportional system for the election of the National Council made it possible for smaller groups to gain representation in parliament. The referendum on international treaties (introduced in 1921, extended in 1977 and 2003) allowed citizens to be involved in decisions on foreign policy. The creation of the so-called "resolutive" referendum in 1949 restricted the ability of the Federal Assembly to protect decisions from exposure to referendum by declaring them to be "emergency measures" (in the 1930s the government had used the emergency clause to systematically avoid referendums). In every case, these innovations were introduced through a national citizens' initiative – proof that direct democracy can use the initiative right to extend (or also restrict) itself.

Popular sovereignty disputed

The Liberals agreed in principle that sovereignty resides in the people, but after 1830 disagreements over how the principle was to be embodied in the institutions of state produced a split between liberal and radical democrats. For the liberal establishment, popular sovereignty was in practice limited to an elective democracy in which the representatives exercised political power on behalf of the people. It rejected a direct participation of the citizens in legislation. This view was reflected in the first democratic cantonal constitutions and in the 1848 federal constitution. Article 1 of the Zurich constitution of 1831 illustrates this: "Sovereignty resides in the people as a whole. It is exercised in accordance with the constitution by the Great Council as the representative of the people."

The ruling liberals justified their model of democracy on the grounds of the political immaturity and incompetence of the common citizen. In their view a person without property and education was not capable of making political decisions based on sound reason and an understanding of the common good. They were afraid that incompetent citizens would make the wrong decisions and endanger progress.

For the radical democrats who opposed them, by contrast, popular sovereignty did not mean that citizens should hand over their sovereignty to their elected representatives, but, quite the contrary, that they should have the last word in the legislative process. It was on this fundamental principle that the radical democrats based their opposition and demanded the appropriate extension of popular rights.

For the radical democrats, the model of indirect democracy simply did not live up to its claim to represent reason and the common good in the best possible way, but rather served to create and extend a new order of privilege for the rich and well-educated, which disadvantaged and even excluded large sections of the population. In the radicals' view, a purely representative system of government primarily served the vested interests of the liberal establishment, and to change this situation required that the citizens be given more political power.

The Democratic Movement forces a change in the system

It took quite a long time before early criticism of the existing ruling order finally coalesced, with the Democratic Movement, into a critique of the "system." The opposition in the constitutional debates of 1830–31 and the popular movements of 1839–41 had demanded the right of veto. The veto can be seen as an institutional precursor of the referendum. It had been institutionalized for the very first time as early as 1831 in the canton St. Gallen, as a concession to protesting farmers and as a means of blocking more wide-ranging demands for participation by the democrats. As an instrument of democracy, however, the veto was hardly user-friendly and presented no threat to the liberal parliamentary democracy; the democratic opposition was still too weak for that. The situation did not change until the 1860s, when the general public had finally become convinced that a just society was impossible without a move to "pure democracy" i.e. through the addition of direct democracy to the existing indirect, representative form of democracy. It now became possible for the Democratic Movement to secure direct democracy.

The Democratic Movement drew its power from the dissatisfaction of large sections of the population with the existing political, social and economic conditions. It accused the government of furthering the interests of the rich instead of the general good. It complained that powerful financial and commercial interests were having a deleterious effect on politics. It demanded direct democracy as a remedy, not solely in order to have greater control over the government, but in order to create greater social and economic equality: "The upwardly striving plutocracy can now be held in check only by shifting the centre of gravity of the legislative process further out, to encompass the entire people; for a few hundred cantonal councillors, i.e. representative democracy, are not powerful enough to resist corruption." With these words, Karl Bürkli expressed the feelings of the whole Democratic Movement.

As with other political changes both before and after, the change of the political system to "pure democracy" was described and legitimated, not as a break with the past, but as the continuation of an ancient tradition of freedom. It was easier to accept something new that came in the guise of venerable tradition. There was, nonetheless, an awareness of the historic importance of the event, as the following quotation from Friedrich Albert Lange reveals: "The 18th April 1869 has given the canton Zurich a constitution which must be considered as one of the most significant phenomena in the field of recent institutions of state. It is, in short, the first consistent attempt to implement the idea of pure popular rule in a form which is appropriate to the modern cultural conditions, and to replace the venerable, but cumbersome, 'Lands gemeinde' (the annual, sovereign assembly of all male citizens which had the right to vote), which is suited only to small-scale situations, by an institution whose cornerstone is the ballot vote in the local communities."

The second democratic revolution – like the first one of 1830–31 – was largely free of violence. Government and opposition continued to speak to one another. Thousands of citizens came together in "Landsgemeinden" (traditional popular assemblies), putting pressure on those in power by presenting similar lists of demands, and forced through a fundamental change in the system of democracy – clearly expressed in the first article of the new cantonal constitution: "The power of the state resides in the people as a whole. It is exercised directly by those citizens who are entitled to vote, and indirectly by the authorities and the officials." Using modern terminology, it could be described as a victory of those who are victims of modernisation against those who stand to gain from modernisation. Today, more than 130 years later, direct democracy has become more topical and relevant than ever, not only at the local and national levels, but also, and that is something fundamentally new, at the level of the European Union.

Sources of Swiss direct democracy

The experience and the ideas of the American and even more of the French Revolutions represented vital sources of inspiration for the development of Swiss direct democracy. French revolutionary law contained many of the direct-democratic instruments which would subsequently be adopted in Switzerland and was carefully studied there.

French ideas on direct democracy had a strong influence on the democratisation of Switzerland, even if this was not openly admitted at the time. However, those ideas were never implemented in France itself where a plebiscitarian tradition developed which serves the interests of those in power. There was one exception: the constitutional referendum, an import from North America, was there to stay. It found its way from France to Switzerland and later spread across Europe, and at present there is a struggle to implement it at the European level in the context of the approval of the draft constitution for the European Union. There is a growing conviction that a constitution which has not been explicitly approved by the citizens is simply undemocratic.

The process of introducing modern direct democracy was also inspired by the experience of pre-modern forms of democracy. The Swiss cantons were bound together by a strongly rooted republican tradition, which set them apart from their monarchical neighbours. There was a living culture of the popular assembly democracy ("Landsgemeindedemokratie") and the federal referendum which went back to the Middle Ages. When the old confederation collapsed, many saw their "home-made" assembly democracy as a more attractive form of democracy and a more secure guarantee of freedom than French-style indirect democracy. This is clearly evidenced by the short-lived "Landsgemeindefrühling" (the "Assembly Democracy Spring") in 1798, as also by the fact that it was only the inhabitants of cantons where the popular assembly was practised (Glarus, Schwyz and Nidwalden) who offered fierce resistance when the troops of the French revolutionary army entered the country.

People were familiar with and trusted their own form of popular assembly democracy. Even more importantly, a shift from the traditional popular assembly ("Landsgemeinde") to a modern representative system meant a loss both of rights of political participation and of material advantages. Both considerations contributed to making popular assembly democracy more attractive.

Social movements repeatedly and consciously hark back to the tradition of assembly democracy and organise their public protests in the form of a "Landsgemeinde". For example, on 22nd November 1830, the liberals organised a popular assembly in Uster to campaign for "the restoration of lost rights of the People" and on 13th December 1867 the Democratic Movement held popular assemblies in Uster, Bülach, Winterthur and Zurich. The Uster assembly of 1830 is still commemorated every year.

Continuity and rupture

Modern direct democracy can be understood as a mixture of completely new ideas and institutions with an old tradition of participation. What is entirely new is the way in which modern democracy has been thought of since the American and French Revolutions. Democracy and freedom are no longer presented as the historic privilege of a particular group which had its origin in the resistance to an unjust tyranny (William Tell) – but as a natural right of every individual. The ideal of modern democracy – that all people should be free and equal – is irreconcilable with any situation in which some are subject to the will of others. The pre-modern form of democracy, which was seen as a group privilege, did not exclude the possibility of oppressing others, something which was quite common in the old confederation.

What is quite old is the conviction that a citizen's freedom depends on his ability and desire to participate in political decision-making. It is one of the central ideas of republicanism and corresponds to the practice of popular assembly democracy. Unlike the purely parliamentarian democracy, modern direct democracy continues this centuries-old tradition of the pre-modern democracy. It is doing this with the new instruments of the initiative and the referendum.

Related information [F=Factsheet, S=Survey]
F3 Differences between pre-modern and modern democracy
F9 Constitutional extracts from 1798, 1848, 1874 and 1999
F10 On the development of direct democracy at the level of the Swiss federal state
F25 The expectations of the Swiss direct democracy movement in the 19th century
S1 All popular votes in Switzerland since 1848
S4 Glossary of direct-democracy terms

Compared with other European countries, Switzerland is seen as having particularly progressive legislation on water protection — thanks not least to the legislative process set in train by the popular initiative.

4

As centralised as necessary, as decentralised as possible

In a democracy, every vote has the same value. In the Swiss federal system, each canton's vote has the same value. Taken together, these two facts mean that in the smaller cantons the citizens' votes have greater weight. Look at the long battle over the protection of water resources. This shows the interplay between federalism and direct democracy, and that differences of opinion do not have to divide people: on the contrary.

On 17th May 1992, Swiss voters were able to vote on seven federal proposals. For example, they voted in favour of Swiss accession to the "Bretton Woods" international financial institutions (World Bank and IMF) and supported the introduction of a civil alternative to compulsory military service. They also had to decide on a popular initiative launched by environmental groups to "Save our Water Resources", and on the revised law on the protection of the same, which had been passed by the government and parliament, but was being opposed by the owners of small electri city generating stations, who were using the optional referendum option to challenge the new law.

Water is an extremely precious resource – one of the most important resources for humans, animals and plants. Formal protection of water sources had been written into the federal constitution in 1953 and had come under statutory federal regulation two years later in the form of a federal law. In 1975, Art. 24bis created the constitutional basis for the conservation of water stocks and especially for ensuring that there were adequate water reserves in Switzerland. This article (Art. 76 in the new Swiss constitution) requires that all the various – and often competing – interests in a specific water resource (river, lake) be taken into account.

The Swiss federal constitution permits the central organs of the state (such as the government and parliament) to issue general guidelines, but leaves it to the 26 individual cantons to decide on their own specific legal provisions – thus giving them considerable power to determine the way they wish to handle matters. The Federation principally takes on those tasks which require uniformity of provision. The rest is within the power of the cantons themselves. Put another way: Swiss government is (only) as centralised as is necessary – and as decentralised as is possible. The decisive distinction between the Swiss concept of federalism and the so-called "principle of subsidiarity" in the European Union is that in Switzerland the central state power can only impose as a uniform rule what has previously been approved by a majority of the citizens and of the cantons in an obligatory constitutional referendum.

It is especially true in the case of water usage that the cantons – many of which have their own hydro-electric power stations – have a considerable interest in keeping restrictions to a minimum. It is this background – of the clash of interests between those who want to protect water resources and those who want to exploit them, and between the powers of the Federation and those of the cantons – which makes the history of the "Save our Water Resources" popular initiative and the controversial revision of the law on protection of water such an instructive lesson on federalism and direct democracy. The main actors in the drama come from the environmental and water conservation camp on the one hand, and from the water users – in this instance the owners of the small hydro-power station – on the other. In addition, the interests of the mountain cantons in particular also played an important role.

The environmentalists launched their "Save Our Water Resources" initiative in the summer of 1983. The initiative committee included representatives of nine national environmental and commercial fishing organisations. Within 18 months, they had collected sufficient signatures to proceed: the initiative was formally presented with 176,887 supporting signatures on 9th October 1984 (the rules require a minimum of 100,000 signatures to be gathered within 18 months).

What is the division of powers between Federation and cantons?

In the case of the "Save Our Water Resources" initiative, the initiative committee had produced a detailed draft law which was to add an Art. 24 to the federal constitution. The government responded in April 1987, recommending that the initiative be rejected. Although it viewed the goals of the initiative as fundamentally right in principle, it found that the exclusive focus on protection – with its considerable economic repercussions – meant that other important interests, especially those of water users, were given insufficient weight. The government presented proposals for a revision of the law on the protection of water resources as an indirect counter-proposal to the initiative. To a large extent, the revised law simply provided general guidelines and left it to the cantons to work out their own detailed legislative measures. The government's draft law was then debated in both chambers of the Swiss Parliament.

Parliament did not find it at all easy to deal with the initiative and the proposed new law. Both chambers extended the period of evaluation of the initiative by a year, in order to allow time to first debate the revision of the existing law on water protection which was to be presented as an indirect counter-proposal. It was the intention to take some of the initiative's concerns into account in drafting the amended law. The new (revised) law on the protection of water resources was passed by the Council of States, as the first of the two chambers, in October 1988.

The Council of States, with 46 members, is the smaller of the two chambers and represents the cantons. Twenty of the cantons – regardless of how big or small they are (as big as Zurich, with more than 1.2 million inhabitants;

or as small as Uri, with only 35,000) – have exactly the same number of representatives (two each), while for historical reasons six cantons (Basel City, Basel Country, Obwalden, Nidwalden, Appenzell Outer-Rhodes and Appenzell Inner-Rhodes) have one representative each. This is a "federalistic" way of supplementing the basic principle of "one man, one vote" and the simple majority rule in favour of the smaller units.

The larger chamber – the National Council – has 200 members and represents "the People" i.e. Swiss citizens in general. Here, the most highly populated canton, Zurich, has 34 representatives and the least populated, Uri, only one. Both chambers have identical powers and responsibilities and normally handle parliamentary business (federal laws, budgetary decrees, conclusion of international treaties etc.) separately. A parliamentary decree or statute is valid only if both chambers have approved it.

In the case in question, there was disagreement over the real heart of the matter – changes to the law on water reserves. A proposal by representatives of the mountain cantons to abolish the Federation's right to prescribe minimum reserve levels and to delegate regulation of the restrictions on water usage to the cantonal authorities failed to win sufficient support and the Council of States ultimately approved the government's plans. However, the prescriptions on minimum quantities of water reserves were reduced to mere guidelines. Two proposals for compensatory payments (known as the "Landschaftrappen" – the "Countryside Penny"), in cases where a community was prepared voluntarily to refrain from exploiting water power in the interests of the environment, were viewed favourably by all parties. However, the Council of States decided not to make a decision on this matter at the time. In the 1989 summer session of parliament, the National Council attached significant amendments: the "Landschaftsrappen" should be used to compensate mountainous areas which refrained from exploiting hydroelectric power on environmental grounds.

Seeking the middle way

At the second reading of the law on protection of water in December 1989, the Council of States voted by a majority to stand by its earlier decisions. The "Landschaftsrappen" – even in a watered-down form – was once again rejected. In March 1990, the National Council stuck to its guns as regards the central issues of the minimum reserve quantity and the retention of the Landschaftsrappen. After further significant differences of opinion between the two Councils had been expressed in a third reading, a breakthrough was finally achieved in November 1990 at the fourth reading of the law in the Council of States, which abandoned its opposition to the inclusion of hard-and-fast water reserve prescriptions in the water protection law. In addition, it now expressed support for compensatory payments from the Federation to those communities which refrained from exploiting water for power on environmental grounds. As a response to the Council of States' compromise, the National Council dropped the last major stumbling block – the proposal for the "Landschaftsrappen". After more than two years of negotiations, the two Councils were finally able to agree on the wording of the amendment of the water protection law – thereby creating the indirect counter-proposal to the original initiative.

In the view of the initiative committee, however, this counter-proposal simply did not go far enough: they therefore decided not to use the option of withdrawing their original proposal. At the other end of the spectrum of interests, the ISKB (the association of owners of small power stations) viewed the proposed amendments to the law as going too far – in particular in relation to the fixing of minimum water reserves – and availed themselves of the option of the facultative (optional) legislative referendum. The power station owners claimed that if the law were to be implemented, most of the power stations producing less than 300 KW would have to close down. This kind of referendum is directly connected to representative democracy, because the referendum vote is on decisions which have been reached by parliament, and which have to be either approved or rejected.

This political battle – lasting for over a decade – on the protection of water shows just how difficult it can be to reconcile such conflicting interests as those of the environmentalists, the cantons and the commercial users. In this instance, reconciliation proved so difficult that when the issue finally came to the decisive vote on 17th May 1992, there were two parallel ballots on the same subject. The popular initiative "Save our Water Resources" failed to win a majority of the votes in any of the cantons and was rejected by 62.9% of the voters overall. For it to have been accepted would have required a double majority of both cantons and registered voters. By contrast, the ballot on the amendment to the water protection law had it comparatively easy: a simple majority of the total vote was all that was required, and the new law was passed by a clear majority of just over 66% of the voters. It came into force on 1st January 1993. As a consequence, the cantons had to adjust their regulations to the new guidelines. Compared with other European countries, Switzerland is seen as having particularly progressive legislation on water protection – thanks not least to the legislative process set in train by the popular initiative. On the other hand, the cantons are still having difficulties implementing the provisions of the new legislation. Commercial interests often carry more weight than environmental considerations.

Co-determination instead of veto

Although the individual cantons play a very strong role within the Swiss Confederation, no canton has a right of veto over decisions made collectively – as is quite common in the EU. The consensus rule was abandoned as long ago as 1848, when the modern state of Switzerland came into being: 15 1/2 cantons approved the new constitution, 6 1/2 rejected it. Despite this, the constitutional assembly of the time – the Diète – decided to implement the new federal constitution, thus replacing the principle of uniformity by that of the double majority for constitutional referendums.

The principle of dual legitimacy (people and cantons) was retained during the subsequent development of the instruments of direct democracy. The first total revision of the federal constitution in 1874 introduced both the so-called popular referendum for federal laws, and also the cantonal referendum. Whereas the popular referendum requires the collecting of at least 50,000 signatures within 100 days of the official announcement of a new law, the cantonal referendum requires the signatures of at least eight cantonal governments.

It was to be more than a century, however, before the first canton actually submitted a cantonal referendum in 1981. The canton Ticino was opposed to a planned change in penal law. Of all the cantons it approached to support its opposition, it received a response from only one: but the parliament of Basel City missed the deadline for a legally effective response.

Another 22 years were to pass before the instrument would finally be used. The first cantonal referendum to satisfy all the criteria and actually go ahead was against the package of tax measures approved by parliament in summer 2003, which would have produced losses in cantonal income of about 510 million Swiss francs. The finance minister of the canton Vaud, Pascal Broulis – one of the spokespersons of the group of cantons opposed to the plans – declared: "If the Federation wants to lower its own taxes, that's its own business; but if the Federation wants to lower the cantonal taxes, that's something else altogether – a first in the history of the Confederation." But before that there was a different kind of premiere: by the end of September 2003, no fewer than 11 cantons had signed the referendum: Basel-City, Bern, Glarus, Graubünden, Jura, Obwalden, Schaffhausen, Solothurn, St. Gallen, Wallis and Vaud. On 16th May 2004 more than two thirds of the participating voters (67.2%) turned down the tax package proposal.

Protecting minorities, promoting compromise

Decisive for the practice of Swiss federalism is the way that the decisions taken by government and parliament at various levels are pegged back to the democratic principle. Thanks to the tools of direct democracy, in the most important cases it is the citizens who have the last word. This helps to promote greater respect for the citizens among the organs of the state and the elected politicians. At the same time, the processes of direct democracy are embedded in a national political system which protects minorities, promotes compromise and fosters collective learning processes.

The example of the conflict over the protection of water resources shows clearly that differences of opinion do not have to divide people. On the contrary: a society which is always prepared to reconsider and debate even what everyone seems to agree on will always be able to integrate opposing views and reach agreements on what needs to be done for the immediate future – at least on a provisional basis. The institutions and procedures which make this possible in Switzerland are federalism and direct democracy.

Related information [F=Factsheet, S=Survey]
F4 How the cantons can influence the writing of a new law
F5 Five stages in the genesis of a new law
F23 The law on the protection of water resources (1983–92)
S1 All popular votes in Switzerland since 1848
S4 Glossary of direct-democracy terms

WANDELHALLE

Direct democracy is far less a disrupting element in politics than it is a way of enlivening it and keeping it on its toes. Much more is expected of all parts of society than in a purely parliamentary system.

The land of the contented losers

Direct democracy reveals where in society the shoe pinches. Although the government wins most referendums on the national level, the authorities have a harder time of it in the cantons, and even more so in the communes. And yet, take note, the system produces on the whole contented losers.

It's late afternoon on the Sunday of a national referendum day. Happy faces all around. Representatives of the government are holding a press conference to explain the reasons why the vote went their way. "This is a victory for the Centre," say Justice Minister Ruth Metzler and Economy Minister Joseph Deiss, after the voters had accepted – by a clear two to one majority – both a reform of citizens' rights and a hospital finance bill on 8th February 2003. Three months later, the voters' support for the government's recommendations was even more striking: on 18th May 2003, they rejected no fewer than seven of the popular initiatives coming from the Left-Green camp, while approving the proposed reform of security policy. Not only that: as Pascal Couchepin, Federal President for that year, noted: "The above-average high turnout shows that citizens do not feel over-burdened." What also pleased the Liberal Couchepin was the fact that the voting figures for the nine ballots were almost identical across the cantons.

There was no trace of pleasure, let alone schadenfreude, at the ballot debacle of their political opponents in the comments of the government representatives. After the clear rejection of the two nuclear power initiatives – the one aimed at extending the moratorium on the building of new nuclear power stations by a further ten years, the other demanding a change in energy policy and the progressive decommissioning of all the existing nuclear stations – energy Minister Moritz Leuenberger pointed out that the "No" vote on the two initiatives should really be seen as a "Yes" vote on the government's indirect counter-proposals. The new law on nuclear power which would enter into force on 1st January 2004 would offer more public involvement in decisions on new nuclear power stations and a halt to the reprocessing of fuel rods. Justice Minister Metzler argued along the same lines in respect of the "No" vote on the "Disabled Initiative": the rejection of the initiative should not be seen as a rejection of the concerns of disabled people. Metzler praised the "losers", saying: "You achieved a lot with your initiative," and drew attention to the new law on the disabled which had the same aim of bringing about equality of treatment – only not quite so comprehensively or expensively.

After so much praise and encouragement from the government, even those on the losing side – a few at first, then in increasing numbers – expressed their satisfaction with the results of the 18th May votes. "The government now has a good basis for instituting a car-free Sunday," said Rahel Häsler, co-president of the Sunday Initiative, whose demand for four car-free Sundays per year had been supported by 37.6% of the voters. Adrian Schmid, director of traffic policies at the Swiss Verkehrsclub – a transport association committed to environmentally-friendly principles – reinforced this view:

"Parliament must now accept the electorate's desire for more public space free from private motor traffic."

Direct democracy is not a disturbing element

Although nine out of ten citizens' initiatives fail at the ballot box, new initiatives are constantly being launched. This stirs up the daily round of politics, challenging the majority consensus and stimulating public debate. Initiative sponsors know from experience that they can achieve an effect, even if their proposal is ultimately defeated in the referendum. Citizens' initiatives are not zero-sum games in which one side gets everything and the other nothing. Opinion polls show that 9 out of 10 Swiss citizens are not prepared to have their statutory direct-democratic rights to participate in decision-making curtailed in any way.

If a party backs the "wrong" side in an initiative and "loses" the referendum, that doesn't affect their chances of being elected. In fact, those who win elections have frequently been on the losing side in important referendums. Losing a referendum seems to give political parties a clear profile which fixes them in the mind of the voters.

The truth is that direct democracy in Switzerland is far less a disrupting element in politics than it is a way of enlivening it and keeping it on its toes. Much more is expected of all parts of society than in a purely parliamentary system: the authorities cannot count on a general background level of popular support between elections, but have to be able to get majorities on a number of specific substantive issues. This increases the pressure on government and parliament to provide information and explain their policies. Regular popular ballots on specific issues promote a political culture which is characterised by participation. This in turn leads to an increased level of interest in politics – including in the media – and to greater levels of political awareness and competence among the general public. When citizens involve themselves with legislation or amendments to the constitution, they increase their knowledge of the law. Ultimately, direct democracy increases the legitimacy of political decision-making. The possibility of launching initiatives and referendums and forcing votes on real issues also serves as a kind of mirror to society, giving it a sense of itself and revealing where the shoe pinches.

Frequent voting issues

One thing which becomes clear from a longer-term historical perspective is that at times of greater economic difficulty (for example between the two World Wars and at the end of the 20th century), issues of social policy and immigration quite frequently feature as the subject of popular initiatives. Votes on the form of the state and the shape of democracy have been a regular part of the calendar, as have policies on national security and issues relating to the family.

Over the last three decades, an increasing number of initiatives have concerned environmental and traffic policy issues and it was in these areas that popular initiatives have been able to record their most significant direct successes. Recent examples include the initiative for the protection of the upland moors (primarily directed against the creation of a military training area near Rothenturm in the canton Schwyz) which in 1987 won majorities of both the voters and the cantons. Seven years later, double majorities were again recorded for the so-called "Alpine Initiative", which made it a constitutional stipulation that goods transit traffic through Switzerland would be transferred completely to the more environmentally-friendly rail by 2010 at the latest. On the other hand, other environmental and traffic initiatives, as well as proposals to reduce the number of foreigners or tighten asylum policy, were rejected. The evidence is that even those issues which are of considerable concern and which might be expected to command majorities often attract only minority support at the ballot box due to the particular (often very radical) solutions being proposed.

Federal authorities win most of the citizens' initiative referendums

540 popular votes were held on the federal level from 1848 to 2006 (until 24.09.2006): 161 popular initiatives, 188 obligatory referendums, 158 popular referendums and 33 counter proposals of the parliament.

If one considers the whole period from 1848 to 2006 and compares it with the period from 1990 to 2006 the following picture arises:

Out of 160 popular initiatives only 15 (9%) were approved. From 1990 to 2006 (until 21.05.2006) only 5 out of 60 popular initiatives were approved. Among them was the initiative "For Switzerland's membership of the United Nations" which was supported by government and parliament.

In addition to the citizens' initiatives, any amendment to the constitution proposed by the government or parliament must be put to referendum. Of the 188 obligatory referendums held so far, 140 were approved by the voters and by a majority of the cantons. Thus the voters agreed with the parliament in 74% of cases. Only 7 of the 38 obligatory referendums held between 1990 and 2006 were rejected, the remainder (82%) being accepted.

The situation is different with the facultative or popular referendums, which are the most difficult for the authorities to control. Of the total of 156 popular referendums, 83 (53%) have been accepted and 73 rejected. Since 1990, the authorities' "success rate" has significantly improved: of the 54 popular referendums held between 1990 and 2006 (until 21.05.2006), the official proposal was accepted on 38 occasions (70%).

In recent years, the referendum has been used to oppose the bilateral agreements with the European Union, the deployment of Swiss soldiers in other countries, army reform and the liberalisation of the electricity market, among other issues. Of these, only the new electricity market law failed.

If one takes all the parliamentary referendums, including counter-proposals, across the whole period from 1848 to 2006, the voters agreed with the authorities in 64% of the votes; between 1990 and 2006 the percentage even rose to 71%. The evidence clearly suggests that the gap between voters and the authorities is narrowing further.

It's easier for initiatives in the cantons

The long-term comparison of success rates for initiatives and referendums at the federal level produces some interesting differences – and especially if one then compares these figures with the results in the 26 cantons and approximately 2800 communes (local authority areas). Big differences are apparent here. In the early years of direct democracy, four out of every five ballots were lost (from the point of view of the government and parliament). By the middle of the 20th century, successes and failures were about equal. These developments reflect changes in the composition of the Swiss government, which until 1891 was composed entirely of Liberal members of parliament. Gradually, representatives of other groups in society – such as Catholics, farmers and social democrats – were able to gain seats. The introduction of the "magic formula" – 2:2:2:1 – which has decided the apportioning of places in the government since 1959 laid the foundation for a more successful (from the point of view of the authorities) handling of citizens' rights. The "magic formula", an element of Swiss consensus democracy, says that the composition of the government must correspond to the relative strength of the parties in the Federal Assembly. So from 1959 to 2003, the government was made up of two representatives each from the FDP (Radical Democratic Party), the CVP (Christian Democratic Party) and the SP (Social Democratic Party), and one from the SVP (Swiss People's Party). In 2004, this composition had to be adjusted to the changed relative strengths of the parties and the CVP lost one seat to the SVP.

The authorities have a harder time of it in the cantons, and even more so in the communes, than at the federal level – although the picture across Switzerland is extremely varied. In Graubünden, for example, voters follow the recommendations of the authorities in 88% of all ballots, but in Fribourg the figure is only 60%. The largest general difference between the national and cantonal levels relates to the success rate for popular initiatives. At the national level, only 9% of all popular initiatives have been successful, whereas the proportion in the cantons is 23%. Citizens' initiatives are especially successful in Western Switzerland and Ticino, where 40% of initiatives have been accepted. In these parts of Switzerland, where the use of direct democracy is below average, the authorities appear to have the hardest time. The differences are even greater at the communal level, where the results suggest that the more chances citizens have of using the tools of direct democracy, the more they will actually use them – not least in order to throw a spoke in the authorities' wheels.

The introduction of direct democracy quite unequivocally represents a democratic progress. The number of issues which can be dealt with publicly is far greater. Public debate allows compromises to be worked out and agreed (for example, by means of indirect or direct counter-proposals). The number of those who can get their voices heard in the political process is far greater. These are all advantages of direct democracy by comparison with purely parliamentary systems – regardless both of one's political point of view and of the likelihood of securing a majority with a particular political stance. This is the necessary insight – drawn from experience – which contains the secret of the land of the contented losers.

Related information [F=Factsheet, S=Survey]
F11 Voting behaviour in initiatives & referendums
F12 Popular initiatives, accepted by people and cantons
F20 The major initiators of popular initiatives & referendums
F21 The main issues of initiatives and referendums at the federal level and in the cantons
S1 All popular votes in Switzerland since 1848
S4 Glossary of direct-democracy terms

The creation of the canton Jura is a victory for a model of social integration through the sharing of power. It shows that there is a democratic alternative to nationalism, which has proven itself incapable of solving the relationship problems with minorities.

Jura:
democracy, not nationalism

The centuries-old Jura conflict, and the creation of the new canton of Jura, illustrate the influence of direct democracy on politics and the state. The history of the separatist movement in the Jura demonstrates that quarrels between minorities and majorities which differ politically and culturally from one another do not need to descend into violence. There is a direct-democratic way of dealing with such problems.

"When it became clear that the vote for founding the canton Jura had been won, the rejoicing knew no bounds. People were dancing in the castle courtyard; they were all embracing each other and kissing each other; car horns sounded a fanfare; musicians wandered through the town with drums and trumpets and all the church bells began to ring."

Schwander, Marcel: Jura. Konfliktstoff für Jahrzehnte
[Jura: Object of Decades-long Strife] (Zurich/Köln 1977)

The Jura conflict began after the former Episcopal principality of Basel was merged with the canton Bern at the Congress of Vienna in 1815. The French-speaking, Catholic population of the Jura formed a minority within the mainly German-speaking, Protestant canton of Bern. For most of its life the conflict remained a smouldering fire, from which flames would occasionally leap up; but it did not spread beyond the region.

It was only after the Second World War that the separatist movement in the Jura became a serious problem for the canton Bern, and ultimately for the whole of Switzerland. The three northern (of the six) Jura districts founded the canton of Jura in 1979 and the three southern Jura districts remained with the canton of Bern. This development became possible after the failure of all attempts to integrate the minority Jura population socially into the canton of Bern, and when separatism was the only solution left. The foundation of the canton of Jura represented a significant victory for the much-maligned separatist movement, which still continues to campaign for a unified Jura.

The Jura conflict was never, nor is it today, the problem of a minority, but rather a problem of social relations between a more powerful majority and a weaker minority. It is a typical conflict of 20th century and present-day Europe, but in the case of the Jura, the descent into violence was avoided, not least thanks to direct democracy. The creation of the canton Jura is thus also a victory for a model of social integration through the sharing of power, a model which has a long and successful pedigree in Switzerland. It shows that there is a democratic alternative to nationalism, which has proven itself incapable of solving the relationship problems with minorities.

THE FAILURE OF REGIONAL INTEGRATION

The five Jura protest movements which arose between 1815 and the Second World War were all short-lived. They were unable to mobilise sufficient support because other conflicts took precedence. Despite this, there did emerge a minority awareness in the Jura and a number of associations were formed which fostered and transmitted this awareness. It was out of this tradition of protest that the separatist movement came into being.

According to the separatists, the people of the Jura were experiencing discrimination as a result of their dependence on the canton of Bern and therefore separation was the solution. After the Second World War, the economic marginalisation of the Jura region added significant credibility to this interpretation.

The Jura protest movement really came to life in the post-war period after the Moeckli affair in 1947 (Georges Moeckli was a politician from the Jura, whose appointment to run one of the ministries was blocked by the Bernese parliament solely on the grounds that his mother-tongue was French). Those who wanted autonomy for the Jura while remaining within the canton Bern joined the Comité de Moutier. The Mouvement Séparatiste Jurassien (renamed the Rassemblement Jurassien in 1951) represented those who were campaigning for complete separation from Bern.

Bern rejected a federalisation of the canton, but did make concessions to the demands for autonomy from the Jura. These included constitutional recognition of the separate identity of the people of the Jura, confirmed in a cantonal referendum in 1950. In this initial phase, the conflict between Bern and the Jura was perceived publicly as a regional problem and the separatists were excluded from official negotiations, separation being completely unacceptable to Bern.

Direct democracy makes up for the deficiencies of representation

In September 1957, the Rassemblement Jurassien (RJ) launched a cantonal initiative to ascertain what the people of the Jura thought about the idea of creating a separate canton Jura. The initiative proposal asked: "Do you want the Jura to be given the status of a sovereign canton of the Confederation?" The initiative allowed the separatists to move their campaign on to the political stage and force the media to report it and comment on it. The separatists and their political platform could no longer be ignored. The numerous media reports dealing with the background of the movement focused a great deal of public attention on the RJ, and its existence as a significant player in the Jura issue had to be acknowledged ("The movement is strong and widespread", the Neue Zürcher Zeitung, 15.7.1957).

When the initiative finally went to referendum ballot in July 1959, it was approved by a clear majority only in the three French-speaking, Catholic districts of the North Jura, whereas the three French-speaking, but majority Protestant, districts of the South Jura and the German-speaking, Catholic Laufental remained loyal to Bern. The newspaper headlines declared the death of separatism: "The RJ dream is over!" (Basler Nachrichten, 6.7.1959); "Separatism condemned to die" (Tagwacht, 6.7.1959).

But instead of obliging their critics and falling into their own graves, the separatists changed their tactics and their arguments. In future, they would speak of the unity, not of the whole Jura region, but only of the French-speaking areas and they would abandon the idea that geography and a shared history constituted the basis of their Jura identity and instead emphasize ethnic origin and the French language.

The separatists' "nation" based on language and ethnicity is a pre-political "natural community" which is in stark contrast with the idea of the Swiss nation as a political community. The fear was expressed publicly that the separatists' nationalism would undermine the idea of Switzerland as a nation based not on a common ethnicity or language, but forged out of an active will to unite despite differences ("Willensnation Schweiz"). The separatists sought support for their vision both at home and abroad, discovering a powerful ally in General de Gaulle and his vision of a "Europe des patries".

"No place for violence in politics"

The separatists fed the public with protest actions cleverly staged for maximum media effect and became the main focus of opposition to Bern, which failed in the attempt to silence the separatist cause by sidelining it. Between 1962 and 1964, a small separatist group calling itself the Jura Liberation Front (FLJ) carried out a number of bomb and arson attacks on army barracks and the houses of prominent anti-separatists. But these actions of a few militants actually created less public furore than the "Les Rangiers affair", when – at an event commemorating the Swiss army – the separatists prevented Bernese government minister Virgile Moine and federal government minister Paul Chaudet from speaking.

The scandal created by this protest had a long-lasting effect and marked the turning-point in the public perception of the Jura conflict. Where physical violence had failed (because it cuts off dialogue), symbolic violence succeeded. It challenged the national self-understanding of a now rattled Switzerland and transformed the Jura conflict from a regional issue into a national one. Although it is true that Switzerland's prevailing national self-understanding was deeply challenged by the separatist movement, the fact is that the movement was not engaged in a struggle against the Swiss state. It was not campaigning for secession and did not want to say goodbye to Switzerland, but only to the canton of Bern. In their opinion, the separatists were arguing for a better Switzerland than their opponents. That they had renounced violence as a means of achieving their aims also showed that they did not wish to cut themselves off entirely from the common ground of politics. As Roger Schaffter, leader of the separatist movement along with the charismatic Roland Béguelin, stated: "Violence is not a legitimate tool of politics in Switzerland."

The creation of the new canton did not occur in a single step; it proceeded through several stages and was by no means a foregone conclusion. Once it was realised that separatism as such could not be defeated, there was a greater willingness to ask the people of the Jura region what they thought about a possible separation from Bern. The first stage was to create the legal basis for such a move. The cantonal parliament ("Grosser Rat") of Bern drew up a supplementary article to the Bernese cantonal constitution which provided for both a referendum procedure ("Volksbefragung") and a direct democratic separation process. The amendment to the constitution was accepted in a cantonal popular vote on 1st March 1970, paving the way for self-determination for the Jura.

The referendum of 23rd June 1974

The next stage saw the government in Bern deciding to ask the people of the Jura to vote on the question of separation in a referendum. The question put before them was: "Do you wish to form a new canton?" The popular vote took place on 23rd June 1974. To the surprise of many, the separatists won the vote with 36,802 votes in favour to 34,057 against, in a turnout of 88.7%.

In line with the constitutional amendment of 1970, initiatives in favour of remaining in the canton of Bern were now submitted, first in the districts of South Jura and Laufental, subsequently also in a number of communities along the proposed new cantonal border. The results of the popular votes which took place in March and September of 1975 were as expected: the South Jura districts of Courtelary, Moutier and Neuenstadt voted for Bern. There followed referendums in 13 border communities: 5 majority Protestant districts voted to remain with Bern, but 8 majority Catholic districts opted for the Jura. Laufental initially decided in favour of Bern, but subsequently opted to join Basel Country.

The Jura was now officially split. Voters in the new canton approved a new constitution. After that it was the turn of voters throughout Switzerland to cast their votes. In his New Year address, Swiss federal president Willy Ritschard appealed to his fellow citizens: "On 24th September, a region will be asking the Swiss people for the right to become a separate canton. We want to show that we know how to act as democrats. Democrats respect minorities. They resolve their conflicts in a peaceful and sensible way. I ask you all to give a joyous 'Yes' to the new canton." When it came to the popular vote, all the cantons and a large majority of Swiss voters approved the accession of the new canton to the Confederation.

The history of the separatist movement in the Jura demonstrates that the relationship problems of cultural minorities do not need to descend into violence and that there is a democratic way of dealing with such problems. With the help of direct democracy, the separatists were able to generate a public debate on their political platform and thus compensate for their lack of representation. This directly lessened the likelihood of violence, because it is a well-known fact that it is the lack of a voice and the lack of representation which can easily lead minorities to resort to violence. It was a combination of direct democracy and federalism which made possible the creation of the new canton.

Saying "No" to nationalism

The founding of the Republic and canton Jura, on the one hand, was a great success for the separatist movement, which possessed those attributes which are essential for the effective use of direct democracy: a clearly-defined cause and the ability to fight for it, to organize and to communicate. On the other hand it was a rejection of the separatists' nationalism and a victory instead for the principles of democracy and federalism.

Bern had not only recognised the existence of a people of the Jura and a claim to self-determination, but in its constitutional amendment of 1970 had even set out the conditions under which a process of separation might take place: "The right to demand a referendum ('Volksbefragung') or to take part in it belongs to those citizens who are entitled to vote on cantonal matters and who have their place of residence in a community situated within the area in which the referendum is carried out (…)." This formulation defines the people of the Jura, with their right to self-determination, not as an ethnic community or "ethnos", as the separatists had claimed, but as citizens of a state society or "demos". According to the separatists, this definition of the people violated the fundamental principles of national self-determination.

Within the context of a popular vote on the separation of the Jura from Bern, the answer to the question: "Who belongs to the Jura people?" was, of course, important. The expectation was that the separatists' chances would be increased by a nationalistic definition of the people, and reduced by a democratic one.

On the other hand, we know from experience that the use of nationalistic concepts to divide the population into "natural communities" and grant to each of these peoples its own territory and its own state does not solve the relationship problems of minorities, but rather tends to perpetuate them by creating and excluding new minorities. The greater the fantasy content of these concepts, i.e. the more "ethnically" mixed a population in reality is, the greater will be the amount of force and violence needed to implement them. The break-up of the former Yugoslavia shows to what this can lead.

It makes a decisive difference what sources nourish the we-feeling of a state society, whether people derive their sense of belonging from active participation in the political decision-making (which allows them to say "We in Switzerland"), or from a belief in a given, pre-political nation (which makes them say "We Swiss"), whose existence must be secured by a continual separation of all that is "one's own" from all that is "foreign".

The existence of Switzerland is fundamentally based on a mixture of unity and diversity. Many factors have contributed to ensuring the success – so far – of this unity in diversity. One of those factors is certainly the policy of the sharing of power, which relies on the institutions and procedures of federalism and of direct democracy. It was these procedures, and not separatist nationalism, which made possible the peaceful separation of the Jura from Bern a quarter of a century ago.

RELATED INFORMATION [F=FACTSHEET, S=SURVEY]
F14 Results of popular consultations in the Jura region
F15 Chronology of the Jura conflict (1815-2004)
S1 All popular votes in Switzerland since 1848
S4 Glossary of direct-democracy terms

Direct democracy is currently experiencing a new surge in popularity in Europe. Once again, it is being resisted on the same old grounds by those in power. Ordinary citizens are supposedly incapable of making decisions on complex political issues.

The myth of the incompetent citizen

In a direct democracy the division of political rights is different from that in a purely representative democracy. The exercise of direct democratic rights changes the relationship between politicians and citizens. It influences the political character and habits of both groups. The track record of direct democracy shows that voters can take political decisions as competently as members of parliament can. Political incompetence is not a cause, but an effect, of the fact that in purely representative democracies citizens are not allowed to participate directly in political decision-making on substantive issues.

In 1851 the Zurich radical, Johann Jakob Treichler, presented in his newspaper a critique of liberal "representative democracy" and in a 19-point programme demanded a transition to a "pure democracy" i.e. by supplementing representative democracy with direct democracy. "What the 'Volksblatt' [Treichler's paper] wants," he wrote, "is the greatest possible happiness of the people through the people themselves, the full and entire rule by the people; the first principle must be: Everything for, everything through the people."

At the suggestion of Alfred Escher, Escher's colleague Jakob Dubs composed a response to Treichler's critique which was published in the "Der Landbote" (Winterthur). As representatives of the liberal establishment, Dubs and Escher were no friends of direct democracy. They shared the view of those liberals who held that people without property or formal education were incapable of making use of extended political rights. In this view these people simply lacked everything which the exercise of political governance required: a sense of responsibility (which only those with property and wealth acquire), a knowledge of justice and laws, far-sightedness, a sense of the common good, education, culture and sound judgement.

The image of the uneducated, disinterested and politically immature people, driven by its passions and not guided by the cool light of reason, has accompanied and held back the growth of democracy since its beginnings. Again and again, the image of the politically incompetent ordinary citizen has been used by the powerful and their allies to resist demands for greater democracy. But though the forward march of democracy was slowed, it could not be halted.

Direct democracy is currently experiencing a new surge in popularity in Europe. Once again, it is being resisted on the same old grounds by those in power. Ordinary citizens are supposedly incapable of making decisions on complex political issues. Not infrequently, Switzerland is held up as an example of the dangers of too much "popular vote democracy."

Politics for the people, not with the people
In the mid-19th century, Dubs was already expressing the fear that direct involvement of the people in the making of laws would lead to a flood of bad laws characterized by the selfish interests and the narrow horizons of the common citizen. "Let those who wish drink from this magic beaker of the democratic programme; we are not able to do it; it is in any case not the kind of democracy in which we believe; not the kind of freedom we revere; and least of all is it that true, free humanity to which the future belongs."

Although the Liberals had come to power through the people, they wanted to govern only for the people, and not with it. In their view, ordinary people were immature and incapable of direct participation in political decision-making. From the very beginning, this argument served as a justification for a purely parliamentary democracy. It remained effective in Switzerland until the 1860s; elsewhere it is still being used.

At the dawn of the 21st century, there is a demand for direct democracy to be introduced, not only at the level of the individual nation-state, but also at the European level. There are currently, for example, lively debates in many European countries about the possibility of an europeanwide referendum on a future EU-constitution, and in these debates popular participation is frequently contested with the same arguments which the defenders of purely representative democracy have always used.

For example, Göran Djupsund, professor of political science in Turku (Finland), wrote "that direct democracy does not always produce (…) good results. We can imagine a situation in which there is a popular vote to decide on issues which have hurt the people. The results of public opinion polls would lead one to expect the reintroduction of the death penalty, a reduction in the number of asylum seekers being admitted, and a drastic cut in fuel duties. One might also expect an explosive expansion of the public sector (…) while parts of it would be shrunk to nothing, for example, museum activities, city orchestras and opera houses." Today's debates appear as variations and reformulations in a long and repetitive cycle of the same arguments for and against participative democracy. The faith in the ability of all people to reach sound political judgements is opposed by the contention that this faith is naïve and unrealistic.

In the 19th and 20th centuries, the incompetence argument was used also against democracy and against the extension of the male franchise as well as against equal political rights for women. The general right to elect representatives and equality of political rights for women can now no longer be put in question. But old ideas and arguments continue to be effective in the case of the general right to vote on issues – or direct democracy.

The argument of incompetence can be sustained only by those who ignore the evidence which contradicts it. If it were true, the stable direct democracy which has been alive in Switzerland for more than 100 years could not exist, because a referendum democracy should be self-destructive, it would – according to Giovanni Sartori's prediction – have come to a rapid and catastrophic end on the reefs of cognitive incapacity.

The technological and educational pre-conditions for democracy have probably never before been as well satisfied as they are today. There are no reasonable grounds for maintaining that one category of people (politicians or the political elite) is better equipped to decide public affairs than the other (the so-called "ordinary citizens"). Despite this, the idea persists: not only does it explain nothing, it is itself in need of explanation.

Parliamentary and direct democracy

Citizens and politicians in a parliamentary democracy do not have access to the same political tools, nor do they fulfil the same roles, as in a modern direct democracy. The relationship between politicians and citizens is different in the two systems. For both politicians and citizens the freedom to act politically and the opportunities to learn how to play the political game and to become good players vary in the two systems. To exercise politics contributes to the shaping of personality. However, parliamentary democracy shapes the personality of politicians and citizens in a different way than direct democracy does. For a better understanding of these differences the political organisation of democracy and the relationship between politicians and citizens can be usefully seen in terms of relations between those who are established and those who are outsiders.

The specific dynamic of such relations derives from the way in which two groups, the established and the outsiders, are in fact inter-related and mutually dependent on each other. Established-outsiders relations can be observed not only between politicians and citizens but everywhere and at all times, for example between groups categorized as men and women, blacks and whites, national citizens and foreigners, settled and newcomers.

Though there are many differences, certain regularities can be observed in all the various manifestations. The established groups always seek to monopolise the opportunities for power and status which are important to them. There is a typical tendency to stigmatise (and counter-stigmatise in return): i.e. the more powerful groups tend to perceive the outsiders who are dependent on them as of lesser worth than they themselves are – and to treat them accordingly. Cause and effect are routinely confused.

At the heart of every established-outsiders relationship is, according to Norbert Elias, an imbalance of power, with its resultant social tensions. This is the decisive factor which allows an established group to stigmatise an outsider group. The freedom to stigmatise persists as long as the established retain the monopoly of power. As soon as the balance of power shifts towards the outsiders, the established group's freedom to stigmatise begins to be lost.

Monopolising substantive decisions

It is evident that established politicians form a group which can profit from its superior position of power. The collective images they have of themselves and of others can produce different results. They can be used to justify the status quo. They enhance the self-esteem of those who see themselves as the "elite" and lower the self-esteem of the so-called "ordinary citizens" who are classified as not belonging to the charmed circle of the "elite."

In a purely parliamentary democracy, the politicians enjoy a monopoly over a series of important sources of power – above all, the right to make decisions on substantive issues and to determine the political agenda. It is their exclusive access to these sources of power which provides the basis for the imbalance of power between the politicians and the citizens. Their relationship is one of institutionalised categorical inequality. It determines the practical division of roles: citizens elect and politicians decide. It even affects the use of language, as an example from Finland shows: in Finnish, the words for "citizen" (kansalainen) and "decision-maker" (päättäjä) describe two mutually exclusive categories of people.

The image of the politically incompetent citizen can be understood as an expression of the superior power of politicians over "ordinary citizens". In a purely parliamentary democracy, the individual citizen's access to political decisions is not really denied because of his/her individual lack of political skills and competence, but because he/she belongs to that group of people who are categorized as ordinary citizens. The question, whether in reality citizens are politically competent or not, does not matter in this context. The important question is: under what conditions do politicians feel the need and are able to represent and treat citizens as incompetent outsiders?

What the Swiss writer Iris von Roten wrote about the relationship between men and women before equal political rights were established can be seen as applying equally to the relationship between citizens and politicians in a parliamentary democracy, and therefore as an answer to that question: "Without equal political rights for both sexes, men are held to be more important than women, are able – at the expense of women – to enjoy more of worldly life, and naturally wish to continue to be and to get more. For regardless of whether we are talking of power, influence, freedom, wealth and possessions, self-confidence, prestige and comfort – however much control is handed over to women must represent an equivalent loss to men. And men want to avoid that at all costs."

In a direct democracy, citizens and politicians are inter-connected and interdependent in a fundamentally different way than in a purely parliamentary democracy. In a direct democracy, citizens share in decision-making and often have the final word. They repeatedly have opportunities to act in effect as politicians and to become what Max Weber called "occasional politicians". Thanks to their rights to initiative and referendum, voters have access to political decision-making and to determining the political agenda. The elected politicians are unable to monopolise the power to make political decisions, but have to share it with the citizens. The concentration of political capital or political sources of power in the hands of a small minority of established politicians is thus severely restricted.

In turn, the more even balance of power affects the way politicians and citizens are viewed. The old image of the incompetent citizen fades into the past and is replaced by an image of the citizen as someone who is more mature, more responsible, more politically competent and more self-confident. At the same time the image of the politicians also changes; from nobler spheres they are brought down to share the same earthly reality with everyone else. Politicians will experience this change probably not only as a loss of power and status but as a gain in empathy and humanity as well.

In the Swiss system of direct democracy, the institutionalised relationship between citizens and politicians is different from that in parliamentary democracies. The absence of the categorical inequality referred to earlier also comes to expression in the language. The concept of the "citizen" very much includes the idea of the right to direct involvement in political decisions. Citizens and legislators cannot be seen as two opposing principles – for it is the citizens who are the sovereign power.

"LEARNING BY DOING"

It is common knowledge that we learn by doing. The skills required to be a legislator are best learned by being involved in the legislative process. The referendum and initiative procedures in a direct democracy make it easier to do this here than in a representative democracy, where the lack of suitable procedures prevents people from developing the sort of political skills they need as legislators.

Matthias Benz and Alois Stutzer, two political scientists at the University of Zurich, have shown that citizens who have greater rights of participation are also better informed politically. The referendum and initiative rights enjoyed by Swiss citizens give them a decision-making power which is independent of government and which allows them not only to object and resist but to participate constructively in the shaping of state and society, and overcome log-jams in the representative system. Direct-democratic procedures empower voters and serve (together with federalism and proportional representation) as mechanisms of power-sharing. This is especially important for those minorities whose interests are represented either inadequately or not at all through the representative organs i.e. government and parliament.

To be sure, citizens have to organise themselves and work together if they want to achieve something. They can, for example, launch an initiative. In doing so, they develop their self-organisational skills and learn how to run a referendum campaign, with everything which that involves: getting resources (financial, human and physical), information, publicity, public debates, dissent, forming alliances, reaching compromises, collective learning, dealing with political power, winning and losing and much more. Direct democracy means hard political work and people can get involved in a variety of different ways and with whatever level of commitment they wish to give to it.

Direct democracy gives citizens additional possibilities of making proposals and of political control, independently of the wishes of government and parliament. It is thus better equipped to ensure that "lies are exposed and contracts adhered to, favouritism prevented and emergencies met". This builds up mutual trust between citizens and helps to strengthen social cohesion. In short, direct democracy is also an institutionalised way of creating political trust between citizens. It belongs among those basic institutions whose vital "reinforcement and defence" remains, according to Claus Offe, a "challenge to democracy and the precondition for its continued existence".

Related information [F=Factsheet, S=Survey]
F13 Bandwidths of indirect and direct democracy
S1 All popular votes in Switzerland since 1848
S4 Glossary of direct-democracy terms

Direct democracy has important implications for the behaviour of the media. Referendum campaigns differ from elections in that a much larger number of interested parties are trying to get across their point of view. Instead of presenting the various electoral manifestos, they are focused on putting forward specific proposals for resolving specific problems.

8

Out loud

When the daily papers make lots more space available for readers' letters, when the volume of conversation rises steadily in restaurants, when complete strangers suddenly start talking to each other in trains and buses — and when, finally, the official "voters' booklet" lands in the letter box — then you know that the country is once again heading for a referendum.

Hair-stylist Andrea G. is always happy when she finds the referendum booklet from the government in her letterbox: "That means there's going to be another referendum," says the 27-year-old from Bern. She gets as much information as she can on all the referendum issues from all the available media and regularly arranges special referendum dinners. "We always meet in a larger group before every vote to discuss the forthcoming referendum questions. I don't feel that I can come to a clear decision for myself until I have checked my views against everyone else's."

Andrea G. is not an exception. In surveys of Swiss citizens conducted by the University of Bern, 60% of those asked described themselves as "well informed" politically. That doesn't mean that everyone always goes to vote; but the confidence in being well informed reflects the degree to which every citizen is taken seriously by the institutions of state in Swiss democracy. It is clear that this is more likely to happen in a democracy which has been strengthened by the addition of instruments of direct democracy than in one in which the citizens' involvement is limited to voting in parliamentary elections: in Austria, for example, only around 30% of citizens consider themselves to be "well informed".

The ancient Greeks already knew of this difference. Writing 2,500 years ago, Pericles observed: "In a democracy, public debate does not serve as a brake on politics, but is rather the indispensable prerequisite for all wise decisions." Even in this Internet age, face-to-face debate with friends and acquaintances remains the most important source of information: in a recent survey in Switzerland, 24% named this as their primary source. The media in general were placed only second in importance – by 22% of those asked. After that came the recommendations of the political parties and, lowest of all, the official "referendum booklet", in which both the authorities (at the federal level, the parliament and government) and the initiative and referendum committees are able to present their main arguments.

The referendum booklet is the only source of information which is guaranteed to reach every voter before a referendum. This is not surprising, since in the majority of cantons the modest little booklet is mailed out to all registered voters, together with the voting slips and the certificate of entitlement to vote, three to four weeks before every referendum ballot. In addition to the federal booklet, more than 5 million copies of which are printed in four different languages (Italian, French, German and Rhaeto-Romanic), there are often cantonal and communal referendum booklets, which might contain the regional or local authorities' annual budget proposals or the design sketches for a new local hospital.

The history of the referendum booklet – officially known as the "Government's Explanations" – goes back to the 19th-century official "proclamations" by the authorities before referendums on a complete revision of the constitution. But it took another 100 years for the referendum booklet to become a firm and statutorily guaranteed institution. It was in 1972 that the government first decided to summarise and explain to non-specialists the text of a 1,500-page free trade agreement.

The right to oppose

For the first two decades in the life of this new medium of information, it was the government which summarised the arguments both for and against a proposal. In practice since 1983, and in law since 1994, initiative and referendum committees have been able to draft their own arguments and have them included in the booklet. The government can intervene only if the text is defamatory or too long. There is, however, no equivalent right to object to the government's arguments – whether or not they are defamatory, untrue or too long! Fortunately, crass errors – such as that which occurred in 1993, when, in the run-up to a national referendum vote on which canton the Laufental should belong to, the government got the borders between France, Germany and Switzerland wrong – are rare.

The practice of direct democracy presents not only a didactic challenge for government, but also tests the ability of politicians to communicate successfully and persuade voters to agree with them. In the run-up to referendum votes, the elected representatives often form themselves into cross-party committees, write newspaper articles and appear as panel members in public debates on the referendum issues. The political parties organise public debates in restaurants and sports centres. The print and electronic media go out of their way to shed light on the most varied aspects of the referendum proposals in as professional, open and balanced a way as possible – not least for quite selfish reasons, since they want to hold on to their customer base, whatever the outcome of the vote.

Well-informed citizens

The public broadcasting stations are in a rather special position as regards their reporting of referendums: unlike in the private media, the chief editors of the three national radio and TV stations make no specific recommendations. Although there is no advertising at all on public radio, TV is partially financed by advertising. But in Switzerland – in contrast to the USA, for example – political adverts are banned. In their dealings with initiatives and referendums, the public broadcast media follow an internally devised code of conduct – the "handbook of journalism" – which is designed to ensure accuracy, impartiality and fairness.

Direct democracy has important implications for the behaviour of the media. Referendum campaigns differ from elections in that a much larger number of interested parties are trying to get across their point of view. Instead of presenting the various electoral manifestos, they are focused on putting forward specific proposals for resolving specific problems. Citizens' expectations also differ: whereas after elections the concern is only to ensure that electoral promises are kept, after referendum votes citizens expect approved measures to be incorporated into law and fully implemented.

In a modern direct democracy there are far greater incentives, for both providers and users of information, to communicate and/or take it up. Everyone benefits, everyone's knowledge and skill are increased. The result is that the average Swiss voter is better and more comprehensively informed when he or she comes to vote on an issue than the average German member of parliament, who is after all paid to do the job – a rather sobering finding for all those who routinely assert the technical superiority of a purely parliamentary democracy over a direct democracy. In short, in a modern direct democracy there is not only a greater demand for political information, but a far richer and more competently provided supply. When we compare the various forms of media, we find that the editorial sections of the print press are of primary importance as a source of information for the individual voter. After that come the referendum booklet and the electronic media. Readers' letters are surprisingly highly rated: a survey by political scientist Hanspeter Kriesi found that around 25% of voters view them as an important source of information. The role of the political parties should also not be underestimated: the parties' voting recommendations are significant for about 12% of all voters. What is clear is that citizens are not influenced by a single source, but make use of information coming from a variety of media, political and other sources in reaching their decisions.

The wooing of the Swiss abroad

Increasing efforts are being made by the authorities, the media and the political parties to include registered Swiss voters abroad in the process of opinion-forming before elections and referendum votes. About a fifth of the roughly 450,000 Swiss citizens living abroad who are entitled to vote take advantage of the option of postal voting. Swiss voters abroad repeatedly play a decisive role in certain highly contested issues. In addition to the referendum booklet, they have access to special foreign editions of the major daily newspapers, are sent free tape recordings or CDs of radio debates and can also view special Web pages devoted to the referendums. If they wish, expatriate Swiss can have a special mailing and SMS alerts sent to them before a vote, giving them information on the current referendum debate and advising them of forthcoming voting days. In the last parliamentary elections in October 2003, a number of parties produced for the very first time separate lists of Swiss voters abroad.

In debates on the options for the expansion or improvement of democracy, people regularly point to the absence of the necessary preconditions: the voters are supposedly ill-equipped, the media too superficial, the political class averse to or incapable of discussing issues with citizens on an equal footing. The Swiss example shows that the relationship between those preconditions and the growth of democracy is not a one-way street: an increase in democracy can improve the preconditions for democracy. The tools and the practice of direct democracy can help to increase the knowledge and skill levels of the voters, promote the need for high-quality, informative media and force politicians and political parties to take voters seriously all the time, and not just before elections. The connection between the development of democracy and the preconditions for democracy is especially important for highly complex, multilingual communities such as the European Union.

The Swiss experience also shows that not every citizen is equally engaged in the political decision-forming process. Political scientist Claude Longchamp from Bern distinguishes five different types of citizens: the isolated ones, who are completely cut off; the passive consumers of the mass media; the debaters, who also get involved in public discussion; the "media multiplicators", who are actively engaged in making up their own minds; and the "agenda setters", who also generate issues. Newspapers, radio and TV – all of them play an important role in Swiss direct democracy. But not even the best media productions are sufficient by themselves: what is of greatest importance is open debate and the face-to-face sharing of views between citizens. In the run-up to the referendum vote – the decisive phase in every initiative and referendum process – such crucial meetings take place at special referendum dinners, around the kitchen table, in the workplace, on the train, in cafés and restaurants. Many Swiss know that they will be able to decide what they themselves think only once they have also listened to what others think – out loud.

RELATED INFORMATION [F=FACTSHEET, S=SURVEY]
F6   Postal voting
F29 Voting rights of Swiss citizens living or staying abroad
S1   All popular votes in Switzerland since 1848
S4   Glossary of direct-democracy terms

In the debate on the potential and the limitations of direct democracy, it is often argued that the general public is incapable of balancing (short-term) costs against (longer-term) benefits when it comes to public finances. Swiss experience contradicts this contention.

Added-value voting

For years, direct democracy was accused of putting a brake on economic progress. We now know that initiatives and referendums promote economic growth, strengthen society, and so help to make people happier. A system in which citizens have a direct influence on the making of major decisions produces much more pragmatic and cost-efficient results than a purely parliamentary democracy where powerful groups may realize their particular interests more easily, and at the cost of the general public.

The Swiss were amazed when, in the summer of 2002, economiesuisse, the umbrella organisation for Swiss business, produced a position paper on public finance in which this most influential body stated clearly and simply: "Direct democracy should be promoted at all levels of the state." The amazement came from the fact that leading industry spokespersons and financial experts had until then consistently claimed that the wide-ranging rights of participation enjoyed by Swiss citizens stifled innovation and damaged the economy. At the close of the 20th century, Walter Wittman, Professor of Economics at Fribourg University, had written that "Switzerland must abandon its direct democracy and turn to parliamentary democracy, just like other countries". If it failed to do so, "direct democracy in general, and the referendum in particular, will ruin the Swiss economy".

There were repeated calls during the 1990s for Switzerland to "get real" about its direct democracy: i.e. to restrict participatory rights by, for example, raising the signature quorum for initiatives and optional referendums and excluding certain issues – such as public finances – from being put to referendum. A significant number of leading figures in the economy had allied themselves to this position after what they had seen as referendum "defeats" in the 1992 decision not to join the EEC and the rejection of liberalised employment law. The then head of the major bank Credit Suisse, Lukas Mühlemann, had demanded as late as 2001 "a restriction of direct-democratic rights". Less than a year later, it appeared that business leaders – under the mantle of economiesuisse – had changed their minds and now believed that the tools of direct democracy were worthy of support because they actually benefited the economy. What had caused this volte-face?

At the end of the 1990s, the routine criticism of direct democracy coming from both academic and business circles had inspired a series of leading academics to have a closer, more empirical, look at the links between direct democracy and economic growth. These academics were able to examine evidence from the USA, where initiatives and referendums have been enthusiastically used for around 100 years in many of the individual states, but they found in Switzerland itself an ideal source of data for comparative research – ideal, because there are significant differences between the various cantons and communities in the way that direct democracy is instituted and practised, i.e. in its relative user-friendliness. Thus, every canton except Vaud uses the finance referendum, which requires all decisions on public spending, loans and other expenditure to be submitted to either obligatory or optional referendum. Some of the other important variables are the signature quorums for popular initiatives and referendums – which vary between 0.9% (in Basel Country) and 5.7% (in Neuchâtel) of the total electorate – and the length of time allowed to the initiative committees for the collection of signatures, ranging from 2 months in Ticino to an unlimited period of time in Basel Country. The range of variability in the possibilities for direct-democratic participation is even greater at the local (communal) level – between extensive participatory rights and virtually none at all.

Cheaper, more honest, better off

A study by Zurich University economists Bruno Frey and Alois Stutzer showed that the cantons of Aargau, Basel Country, Glarus, Zurich and the two Appenzell cantons are among the most democratic in Switzerland. In 2003, Geneva-based lawyers Michael Bützer and Sébastien Micotti produced a comparative study of direct democracy at the local (communal) level. It concluded that communities in eastern and central Switzerland enjoy considerably greater institutional autonomy than those in western Switzerland and Ticino.

Including earlier research in their investigation, St. Gallen economists Gebhard Kirchgässner and Lars Feld – now a professor at Marburg University in Germany – made a statistical analysis of the influence of direct democracy on economic growth. The results were striking:

1. In cantons with stronger rights of participation on financial issues, economic performance is 15% higher (in terms of GDP per head).

2. In cantons where citizens can vote on the budget, there is 30% less tax-avoidance – on average 1,500 Swiss francs per taxpayer. Cantonal debt is correspondingly lower. The possible explanation: people are more prepared to support public expenditure when they are involved in deciding how their money is spent.

3. In communities where the budget has to be approved by referendum, public expenditure is 10% lower per head than in places where residents have no such rights. It appears that citizens are more careful with the money taken from them in taxes than the politicians are.

4. Communities which have the finance referendum have 25% lower public debt (5,800 Swiss francs per taxpayer) – the direct result of lower expenditure and greater tax income.

5. Public services cost less in towns and cities with direct democracy: refuse disposal is almost 20% cheaper.

Professor Kirchgässner and his colleagues conclude: "In economic terms, everything is in favour of direct democracy – nothing against." They therefore argue that direct democracy should be extended, rather than restricted. In their view, direct democracy is "up-to-date, successful, exportable and has the potential for further development".

The results of public opinion polls support these conclusions. When the Swiss cantons were compared, it was found that the more people were involved directly in politics through initiatives and referendums, the more contented they were with their lives. According to a study by Frey and Stutzer, the degree of political participation was "even more significant than the level of personal income." This rather tends to undermine the common claim that people are primarily interested in earning money.

Citizens in favour of specific tax increases

In the debate on the potential and the limitations of direct democracy, it is often argued – especially outside Switzerland – that the general public is incapable of balancing (short-term) costs against (longer-term) benefits when it comes to public finances. Swiss experience contradicts this contention, not only in the cantons and communities, where people have a closer relationship with political affairs, but even at the federal level.

In a referendum on 7th March 1993, 54.5% of voters approved an increase in the price of petrol and diesel of 21 Swiss cents [about 14 Euro cents] per litre. The main issue in the referendum campaign was not environmental protection, but the need to bolster the public purse. Five years later, more than 57% voted in favour of introducing a distance-related heavy vehicle duty which would increase the cost of transporting goods by road. Again in 1993, two-thirds of voters had agreed to introduce national VAT and to use a future rise to benefit old-age pensions. Similar proposals by both government and parliament between 1977 and 1991 had been rejected, because voters had been asked to approve whole packages of measures rather than specific individual proposals. When the politicians finally came clean and explained to people why there was a need to raise extra money, they were able to secure public approval not only for the change in the system, but also for the tax rise.

The costs of direct democracy have not so far been an issue in cost-conscious Switzerland. That has to do on the one hand with the country's political culture, where active public participation is accepted as a fundamental right, and on the other with the wide-ranging benefits for society (including the economic ones) of direct democracy. As there are referendum votes every three or four months at local, cantonal and federal levels, it would be difficult to assess the cost to the administration of its referendum-related work.

There has been much more debate in recent years over the financing of referendum campaigns. According to political scientist Claude Longchamp, it takes "around 10 million francs" to organise a professional national citizens' initiative from the initial launch through the campaign to tying up all the loose ends after the vote. On the other hand, the example of the "Sunday Initiative" shows that it can be done with considerably less money: though the group campaigning for "four car-free Sundays per year" had no more than 50,000 francs to play with, they still managed to get 37.6% of the votes. The same day saw a vote on putting a stop to Switzerland's nuclear power programme. The environmental organisation campaigning for this had managed to raise 3.5 million francs – but only got 33.7% of the vote. In Longchamp's view, this clearly shows that in Switzerland referendum results cannot be bought. Another example which shows that success and modest financial resources are not mutually exclusive is the initiative on "Life-long custody for non-curable, extremely dangerous sex offenders and violent criminals," which was accepted in the referendum of 8th February 2004.

Money alone is not enough
Even in those cases where wealthy interest groups are involved, there is no evidence that money can directly influence referendum results in Switzerland. Quite the opposite: there are plenty of cases where, despite the spending of large amounts of money, voters went against the majority of the political or financial elites. This was so in the case of the price monitoring initiative of 1982, which was accepted against the wishes of the authorities and the business world. Likewise with the introduction of the heavy goods vehicle duty and the motorway card (an annual fee for using motorways), which had been opposed by such influential and wealthy groups as the Touring Club of Switzerland, the Business Federation and tour operators. EEC accession was rejected in 1993, even though the commercial world had spent millions in promoting it.

In larger political entities with direct-democratic instruments – such as the American state of California (population 35 million) – extensive studies have shown that having greater financial resources is not usually sufficient to win over voters. It can, however, be an effective means of wrecking a proposal.

Political scientist Elisabeth R. Gerber from the University of San Diego found that citizens' groups appeared to do better overall in initiatives and referendums than wealthy interest groups. For example, Californians voted for a ban on smoking in all closed public areas, despite the multi-million dollar campaign waged by the tobacco companies.

From an economic point of view, therefore, there are virtually no arguments against direct democracy. Rather is it the case that a form of politics based on the principle of consensus, in which citizens have a direct influence on the making of decisions on substantive issues, produces much more pragmatic results than the kind of knee-jerk response common in purely parliamentary democracies, where the response is often excessive and has to be undone later at great cost.

Related information [F=Factsheet, S=Survey]
F12 Popular initiatives, accepted by people and cantons
F21 The main issues of initiatives and referendums at the federal level and in the cantons
F27 The economic effects of the use of direct democracy
S2 Direct-democratic procedures and plebiscites in the constitutions of 32 European states
S4 Glossary of direct-democracy terms

In a direct democracy, the constitution and the law clearly define when it is mandatory for the citizens to be consulted, and when they can decide for themselves that they have to be consulted. The quality of the direct-democratic procedures in place is crucially important for the use of direct democracy and for the quality of the decisions reached.

10

Design determines the quality

The quality of direct democracy is determined by the design of the procedures: Who is able to control them? Are they citizen-friendly? What is their scope? More important than the number of popular votes is the way in which they come about. Only a well-designed direct democracy can fulfill its tasks and have the desired effects.

A popular initiative or a referendum is launched every week somewhere in Switzerland. In the Upper Engadine (a county within the canton Graubünden) for example, on 11th November 2003, at 11.11 in the morning, a 27-member initiative committee began the collection of signatures for a district initiative aimed at "limiting the number of second homes being built". At the presentation of the initiative in Samedan, not far from the well-known winter sports resort of St. Moritz, committee member Romedi Arquint explained the reason for the campaign: "We want to put pressure on politicians to finally take the issue seriously." In recent years, numerous financial institutions have invested part of their funds in property in such holiday regions as the Upper Engadine – sparking off not only a building boom, but an above-average increase in the price of land.

This has adversely affected the local people, who hope to reverse the trend through their popular initiative and restrict new building to 100 second homes a year. 800 signatures are required to validate the initiative and there is no fixed time limit for collection. If the required number of signatures can be gathered, the initiative will be placed on the ballot and the voters of the Upper Engadine will be able to decide the issue by popular vote within a year.

Wide diversity of form

Switzerland is a political entity with very marked diversity. This is true especially of direct democracy, both in its practice and also in the way participatory rights are designed. For instance, the number of signatures required to validate an initiative ranges from 0.9% of the registered voters in the canton Aargau, to 5.7% – six times as many– in the canton Neuchâtel. For federal initiatives, around 2% are required. If we look beyond the borders of Switzerland, the range is far greater. In the Free State of Bavaria of the German Federal Republic, for example, a minimum of 10% of the electorate must give their signatures in support of a popular initiative (in Germany called "Volksbegehren", popular demand), and in Saarland the signature threshold is even 20%. It is no surprise, therefore, that with preconditions such as these very few initiatives ever get as far as the ballot box: despite the fact that the right of initiative is inscribed in the constitutions of all 16 federal states of Germany, there have been only 10 popular votes at this level since 1945.

When we come to consider how initiative and referendum rights are formulated, it isn't just a question of the "admission price" (the number of signatures required), but also of the amount of time the initiative group has in which to collect the signatures. In Switzerland, the time allowed for initiatives is generally longer than that for referendums. At the federal level, initiative committees are allowed 18 months to collect the 100,000 signatures required; referendum committees, on the other hand, must speed up to obtain at least 50,000 signatures within 100 days after the publication of the parliamentary bill. At the cantonal level, the requirements vary considerably. In the canton Ticino, initiatives are given two months to collect signatures, whereas referendum requests have to be submitted within 30 days. In the canton Aargau, initiatives have a full 12 months and referendums 90 days. There are no time limits at all for initiatives in the canton Schaffhausen.

Quite different signature collection periods exist in other states. In the Free State of Bavaria, nearly 1 million signatures (10% of the electorate) have to be collected within 14 days – and not just anywhere, but only in state offices. In Austria, anyone wanting to submit an initiative to parliament has only seven days to collect 100,000 signatures (according to §10 of the 1973 law on citizens' initiatives, those wishing to sign can do so only in specified places and at specified times). In Venezuela, the people who wanted to remove the incumbent President Hugo Chavez in 2004 had only four days to obtain the signatures of 20% of the entire electorate. Under such extreme conditions, it is only very rarely – as in the case of Venezuela – that the instrument of initiative and referendum is able to be used.

The design of direct democracy is somewhat more user-friendly in the states of the USA and in Italy. In the United States signature thresholds vary from a high of 15% of qualified voters based on votes cast in the last general election in Wyoming to a low of 2% of the state's resident population in North Dakota; in Italy, 500,000 signatures are enough to secure a national referendum to repeal a law. However, such referendums are valid only if at least 50% of the electorate actually turns out to vote.

An international comparison of citizens' rights also reveals significant differences in their legal consequences. Whereas in Austria a "citizens demand" never leads to a popular vote, the Swiss citizens' initiative always leads to a binding popular vote, provided the initiative committee does not withdraw the initiative.

Protection of minorities and communication
It is clear from Swiss experience that the benefits which can accrue from direct democracy materialise only if the procedures are regularly used in political practice. However, it is also true that under democratic conditions the mere existence of well-designed direct-democratic procedures has a

The quoting of bad experiences with plebiscites, often done in a ritual and repetitive manner, is not a valid argument against direct democracy. On the contrary, the fact that all kinds of dictators have used the plebiscite to justify their use of power ought to be a warning to us that plebiscites can be used to turn democracy into its opposite.

Failing to distinguish between democracy and dictatorship is a fatal error. Good democracy – and especially direct democracy – hardly allows tyrants of Hitler's ilk to flourish. On the contrary: dictatorships and totalitarianism can only flourish where democracy does not exist or has ceased to exist: Germany at the time of Hitler's accession to power is a striking example of this.

The design of direct democracy

In a genuine direct democracy, the constitution and the law clearly define when it is mandatory for the citizens to be consulted, and when they can decide for themselves that they have to be consulted. The quality of the direct-democratic procedures in place is crucially important for the use of direct democracy and for the quality of the decisions reached. When initiative and referendum procedures are being drawn up, a number of factors have to be taken into account:

- **Signature thresholds:** how many voters' signatures are required in order to trigger a citizens' initiative or a referendum?

- **Time allowances:** how much time is allowed for each stage of the process (collection of signatures, government response, parliamentary debate including a possible counter-proposal, referendum campaign)?

- **How the signatures are collected:** can signatures be freely collected (on the street, for example) and thereby generate discussions, or are discussions prevented by restrictive collection rules (e.g. that signatures can be given only in designated official centres)?

- **How well direct democracy is embedded in the overall political system:** what rules exist for the involvement of government and parliament?

- **Majority requirements and minimum turnout quorums:** is there a prescribed minimum "Yes" vote or turnout quorum (as a percentage of the electorate) in addition to the simple majority rule?

- INFORMATION FOR CITIZENS AND PUBLIC DEBATE: are citizens properly, objectively and adequately informed? How is public debate promoted and supported?

- RESTRICTION OF SUBJECT-MATTER: what issues are citizens NOT allowed to decide direct-democratically?

- LEGAL CONSEQUENCES: what are the legal consequences of a valid citizens' initiative (i.e. one which has satisfied the legal requirements)?

- THE PROCESS AS A WHOLE: do the direct-democratic procedures form a coherent whole which cannot be subverted by the authorities, government or parliament?

The number of popular votes has increased significantly in recent decades: during the 1990s, on the national level, there was an increase of around 35% in Switzerland and more than 100% in Europe as a whole. There are even more impressive figures at the local level: in Bavaria alone, more than 1,000 popular votes took place within a ten-year period. Worldwide, more and more people are now able to vote on an increasing number of issues.

After this quantitative breakthrough towards direct democracy since 1989, the future of direct democracy now depends on qualitative improvements, in Switzerland as elsewhere, and there is a need to bid farewell once and for all to all plebiscitary procedures.

GUIDELINES FOR (MORE) DEMOCRACY

In order to get an (even) better design of direct-democratic procedures, the following guidelines would need to be taken into account:

The procedures of direct democracy should be so designed as to encourage, rather than prevent, unimpeded communication at all levels. Setting thresholds for participation (turnout) and approval only encourages those who want to preserve the status quo to avoid communication. It is often easier to prevent supporters of a reform from reaching a quorum by blocking debate and persuading people not to vote than by securing an honest majority in the referendum ballot.

Reflection, discussion, meetings and interactions all need time. So do efforts to reach mutual understanding or compromise between those representing differing interests and organisations. If the necessary time is not granted, the procedures tend to favour the established interests, who generally want to avoid being challenged in any case – quite apart from the fact that without sufficient time it is impossible to strengthen social integration. So the amount of time allowed for each stage of the process should be arranged with these considerations in mind. If only 14 days are allowed for the collection of what is in any case usually too large a number of signatures, then organisations which are not already established and well-organised are scarcely able to make successful use of the direct-democratic instruments designed primarily for them. It would be much more helpful to allow a collection period for signatures of between at least six months and a year.

The same applies to the time allowances and procedures granted to the administration, the organised interests and their associations, the political parties and parliament. Citizens' initiatives in California bypass parliament completely, whereas in Switzerland, once the required number of signatures has been handed in, a very diverse and extensive process of consultation and negotiation begins. If the system is to produce a high quality of discussion, with a genuine attempt to reach an understanding of each other's different positions, then it is vital not to hold the referendum vote too soon, perhaps only six months after the signatures have been handed in. The institutions should be allowed a minimum of a year, perhaps even 18 months. This has nothing to do with stalling or dragging one's heels, it is an effort to take those who launch initiatives seriously and to increase the reasonableness of the system and its procedures as well as the chances of finding an acceptable compromise. Direct democracy is much more than a "fast food", opinion-poll pseudo-democracy based on knee-jerk, emotionalreactions to the concerns of the moment. What people are prepared to accept and be bound by has to be worked out democratically every time anew for each new issue.

Improving and guaranteeing the quality of direct democracy is not an end in itself. Only well-motivated and self-confident citizens, who have had a positive experience of politics at local, regional and national levels, will have the courage and confidence to demand elements of direct-democracy where they are most needed – in relation to the European integration process. It is not only that Europe is in need of more democracy. Democracy itself is today in need of being firmly rooted at the transnational level.

Related information [F=Factsheet, S=Survey]
- **F8** Direct democracy in the cantons
- **F18** Citizens' rights at the federal level in Switzerland
- **F26** Key points for free and fair referendums in Europe
- **F28** Important factors in the shaping of direct-democratic procedures
- **S2** Direct-democratic procedures and plebiscites in the constitutions of 32 European states
- **S3** Global Overview of Direct Democracy in selected regions of the world
- **S4** Glossary of direct-democracy terms

Direct democracy plays a central role in Swiss people's attitude to European integration. Many people consider that citizens' rights would be threatened if Switzerland were to join the EU. Others view accession as a chance to bring direct democracy to the European level, where many of today's political decisions are being made.

The democratisation of democracy

Over the past 150 years, direct democracy in Switzerland has gradually become more mature, and more sophisticated. But there have also been setbacks. Current weaknesses include criticism, both at home and abroad, of how the country deals with immigration and of a lack of political education in schools. And what about the fairness of the political process in Switzerland?

In April 2005, the voters of the canton of Geneva (where 38% of the population are foreigners) decided to give the right to vote, but not the right to be elected, to foreigners who have been residents of the canton for at least 8 years. Geneva thus became the sixth canton to introduce voting rights for foreigners at the communal level, joining the cantons of Neuchâtel, Jura, Appenzell Outer-Rhodes, Vaud and Fribourg. But the six cantons are still the exception: in the past, attempts in numerous Swiss communities and cantons to introduce voting rights for residents who do not hold a Swiss passport had failed to get majority support in the referendum ballots. There is also currently a wide-ranging political and legal debate on what to do with the applications of those foreign residents who wish to acquire Swiss citizenship. One thing is certain: Switzerland is still making heavy weather of the issue of integration at home. Citizens' rights play a central role in this. They are the tools which those who already enjoy full rights of political participation can use to integrate those others who are still partly excluded – or not, as the case may be.

But the instruments of direct democracy are also the means by which direct democracy itself is reformed. Popular initiatives dealing with direct democracy are regularly launched at all levels – local, cantonal and federal – and proposals for the reform of citizens' rights are regularly voted on in referendum ballots. On 9th February 2003, more than 70% of those who voted indicated their support for the so-called "citizens' rights proposal" put forward by government and parliament – a proposal which in the run-up to the vote had been branded a "pseudo-reform" by members of both right and left wings of the political spectrum, and which the Neue Zürcher Zeitung afterwards said was "badly designed", though it conceded that "if it is used sensibly, it probably won't do any harm".

Although reform of direct democracy is one of the issues which turns up most frequently in referendums at the local and regional levels, there is a more cautious approach to reform at the national (federal) level. Nonetheless, there have been a number of important referendums aimed at extending participatory rights over the past few decades. In 1987, for example, both people and cantons voted to introduce the "double yes" for popular initiatives where there is an official counter-proposal. However, a citizens' initiative which went to ballot in 2000 and which aimed at giving citizens the right to present a counter-proposal (the so-called "constructive referendum") was rejected.

There have also been repeated attempts in recent years to dismantle citizens' rights. The government proposed a raising of the signature quorums for initiatives and referendums, and initiative committees demanded a shortening of the time allowed to the authorities to process initiatives. Although the proposal to cut the time allowances suffered a clear defeat at the ballot box, the plan to increase the signature quorums did not even get through parliament. Although the signature quorum remained the same, it has not become any easier to collect the 100,000 signatures required for a national citizens' initiative. Quite the opposite: it has actually become harder. Hans-Urs Wili, civil rights expert at the Federal Chancellery, is convinced that "the trend towards more postal voting has adversely affected the traditional collection of signatures outside the voting centres". This perhaps explains why as of January 2004 there were only 6 popular initiatives waiting to go to ballot – fewer than at any time since the 1970s.

The Federal Court can intervene

It remains an open question whether the introduction of the "general popular initiative" approved in February 2003, which creates a new form of initiative at the federal level, will significantly affect the practice of direct democracy. The new instrument will come into force in 2007. It will allow those initiative committees which are able to raise the required 100,000 signatures to present a general proposal to parliament. It will then be left to the members of parliament to decide in what form the proposal should be processed – either as legislation or as an amendment to the constitution. A measure of control on the process will be afforded by giving dissatisfied initiative groups the right to present a formal complaint to the Federal Court if they believe that either the content or the purpose of their initiative has been disregarded.

The highest court of the land has intervened in the past when the implementation of direct-democratic rights called into question other fundamental rights embedded in the constitution. In 1991, for example, the Lausanne-based court prohibited the voters of Appenzell Inner-Rhodes from continuing their exclusion of women from the vote. In summer 2003, it made it illegal for decisions on acquiring Swiss citizenship to be made by secret referendum vote – thereby initiating an important public debate on the options and limits of direct democracy. "Granting citizenship is not a political decision, but an administrative act," declared the federal court. It criticised the fact that when decisions on citizenship were made through the ballot box, there was no obligation to provide an explanation. The judges' ruling brought about changes in the handling of citizenship applications throughout Switzerland. Many decisions on citizenship were simply shelved until the matter was finally resolved. In May 2004, the Swiss People's Party (SVP) launched a citizens' initiative to establish a constitutional right to decide by the people which organ shall decide on citizenship. Ultimately, the SVP wants to establish a right to decide on citizenship by popular ballot. The Council of States – the smaller of the two chambers of parliament – wants it to be left to the cantons to decide for themselves how they deal with applications for citizenship.

CITIZENS' RIGHTS – POPULAR, BUT A SOURCE OF CONTENTION

The public debate on the most recent reform of direct democracy has shown that, although most Swiss like their citizens' rights, they are also constantly arguing about them.

For instance, the main reason why the Social Democratic Party (SP) opposed the new general initiative was that the same high threshold of 100,000 signatures was being required as for the binding constitutional initiative. At an earlier stage, when the bill was being drafted, it was thought that 50,000 signatures would be sufficient. The SP announced that it would be proposing measures to reduce the signature quorums for initiatives and referendums.

The SVP, on the other hand, opposed the reform because of the extension of the referendum on international treaties, which the SVP claimed was "too complicated" and represented an "enfeebling of the people." The SVP is also campaigning for the direct popular election of the government and for a national finance referendum.

For the other two parties represented in the government – the Liberal Democratic Party (FDP) and the Christian People's Party (CVP) – the two new instruments signalled "a small, but essential step in the expansion of civil rights" (FDP) and "a logical strengthening of the democratic system" (CVP).

In terms of the modernisation of direct democracy, the government is looking especially at the possibility of using the Internet. The first regular referendum ballot at which e-voting was allowed took place on 14th January 2003 in the small community of Anières in the canton Geneva. In a vote on the renovation of a public building, 44% of voters used the Internet, 46% voted by post – and only 10% went to vote in person. On 26th September 2004 the first e-vote on national referendums took place in the communities of Anières, Cologny, Carouge and Meyrin in the canton Geneva. On 28th November 2004 (8 communes in Geneva), 25th September 2005 (restricted number of voters in Neuchatel) and 27th November 2005 (restricted number of voters in Neuchatel and 3 communes in Zurich) e-voting was used again in national referendums., These e-voting experiences are currently being evaluated by the Federal Council and the Parliament. The cantons and communities of Switzerland also have a tradition of reforming their citizens' rights. The instruments of direct democracy are used even more at the cantonal level than at the national level to increase direct-democratic rights. As Adrian Vatter notes in his "Kantonale Demokratien im Vergleich" ("A Comparison of Democracy in the cantons"), citizens' initiatives aimed at introducing voting rights for foreigners and for reducing the voting age to 18 were particularly common in the cantons. There were also many initiatives which demanded greater public involvement in important decisions on such matters as the building of new roads and nuclear power stations. Most of these initiatives failed to get a majority in the referendum vote.

WHO BELONGS TO "THE PEOPLE"?

This question has always played a central role in the history of Swiss democracy. Before women were finally given the right to vote in national elections and referendums in 1971, men had voted against this long-overdue measure in numerous national and cantonal ballots. Since then, there have been many referendum ballots on voting rights for citizens who are not Swiss nationals and on the means by which foreign residents can acquire Swiss citizenship. Both these cases are a reminder of the contrast between the pre-modern understanding of the right to vote as a privilege, and the modern conception of it as a human right. As with the question of women's voting rights, there are big differences between the cantons on voting rights for foreigners and on naturalisation. The government is proposing a new reform measure whereby all those who were born in Switzerland, but who for various reasons do not yet have a Swiss passport, would be able to vote.

In addition to the battles over the strengthening or dismantling of direct democracy, the question of the fairness of the political process has come more and more to the fore in recent years. Questions are being asked about

- the money, from various sources, used in the direct-democratic process
- the honesty of the arguments used in referendum campaigns
- the role of the government in the whole process

On the first point, there is a debate on whether to make disclosure of all monies spent on referendum campaigns mandatory. As regards the second point, proposals have been put forward for an ombudsman's office which would publicise any clearly false information – but would have no power to impose any legal sanction. And on the third question, a citizens' initiative was launched early in 2003 under the slogan: "People's sovereignty instead of authorities' propaganda."

WHAT ABOUT POLITICAL EDUCATION IN SCHOOLS?

One of the weaknesses in Swiss democracy is the absence of political education in primary and secondary schools. Young people under 16 in Switzerland fall below the average internationally in this respect. They have a very clear idea of democracy, but their knowledge of politics and their willingness to be involved practically in democracy are very weak. These are the findings of a comparative study by the "International Association for the Evaluation of Educational Achievement" (IEA), which questioned 90,000 14- and 15-year olds in 28 countries. For Fribourg University professors Fritz Oser and Horst Biedermann, the sobering analysis points up the widespread lack of political education in Swiss schools. Urgent action would seem to be necessary.

Direct democracy also plays a central role in Swiss people's attitude to European integration. A majority of people consider that citizens' rights would be threatened if Switzerland were to join the EU. A minority view accession as a chance to bring direct democracy to the European level, where many of today's political decisions are being made.

A study by Professor Dietrich Schindler from the University of Zurich found that 3 of the 40 bills and citizens' initiatives subject to mandatory referendum in the first half of the 1990s would have been entirely covered by EU law and 14 popular referendums would have "partially" affected EU law. Overall, Schindler believes that around 10% of the national referendum ballots would have been impossible under EU law (at least in part). The loss of civil rights would have been even less at the cantonal and communal levels. This puts into perspective the claim that European integration would inevitably bring about a wholesale loss of popular rights. Looking into the future, initiatives and referendums are about to play a significant role for the first time in the context of the European integration process: in most countries, any adoption of a new constitutional treaty will depend on securing popular approval. The 2004 constitutional draft includes a right of initiative (on a par with that of the European Parliament).

The development of Swiss citizens' rights shows that the democratisation of democracy is not a one-way street. Sometimes there is progress, sometimes there are setbacks. In UN Secretary-General Kofi Annan's words: "Obstacles to democracy have little to do with culture or religion, and much more to do with the desire of those in power to maintain their positions at any cost."

RELATED INFORMATION [F=FACTSHEET, S=SURVEY]
F6 Postal voting
F7 Electronic voting – the first real practice
F22 Referendum votes on issues relating to foreigners in the Federation
F24 Restrictions on the constitutional initiative in Switzerland
S1 All popular votes in Switzerland since 1848
S4 Glossary of direct-democracy terms

The 21st century will see the part-time democracy of the past replaced by a full democracy, in which citizens will have the right to have their say on substantive issues. This is the only way for representative democracy to become truly representative. Citizens' rights can turn the utopia of yesterday into the reality of tomorrow.

12

Utopia becomes reality

Initiatives and referendums are playing a growing role everywhere. Since 1991, the number of national referendums and plebiscites around the world has doubled. From Norway to Taiwan and from New Zealand to Bermuda, direct democracy is being strengthened at both the national and the local level. And the proposal for an EU Constitution contains a provision for the very first transnational citizens' initiative. An overview.

Jean Jacques Rousseau's idea was as simple as can be imagined: people need laws to govern public life; if everyone is involved in drawing up those laws, then in the final analysis, everyone has to obey only himself/herself. The result: self-regulation instead of the dominance of some over others.

This utopian dream of yesterday is more and more becoming the reality of today. In fact it isn't so long ago that only a minority of the world's population was living in countries with basic democratic rights. In 1980, only 46% of the world's population, in 54 countries, enjoyed the benefits of democracy. Today, more than two-thirds of people – 72%, in 133 countries – belong to the "democratic" world. This process of democratisation applies especially to Europe, where it is now only in Belarus that "democracy" remains a swear word.

In a recent report the United Nations Development Programme (UNDP) described the democratisation of societies as one of the most important positive trends. At the same time, the UN experts define the further democratisation of democracy as the greatest challenge of our time and make it clear that "True democratisation means more than elections. People's dignity requires that they be free – and able – to participate in the formation and stewardship of the rules and institutions that govern them."

The Swiss had realised this as early as in the 19th century and had successfully fought for the introduction of direct democracy. The rest of Europe and the world are now catching up: since 1991, the number of national referendums and plebiscites has doubled. Of the total of 560 documented national popular votes worldwide between 1991 and 2006, 98 were in the Americas, 62 in Africa, 38 in Asia and 30 in Oceania. By far the largest number – 332 – were in Europe. In the preceding decade, the total was only 129.

Two developments in particular highlight this clear trend towards more (direct) democracy. First, the democratic revolutions in Eastern Europe led to no fewer than 27 new constitutions, most of which were approved by the people in referendums. Second, the acceleration of integration within the EU opened the floodgates to a wave of direct democracy with transnational implications: 36 of the 45 national popular votes in Europe and about Europe have happened since 1992.

The institution of the constitutional referendum was born in revolutionary America. The first vote took place in 1639, in the then independent American colony of Connecticut. However, the constitution-making efforts in Massachusetts and New Hampshire of 1778-1780 were of a particularly formative importance.

In Europe, it was the French who took up this American invention. The National Assembly declaredthat a constitution has to be decided by the people. In August 1793, six million French voters were asked to decide on the new democratic national constitution (the Montagnard constitution). Almost 90% of them voted in favour of the revolutionary new rules, which included the right of 10% of the electorate to demand a referendum.

Direct popular rights were developed further in Switzerland and not in France, where they did not survive Napoleon. From Europe they returned to the Americas: in the late 19th century to the north-western states of the USA and at the beginning of the 20th century to Uruguay. It was only after the Second World War that instruments of direct democracy became important in many other countries of the world – in Italy, Australia, South Africa and Ecuador, for example. Over the last 200 years, 1380 national referendums have been held worldwide – almost half of them in the last 15 years.

Direct democracy as a complement to indirect democracy is neither a silly idealistic notion from the past, nor the hobby-horse of a small group of out-of-touch fantasists. It has shown itself to be, on the contrary, an extremely practical idea – not least at the local level. In 2003, almost 10,000 referendums were recorded in American communities alone, and since the introduction of the local referendum in the southern German state of Bavaria in 1995, there have been more than 1,000 popular ballots. There is obviously no shortage of either issues or active citizens in Bavaria: local politics has been invigorated, as a member of the Bavarian parliament, Klaus Hahnzog, documented in his collection of essays entitled: "Mehr Demokratie wagen" ("Let's go for more democracy").

The metamorphosis of Europe

Let's go for more democracy: that's especially true for certain subjects. Across the world, referendums and plebiscites are being held on an enormous range of issues: the growth of the state, the constitution, road-building projects, moral issues, town planning, taxes. But the one issue which dominates above all is the question of European integration. No-one could have predicted it.

The founding fathers of the EU didn't think much of the idea of involving citizens directly in decision-making at the European political level. It was less the experience of the 1939–45 war than the growing threat from the Cold War which meant that the ideas for a democratic European federation developed in the 1940s were initially consigned to the waste-paper bin. The process of integration during the 1950s was dominated by questions of economy and bureaucracy: the Monnet system did not provide for the direct involvement of the citizen.

It was another great Frenchman – President Charles de Gaulle – who was the first to formulate the challenge of a European referendum at the beginning of the 1960s: "Europe will be born on the day on which the different peoples fundamentally decide to join. It will not suffice for members of parliaments to vote for ratification. It will require popular referendums, preferably held on the same day in all the countries concerned."

Ten years later de Gaulle's successor, Georges Pompidou, finally dared to make a start and let the citizens of his country be the first Europeans to take part in a plebiscite on Europe. On 23rd March 1972, a two-thirds majority voted in favour of extending the then European Community northwards to include Denmark, Great Britain, Ireland and Norway. In retrospect, this decision did not only open the door to the north, but also to more (direct) democracy in Europe. In the same year, voters in both the Irish Republic (10th May) and Denmark (2nd October) decided in favour of joining the EC. That was not the end of the matter: there were popular votes on Europe in both Norway and Switzerland. On September 26th, the Norwegians voted narrowly against accession and the Swiss voted massively in favour of a free trade treaty with the EEC on 10th December, with 72.5% of voters saying "Yes."

This first great year of referendums in the history of the European integration process already clearly revealed the great disparity between popular vote procedures in the different countries: whereas the French plebiscite was called by the French president and the result was merely advisory, the Irish popular decision on accession was prescribed in the constitution and was binding on the political leadership of that country. In Denmark, transfers of sovereignty to international organizations have to be put to referendum only when there is no 5/6ths majority in the national parliament. In Norway and Switzerland, finally, it was parliament (in the former case) and the government (in the latter case) which voluntarily decided to submit the issue of accession to the EC (Norway) and to the EEC Free Trade Treaty (Switzerland) to popular vote.

We have now reached the stage where citizens in 21 of the now 25 member states of the EU have had at least one chance of voting directly on the EU.

Minimum requirements that really work

In many states popular voting procedures show a lack in quality. In Europe, the (full) popular initiative and/or referendum exists only in the following eight countries: Hungary, Italy, Latvia, Liechtenstein, Lithuania, Switzerland and Slovakia (see survey 2). The constitutions of the Netherlands, Austria, Poland, Portugal, Romania, Albania and Spain contain an agenda-initiative. Popular votes in the form of plebiscites exist in Belgium, Bulgaria, Cyprus, Estonia, Finland, France, Great Britain, Greece, Luxembourg, Norway, Sweden and Turkey, and defacto also in the Czech Republic. In these countries the organisation of a popular vote depends exclusively on the will of those in power. In Germany and Malta there are (as yet) no constitutional provisions for a popular vote.

The future of direct democracy in Europe and across the world depends on the free expression and fair use of citizens' rights. The following represent the minimum requirements which must be met:

- Citizens must have the right to launch a popular initiative and referendum process themselves.
- Popular referendums must be binding. Non-binding consultations are often ambiguous; instead of solving problems, they create new ones.
- There must be no minimum turnout quorums: these permit non-voting to be used tactically and increase the likelihood of referendums being declared invalid.

It should also be a requirement for:
- all donations and campaign funds used in the run-up to referendums to be declared in the interests of transparency.
- both sides in a referendum campaign to be given space and time in the media.
- the role of government and of public debates in referendum campaigns to be clearly defined.

Many reforms which are "sold" to citizens as "participatory" or "direct" democracy only reveal their true character when they are measured against the six requirements listed above.

For example, the social-democratic government in Sweden recently proposed the introduction of a new initiative right, which would, however, proceed to a (consultative) referendum only if 10% of the residents of a community and one-third of the members of the local parliament requested it. In 2004, the Taiwanese parliament passed a referendum law which was so complicated and user-unfriendly that one commentator in this country with a population of 23 million declared that it "actually prevents people from having a say". When popular rights are being drawn up, particular attention must be paid to design flaws – whether intentional or unintentional – because any negative experience with direct democracy can result in it being rejected for a long time to come.

Test case: the European Citizens' Initiative

It is for this reason that the possible introduction of the "European Citizens' Initiative" will be such an interesting, but also tricky, test case. The 2004 Draft Treaty establishing a Constitution for Europe included a provision for "no less than one million" citizens to "invite the Commission to submit any appropriate proposal on matters where citizens consider that a legal act of the Union is required for the purpose of implementing this Constitution (…)". The option of proposing a new article of the "constitution", an amendment to a law or merely a new regulation would place citizens on a par with the members of the European Parliament.

Compared with the national rights of initiative, which in some countries are well-developed, the EU provision of an agenda initiative may appear rather modest, for the formal right of initiative will remain with the EU Commission. Nonetheless, there could be enormous indirect consequences if at some time in the future the new citizens' initiative right allows trade unions and other organizations to mobilize millions of people in support of their concerns, whether it is to bring about a new law or new regulations. In addition, the citizens' initiative should give citizens a tool for further extending participatory democracy.

"This direct-democratic instrument will enable citizens to become players at the transnational level," says Jürgen Meyer, German parliament representative in the Convention. Meyer and other experts from the Marburg-based Initiative and Referendum Institute Europe are acting as consultants to the Commission and the member states on the new initiative right to try to ensure, in Meyer's words, that "the whole thing comes out in as citizen-friendly a form as possible".

For Brian Beedham, editor at "The Economist" in London, the worldwide trend to more direct democracy means nothing less than that "the next big step for mankind" lies just ahead. The 21st century will see the "part-time democracy" of the past replaced by a "full democracy", in which citizens will have the right to have their say on substantive issues at any time. This is the only way for representative democracy to become truly representative. Citizens' rights can turn the utopia of yesterday into the reality of tomorrow.

Related information [F=Factsheet, S=Survey]
F26 Key points for free and fair referendums in Europe
S1 Direct-democratic procedures and plebiscites in the constitutions of 32 European states
S3 Global Overview of Direct Democracy in selected regions of the world
S4 Glossary of direct-democracy terms

Resources

FACTSHEETS

1. Election and referendum diary canton Zurich: 2003 — 114
2. Cantonal popular (referendum) votes: 1970-2003 — 119
3. Differences between pre-modern and modern democracy — 120
4. How the cantons can influence the writing of a new law — 122
5. Five stages in the genesis of a new law — 123
6. Postal voting — 125
7. Electronic voting – the first real practice — 129
8. Direct democracy in the cantons — 133
9. Constitutional extracts from 1798, 1848, 1874 and 1999 — 137
10. On the development of direct democracy at the level of the Swiss federal state — 144
11. Voting behaviour in initiatives & referendums — 147
12. Popular initiatives, accepted by people and cantons — 149
13. Bandwidths of indirect and direct democracy — 151
14. Results of popular consultations in the Jura region — 152
15. Chronology of the Jura conflict (1815-2004) — 154
16. The Army XXI referendum on 18 May, 2003 — 158
17. The popular initiative "Equal rights for the disabled" — 159
18. Citizens' rights at the federal level in Switzerland — 161
19. The result of the parliamentary elections in 2003 — 163
20. The major initiators of popular initiatives & referendums — 165
21. The main issues of initiatives and referendums at the federal level and in the cantons — 166
22. Referendum votes on issues relating to foreigners in the Federation — 167
23. The law on the protection of water resources (1983-92) — 169
24. Restrictions on the constitutional initiative in Switzerland — 173
25. The expectations of the Swiss direct democracy movement in the 19th century — 176
26. Key points for free and fair referendums in Europe — 177
27. The economic effects of the use of direct democracy — 178
28. Important factors in the shaping of direct-democratic procedures — 180
29. Voting rights of Swiss citizens living or staying abroad — 186

SURVEYS

1. All popular votes in Switzerland since 1848 — 189
2. Direct-democratic procedures and plebiscites in the constitutions of 32 European states — 232
3. Global Overview of Direct Democracy in selected regions of the world — 265
4. Glossary of direct-democracy terms — 308

INFORMATION

Towards the 1st World Conference on Direct Democracy in 2008 — 321
The Initiative & Referendum Institute Europe — 322
About/Acknowledgements — 324
Index — 326

FACTSHEET
Election and referendum diary
Canton Zurich: 2003

Elections 2003

Level of state		Body elected
Municipality	9 Feb	Renewal of office, Justices of the Peace 2003-2009
Canton	6 Apr	Cantonal council (parliament) 2003–7
	6 Apr	Governing council (Executive) 2003–7 (4 women 3 men)
	18 May	Church synods 2003–7
Federation	19 Oct	National council 2003–7
	19 Oct	Zurich members of Council of States (2) 2003–7

Municipality (city of Zurich): Referendum votes 2003

		Proposal	Result
9 Feb	1	Loan of 75 million francs for buildings for the "Energy Services" division of the Zurich city electricity generating station	ACCEPTED (78.13%) TURNOUT: 31.27%
18 May	2	Reconstruction and renovation of the indoor stadium involving the purchase of land costing 31,448,000 francs, building permit, loan of a maximum 20 million francs and portion of increase in share capital	ACCEPTED (73.5%) TURNOUT: 49.55%
18 May	3	Public design plan for "Sechseläutenplatz-Theaterplatz"	ACCEPTED (69.31%) TURNOUT: 49.68%
7 Sept	4	Subsidy for residential building and pension fund, insurance against potential losses on loan to city of Zurich pension fund, supplement to decision of municipality dated 31st August 1924	ACCEPTED (79.69%) TURNOUT: 32.33%
7 Sept	5	Private development plan for the Zurich stadium with environmental impact study	ACCEPTED (63.26%) TURNOUT: 32.44%

01 FACTSHEET
Election and referendum diary
Canton Zurich: 2003

Municipality (city of Zurich): Referendum votes 2003

		Proposal	Result
7 Sept	6	Approval of 47,666,500 francs for a share in the Zurich Stadium Co. responsible for creating infrastructure for the football stadium. www.stadion-zuerich.ch	ACCEPTED (59.19%) TURNOUT: 33.25%
7 Sept	7	Definitive introduction of block-lessons in the lower classes of the primary school from the 2005/2006 school year, approval of annual recurrent expenditure of 3,650,000 francs	ACCEPTED (72.04%) TURNOUT: 32.72%

Canton Zurich: Referendum votes 2003

		Referendum Question (Cantonal and Executive council recommendation)	Result
9 Feb	1	Do you want to accept the following proposal? Introductory law to the Swiss civil code (amendment) (YES)	ACCEPTED (56.5%) TURNOUT: 32.7% MUNICIPALITIES: YES: 169 / NO: 13
9 Feb	2	Do you want to accept the following proposal? Decision of the cantonal council on approval of a loan for a cantonal contribution to the building of the Glattal railway and also for road building and modification in the central Glattal (YES)	ACCEPTED (66.6%) TURNOUT: 32.9% MUNICIPALITIES: YES: 170 / NO: 12
18 May	3	Do you want to accept the popular initiative "Lower taxes for lower incomes (popular initiative for greater tax fairness in the canton Zurich)"? (NO)	REJECTED (63.9%) TURNOUT: 50.1%
30 Nov	4	Do you want to accept the change in the cantonal constitution regarding the division of duties between canton/communities? (YES)	ACCEPTED (83.42%) TURNOUT: 40.0% MUNICIPALITIES: YES: 182 / NO: 0

01 FACTSHEET
ELECTION AND REFERENDUM DIARY
CANTON ZURICH: 2003

CANTON ZURICH: REFERENDUM VOTES 2003

	REFERENDUM QUESTION (CANTONAL AND EXECUTIVE COUNCIL RECOMMENDATION)	RESULT
30 NOV	5 Do you want to accept the change in the cantonal constitution to reform the relationship between church and state? (YES)	REJECTED (55.01%) TURNOUT: 40.2% MUNICIPALITIES: YES: 14 / NO: 168
30 NOV	6 Do you want to accept the law on churches? (YES)	REJECTED (54.18%) TURNOUT: 40.2% MUNICIPALITIES: YES: 16 / NO: 166
30 NOV	7 Do you want to accept the law on the recognition of religious communities? (YES)	REJECTED (64.06%) TURNOUT: 40.4% MUNICIPALITIES: YES: 8 / NO: 174
30 NOV	8 Do you want to accept the law on a police and judicial center for Zurich? (YES)	ACCEPTED (55.70%) TURNOUT: 40.3% MUNICIPALITIES: YES: 110 / NO: 74
30 NOV	9 Do you want to accept the amendment to the health law relating to the handing over of medicines? (YES)	REJECTED (58.88%) TURNOUT: 40.8% MUNICIPALITIES: YES: 14 / NO: 168
30 NOV	10 Do you want to accept the law on the partial revision of the procedure in criminal cases? (YES)	ACCEPTED (76.27%) TURNOUT: 39.8% MUNICIPALITIES: YES: 182 / NO: 0
30 NOV	11 Do you want to accept the popular initiative "The right of the people to have a say on tax matters"? (maximum tax rate of 98% in the constitution) (NO)	REJECTED (63.77%) TURNOUT: 40.3% MUNICIPALITIES: YES: 11 / NO: 171
30 NOV	12 Do you want to accept the popular initiative "An end to the official raising of housing costs for tenants and owners"? (Abolition of the tax when properties change hands) (CANTONAL COUNCIL: YES / EXECUTIVE COUNCIL: NO)	ACCEPTED (52.06%) TURNOUT: 40.4% MUNICIPALITIES: YES: 155 / NO: 27

01 FACTSHEET
ELECTION AND REFERENDUM DIARY
CANTON ZURICH: 2003

FEDERATION: Referendum votes 2003

		Proposal	Result
9 Feb	1	Federal decree on amendment to citizens' rights	ACCEPTED (70.4%) TURNOUT: 28%
9 Feb	2	Federal law on adjusting canton's contributions to hospital costs	ACCEPTED (77.4%) TURNOUT: 28%
18 May	3	Amendment to federal law on the army and military administration	ACCEPTED (76.0%) TURNOUT: 50%
18 May	4	Federal law on civil protection	ACCEPTED (80.6%) TURNOUT: 50%
18 May	5	Popular initiative "Yes to fair rents for tenants"	REJECTED (67.3%) TURNOUT: 50% CANTONS: YES: 1 / NO: 19 6/2
18 May	6	Popular initiative "For one car-free Sunday per season – a 4-year trial (Sunday Initiative)"	REJECTED (62.4%) TURNOUT: 50% CANTONS: YES: 0 / NO: 20 6/2
18 May	7	Popular initiative "Healthcare must be affordable (Health Initiative)"	REJECTED (72.9%) TURNOUT: 50% CANTONS: YES: 0 / NO: 20 6/2
18 May	8	Popular initiative "Equal rights for the disabled"	REJECTED (62.3%) TURNOUT: 50% CANTONS: YES: 3 / NO: 17 6/2
18 May	9	Popular initiative "Non-nuclear energy – for a change in energy policy and the gradual decommissioning of nuclear power plants (Non-nuclear energy)"	REJECTED (66.3%) TURNOUT: 50% CANTONS: YES: 1/2 (BS) / NO: 20 5/2

01 FACTSHEET
ELECTION AND REFERENDUM DIARY
CANTON ZURICH: 2003

FEDERATION: Referendum votes 2003

	Proposal	Result
18 May	10 Popular initiative "Moratorium Plus – for an extension of the moratorium on nuclear power plant construction and a limitation of the nuclear risk (MoratoriumPlus)"	REJECTED (58.4%) TURNOUT: 50% CANTONS: YES: 2/2 / NO: 20 4/2
18 May	11 Popular initiative "For adequate vocational training (Apprenticeship Initiative)"	REJECTED (68.4%) TURNOUT: 50% CANTONS: YES: 0 / NO: 20 6/2

02 FACTSHEET
Cantonal popular (referendum) votes: 1970-2003

Cantonal referendum votes in 21 cantons

Canton	Total votes 1970-2003	1997-2003
Zurich	457	77
Solothurn	316	47
Basel Country	282	74
Schaffhausen	272	52
Graubünden	262	69
Basel City	242	22
Bern	222	22
Uri	183	29
Aargau	183	50
Thurgau	163	17
Geneva	150	30
Schwyz	142	26
Valais	136	8
Neuchâtel	121	6
St. Gallen	121	20
Lucerne	99	21
Zug	97	25
Vaud	86	23
Fribourg	85	11
Ticino	53	12
Jura (since 1979)	45	4
TOTAL	3,709	645

Source: C2D Research and Documentation Centre on direct democracy, Geneva (http://c2d.unige.ch/)

03 FACTSHEET
DIFFERENCES BETWEEN PRE-MODERN AND MODERN DEMOCRACY

	PRE-MODERN	MODERN
Concept	Classical direct democracy	Modern direct democracy
Model	"Associational democracy": Assembly democracy ("Landsgemeinde" or just "Gemeinde" [popular assembly])	"Individualistic democracy": Referendum and Initiative as a complement to representative democracy
Counter concept	Aristocracy, monarchy	Representative democracy
Political culture, citizens' rights	Group consciousness: democracy, popular sovereignty, freedom, equality for "us" as members of a particular, privileged collective; historical justification for a collective particularism	Individualism: democracy, popular sovereignty, freedom, equality for "ALL" as an inalienable human right; individual human rights based on natural law
Basis or justification	Democracy as the historical privilege of a certain group; origin in resistance to unjust tyranny (William Tell)	Democracy as a natural right
Democracy	Reconcilable with domination of some by others	Irreconcilable with domination of some by others
Freedom	Associational/community or collective freedom	Individual freedom
Equality	Equality between the members of a particular collective	Equality of all humans

03 FACTSHEET
Differences between pre-modern and modern democracy

	PRE-MODERN	MODERN
Political equality	The most important governmental, administrative and judicial posts occupied everywhere by members of eminent families (so-called "heads"), who were clearly distinct from the "common man" economically, socially and culturally – though not legally.	Formal equality linked to inequality in the actual practice of participation in politics
Political practice	Purchase of official posts and votes as a form of social equalization or political participation.	Purchase of official posts and votes held to be corrupt; social equalization through the medium of the welfare state

FACTSHEET
HOW THE CANTONS CAN INFLUENCE THE WRITING OF A NEW LAW

Switzerland is a federal state which emerged out of an earlier confederation of separate, independent states – the cantons. The cantons – frequently referred to in Switzerland as the "Stände", or "states" – are the original states which joined together in a confederation (the "Bund") in 1848, seceding to the confederation a portion of their own sovereignty. The Swiss political system acknowledges this fact by giving the cantons a high degree of autonomy and by involving them deeply in all the stages of political decision-making.

Swiss federalism is distinguished by five elements:
1. The cantons enjoy a substantial number of powers and competences
2. There is extensive cooperation between the "Bund" – the central power – and the cantons; but also between the cantons themselves
3. The cantons enjoy a certain autonomy in the raising and spending of public finances
4. The cantons are autonomous in respect of organisation and procedures
5. The cantons enjoy statutory rights of co-decision making in fundamental decisions of the central power

Article 3 of the federal constitution states:
"The cantons are sovereign, insofar as their sovereignty is not limited by the federal constitution; they exercise all those rights which are not ceded to the Bund."

Switzerland consists of 26 cantons, of which 6 – for historical reasons – have rights which are in certain respects reduced. Each canton has its own constitution, its own parliament, its own government and its own courts. Every canton sends two representatives to the "Council of States", except for Basel City, Basel Country, Obwalden, Nidwalden, Appenzell Outer-Rhodes and Appenzell Inner-Rhodes, all of which send only one.

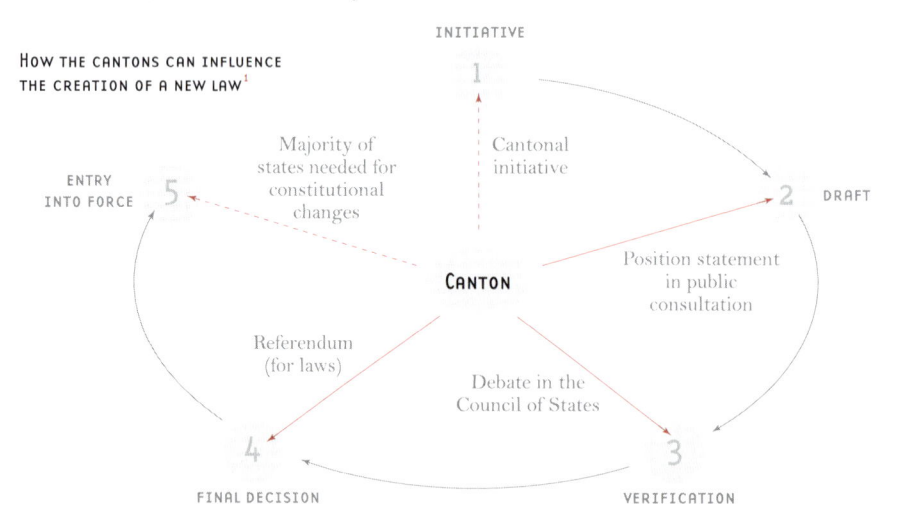

HOW THE CANTONS CAN INFLUENCE THE CREATION OF A NEW LAW[1]

- 1 INITIATIVE — Cantonal initiative
- 2 DRAFT — Position statement in public consultation
- 3 VERIFICATION — Debate in the Council of States
- 4 FINAL DECISION — Referendum (for laws)
- 5 ENTRY INTO FORCE — Majority of states needed for constitutional changes

CANTON

[1] For more information on the 5 phases, see Factsheet 5: Five stages in the genesis of a new law

05 FACTSHEET
FIVE STAGES IN THE GENESIS OF A NEW LAW

The genesis of a law is a complex and often also a lengthy affair. The process takes a minimum of twelve months, but in extreme cases can last for more than a dozen years. Despite this, the number of new laws has increased markedly in recent years. Currently, new laws enter into force at the rate of one per week on average.

The path towards a new law can be divided into five stages:

1. The initial trigger can come, for example, from individual voters or interest groups launching a popular initiative. But it can also come from members of parliament or sections of the administration, from cantons or from the Federal Council.

2. In the second stage, a preliminary draft of the law is worked out. The Federal Council often appoints for this purpose a 10–20 member committee which includes representatives of those who have an interest in the new law. The preliminary draft is then sent out for consultation to the cantons, the political parties, the unions and to other special interest groups. All of these can express a formal opinion on the proposal and also propose changes to it. On the basis of the feedback from the consultation, the federal administration revises the draft law and passes it on to the Federal Council. The Federal Council checks the text and passes it – together with an explanatory memorandum – on to the National Council and the Council of States for parliamentary consideration.

3. The third stage is the parliamentary stage, in which the draft law is debated. The presidents of the two Councils decide in which of the two chambers the draft new law will be debated first. An advisory committee of the chosen council debates the text and then presents it together with its own opinion to the whole council (e.g. the National Council). This procedure is repeated in the second chamber (in this case, the Council of States): the text agreed by the National Council is first debated by an advisory committee of the Council of States.

   If the National Council and the Council of States should come to different decisions, the so-called "resolution of differences" procedure comes into play. The advisory committee of the first chamber examines the individual differences and then makes a proposal to its chamber – to accept the Council of States' version on one point, for example, but to insist on their own version on another point. After the revised draft has been debated and agreed in the first council, the advisory committee of the second council deals with any remaining differences and makes its own proposal to its chamber.

   If after three rounds of debate there are still differences in the agreed drafts, the so-called "agreement conference" is called in order to seek a compromise solution. It consists of members of the two committees of the National Council and the Council of States. The compromise formula goes to both Councils for a final vote.

05 FACTSHEET
FIVE STAGES IN THE GENESIS OF A NEW LAW

4 At the next stage, the electorate has the opportunity to express its opinion on the proposed law. The draft law is subject to the facultative, or optional, referendum i.e. 50,000 eligible voters or eight cantons can demand a popular referendum vote on the law. The demand for a referendum vote must be made within 100 days of the draft law being published. (Changes to the constitution are subject to obligatory referendum).

5 The new law enters into force if 100 days pass without a referendum being called, or if a majority of the voters approves it in the popular vote resulting from the facultative referendum.

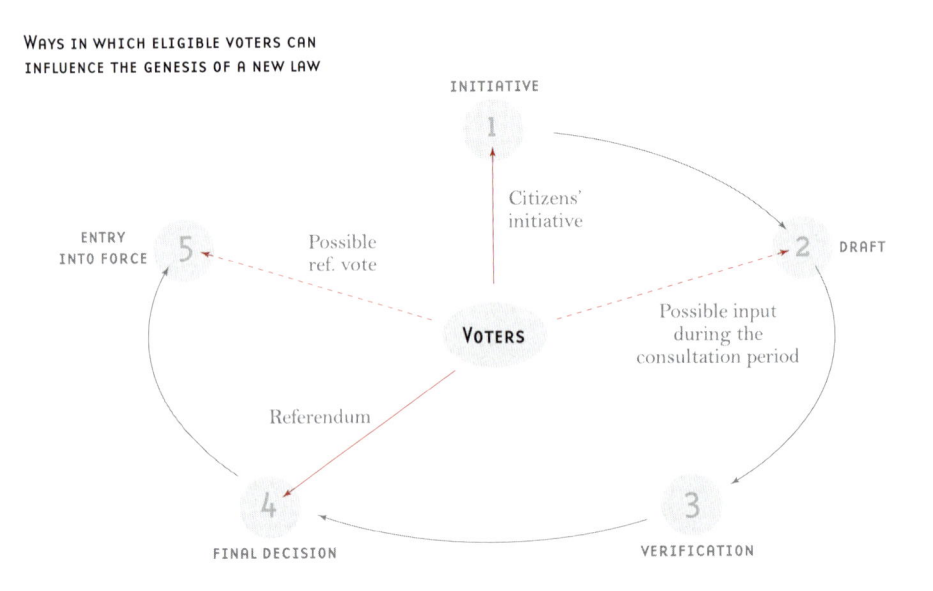

WAYS IN WHICH ELIGIBLE VOTERS CAN INFLUENCE THE GENESIS OF A NEW LAW

```
                          INITIATIVE
                              1
                              ↑
                       Citizens'
                       initiative
   ENTRY      5 ←──Possible──           2   DRAFT
 INTO FORCE      ref. vote
                              Possible input
                    VOTERS    during the
                              consultation period
              Referendum
                      ↓
                      4                  3
                 FINAL DECISION      VERIFICATION
```

SOURCE: Swiss Federal Chancellery: The Path Towards a New Law (www.admin.ch/ch/e/gg/index.html)

06 FACTSHEET
Postal voting

Since 1994 it has been a principle in Switzerland that every voter can decide freely whether to vote in person, or whether to vote by post in federal referendums[1]. Postal voting is easier both in terms of space and time. People who are away from home can mail their vote from anywhere, even from abroad. One is able to vote by post after one has received the documents required under cantonal law to enable one to vote[2]. The specific procedure for postal voting is determined by the cantons. They have to ensure that the process is straightforward and especially that it guarantees control of the entitlement to vote, voting secrecy and the recording of all votes, and that it prevents abuse[3].

There are two different systems of postal voting in Switzerland: the simplified system and the system of postal voting on request. The first of the two systems – the general, or simplified, postal vote – is more common. Voters receive an official mailing of the material for the postal vote. The second system, that of postal voting on request, is now only practised in one canton. Voters can apply to the relevant authorities for permission to vote by post. The application can be for one referendum ballot, for the whole of a legislative session, or for all forthcoming referendum ballots.

Postal voting has become very popular in urban areas. More than 90% of voters in Basel City and Geneva now give their votes by post. But the share of postal voting still varies widely from canton to canton. The level of postal voting seems to depend primarily on the pattern of settlement: people in the more densely settled towns and cities use postal voting more frequently than those who live in villages[4].

---

[1] Federal Law on political rights (BPR) Art. 5 § 3
Available online at: www.admin.ch/ch/e/rs/c161_1.html
[2] BPR Art. 8 § 2
[3] BPR Art. 8 § 1
[4] Further information:
Swiss Federal Chancellery: Survey on postal voting, Bern 1998
Available online at: www.admin.ch/ch/d/pore/va/doku/pdf/enquete_bsa.pdf
Longchamp, Claude: *Popular postal voting* – Main results of the VOX-Analyses of postal voting at federal citizens' referendum ballots, 1998. Online at: www.polittrends.ch/beteiligung/welcome.html
Von Arx, Nicolas: *Postal Democracy, Postal voting in Switzerland*, in: Aktuelle Juristische Praxis 1998, S. 933–950.

06 FACTSHEET
POSTAL VOTING

Introduction of simplified Postal voting according to canton[5]:

Canton	Current legal basis (as of 20.08.2004)	Since
Zurich	Law on political rights, § 69 www.zhlex.zh.ch/	1994
Bern	Law on political rights, Articles 10, 11 and 1 www.sta.be.ch/belex/d/1/141_1.html	1991
Lucerne	Law on voting rights, § 61–63 www.lu.ch/index/staatskanzlei/rechtssammlung.htm	1994
Uri	Law on secret elections, referendum ballots and citizens' rights, Articles 19–23 www.ur.ch/rechtsbuch/start.htm	1995
Schwyz	Law on elections and referendum ballots, § 28 www.sz.ch/gesetze/G100/120_100.pdf	2000
Obwalden	Law on the exercise of political rights, Articles 29–31 www.obwalden.ch/regierung_verwaltung/staatskanzlei/gessamml/pdf/122100.pdf	1995
Nidwalden	Introductory ruling on federal law on political rights, § 32–36 www.navigator.ch/nw/lpext.dll?f=templates&fn=main-h.htm&2.0	1994
Glarus	Law on elections and referendum ballots, Articles 13, 15–17 http://gs.gl.ch/pdf/i/gs_i_d_22_2.pdf	1995
Zug	Law on elections and referendum ballots, § 13, 23, 30–35 www.zug.ch/bgs/data/131-1.pdf	1997
Fribourg	Law on the exercise of political rights, Article 18 www.fr.ch/ofl_bdlf/de/plan_sys/default.htm	1995

---

[5] Further information on ways of making voting easier in the cantons available online at: www.admin.ch/ch/d/pore/nrw03/ste/kt_index.html

06 FACTSHEET
POSTAL VOTING

INTRODUCTION OF SIMPLIFIED POSTAL VOTING ACCORDING TO CANTON[5]:

CANTON	CURRENT LEGAL BASIS (AS OF 20.08.2004)	SINCE
Solothurn	Law on political rights, § 78–85 www.so.ch/extappl/bgs/daten/113/111.pdf	1980
Basel City	Law on elections and referendum ballots, § 6, 8 www.gesetzessammlung.bs.ch/sgmain/default.html	1995
Basel Country	Law on political rights, § 7, 10 www.baselland.ch/docs/recht/sgs_1-1/120.0.htm	1978
Schaffhausen	Law on popular referendum ballots und elections and on the exercise of citizens' rights, Articles 14, 50, 53bis–53quater http://rechtsbuch.sh.ch/	1995
Appenzell Outer-Rhodes	Law on political rights, Articles 13–15 www.bgs.ar.ch/	1988
Appenzell Inner-Rhodes	Ruling by the Great Council concerning political rights, Articles 12–14, 17 www2.ai.ch/_download/lexdb/121.pdf	1979
St. Gallen	Law on voting by ballot, Articles 16–16ter www.gallex.ch/gallex/1/fs125.3.html	1979
Graubünden	Law on political rights in the canton Graubünden, Articles 24, 25, 34 www.navigator.ch/gr/lpext.dll?f=templates&fn=main-h.htm&2.0	1995
Aargau	Law on political rights, § 17 www.ag.ch/sar/output/default.htm?/sar/output/131-100.htm	1993
Thurgau	Law on voting in referendums and elections, § 10 www.rechtsbuch.tg.ch/pdf/100/161_1Zneu.pdf	1985

---

[5] Further information on ways of making voting easier in the cantons available online at: www.admin.ch/ch/d/pore/nrw03/ste/kt_index.html

06 FACTSHEET
Postal voting

Introduction of simplified Postal voting according to canton[5]:

Canton	Current legal basis (as of 20.08.2004)	Since
Ticino	Law on the exercise of political rights, Articles 1, 32–34 www.ti.ch/CAN/temi/rl *(Postal voting on request since 1987)	*
Vaud	Law on the exercise of political rights, Articles 17b, 18, 20, 24 www.rsv.vd.ch	2002
Valais	Law on elections and referendum ballots, Articles 23, 24 www.vs.ch/home2/etatVS/vs_public/public_lois/fr/loishtml/160.1.htm	2004
Neuchâtel	Law on political rights, Articles 9a, 10, 20 www.ne.ch/neat/site/jsp/rubrique/rubrique.jsp?StyleType=bleu&CatId=2151	2003
Geneva	Law on the exercise of political rights, Articles 61, 62, 67 www.ge.ch/legislation/rsg/f/rsg_a5_05.html	1995
Jura	Law on political rights, Articles 18, 19, 21 http://rsju.jura.ch/extranet/groups/public/documents/rsju_page/loi_161.1.hcsp	1999

---

[5] Further information on ways of making voting easier in the cantons available online at: www.admin.ch/ch/d/pore/nrw03/ste/kt_index.html

FACTSHEET
Electronic voting – the first real practice

What is e-voting?
E-voting is short for "electronic voting" and refers to the option of using electronic means (i.e. the Internet, e-mail) to vote in referendums and elections, give signatures for initiatives and referendums and acquire information on elections and referendums from the authorities. In Switzerland, it is planned to use e-voting to complement conventional procedures (voting in person by ballot and postal voting), but not to replace them.

The starting point
A number of proposals were directed by parliament to the Federal Council, asking it to look into whether and how direct democracy in Switzerland could be reinforced by the new information and communication technologies. As a result, the Federal Council commissioned the Federal Chancellery in August 2000 with the task of examining the feasibility of e-voting. To this end, the Chancellery set up a working party composed of federal and cantonal representatives and known as the "Preliminary Project on e-voting", which has delivered a first report on the options, risks and feasibility of e-voting to the Federal Council.[1] The report was approved by the Federal Council in January 2002 and noted in subsequent sessions of parliament. The working party continues to monitor the pilot projects supported by the Chancellery in the cantons of Geneva, Neuchâtel and Zurich, which are designed to clarify the main considerations which would arise if e-voting were to be introduced in Switzerland.

Pros and cons of e-voting
Both supporters and opponents of e-voting list a series of weighty arguments. On the one hand there are the opportunities which the electronic exercise of political rights might bring. E-voting can make voting in elections and referendums easier for many people. The considerable mobility of the Swiss population, the change in communication habits and the daily information overload could further reduce participation in political decision-making. But one might also think of those who are blind or visually impaired, who at present have only limited opportunities of exercising their right to vote in secrecy; or of the Swiss who live abroad, who are often excluded from voting by distance and slow postal services. There is disagreement among experts as to whether e-voting would actually encourage more people to vote or not.

On the other hand, there are potential risks in e-voting, primarily in terms of the possible abuse of the system. Critics fear the unauthorised intervention of third parties in the voting process. There is no guarantee, given the current state of information technology, that a programme could not be manipulated to allow someone to store and print out a different form or document from the one appearing on the screen. With electronic voting it is more difficult to detect and find the source of errors, technical breakdowns etc. than with conventional procedures, and public checking of recounts is less easy. If public doubts about the reliability of electronic forms of voting cannot be removed, the whole functioning of the democratic system may be brought into question.

---

[1] Report on e-voting: options, risks and feasibility of the electronic exercise of political rights, BBl 2002 645. The report, together with addenda and submissions from experts, is available at: www.admin.ch/e-gov (in German, French and Italian)

FACTSHEET
Electronic voting – the first real practice

The pilot projects in Geneva, Neuchâtel and Zurich

A consultation exercise carried out in all the cantons showed that many cantons would like to be involved in the pilot projects which are being partly financed by the Federation[2]. To date, agreements have been reached with Geneva, Neuchâtel and Zurich.

One particular criterion was decisive in the selection of the pilot projects. The three pilot cantons form a set which covers those factors relative to the requirements for e-voting which are of central importance for all the cantons. The canton Geneva[3], for example, already has a centralised administrative structure and a central register of voters. This has still to be created in the canton Zurich[4]. The canton Neuchâtel is examining the implementation of e-voting as an integral part of its "Guichet unique" ("one stop e-counter"), an electronic public office for all cantonal authority matters[5]. The differing requirements and goals, as well as the staggering of the three pilot projects over time will allow the gradual build-up of the know-how necessary for a nationwide solution.

A variety of tests has been carried out in the cantons Geneva, Neuchâtel and Zurich:

Date	Canton	Communes	Number of voters with the opportunity of using e-voting	Number of voters having actually used e-voting	Level of referendum/ election
19.01.2003	Geneva	Anières	1,162	323	communal referendum
30.11.2003	Geneva	Cologny	2,521	432	communal referendum
18.04.2004	Geneva	Carouge	9,049	1,024	communal referendum
13.06.2004	Geneva	Meyrin	9,170	788	communal referendum
26.09.2004	Geneva	Anières, Carouge, Cologny, Meyrin	22,137	2,723	national and cantonal referendums

[2] The survey is available (in German, French and Italian) at: www.admin.ch/e-gov
[3] Further information on the Geneva pilot project is available at: www.geneve.ch/chancellerie/e-government/e-voting.html
[4] Further information on the Zurich pilot project is available at: www.statistik.zh.ch/projekte/evoting/evoting.htm
[5] Further information on the Neuchâtel pilot project is available at: www.ne.ch/gvu

FACTSHEET
Electronic voting – the first real practice

Date	Canton	Communes	Number of voters with the opportunity of using e-voting	Number of voters having actually used e-voting	Level of referendum/election
24.10.2004	Geneva	Vandoeuvres	1,382	240	communal referendum
28.11.2004	Geneva	Anières, Carouge, Cologny, Collonge-Bellerive, Meyrin, Onex, Vandoeuvres, Versoix	41,431	3,755	national and cantonal referendums
24.04.2005	Geneva	Anières, Bernex, Carouge, Chêne-Bourg, Collonge-Bellerive, Cologny, Grand-Saconnex, Lancy, Meyrin, Onex, Thonex, Vandoeuvres, Vernier, Versoix	88,082	7,911	cantonal referendum
25.09.2005	Neuchâtel	users of the "Guichet Unique"	1,732	1,178	national and communal referendums
30.10.2005	Neuchâtel	users of the "Guichet Unique"	2,209	1,194	cantonal election
30.10.2005	Zurich	Bülach	3,919	1,461	communal referendum
27.11.2005	Zurich	Bertschikon, Bülach, Schlieren	16,726	1,397	national, cantonal and communal referendums and communal election
27.11.2005	Neuchâtel	users of the "Guichet Unique"	2,469	1,345	national referendum

FACTSHEET
Electronic voting – the first real practice

Legal basis

Federal law on political rights[6] and the related, similarly-worded decree[7] had to be supplemented in order to give the Federal Council the legal means to permit legally binding studies at the federal level. The legal basis and the practical regulations came into force on 1st January 2003. From then on it was possible for the Federal Council to permit a canton, if it so requested, to carry out e-voting pilot studies limited as to time, place and subject matter.

The federal constitution inscribes the right to free decision-making and secure voting free from counterfeiting. From this result a series of requirements for e-voting which are set out in Articles 27a-27q of the Federal Decree on Political Rights. Voters must be informed about the organisation, the technology used and the temporal sequence of the process of electronic voting. It must be possible to change one's mind and/or to cancel one's vote before it is finally sent off; there must be no on-screen advertising which could influence voters in any way; and there must be a perfectly clear visual indication on the computer or machine being used to register the vote that the vote has been transmitted.

In order to maintain voting secrecy, the electronic vote has to be encoded from the moment of sending until the moment of arrival; it must remain fully anonymous and must not be traceable to the voter. The possibility of a vote getting lost must be technically ruled out, even in the case of a fault or failure in the system. It must be possible to reconstruct every individual use of the system and every vote given even if there is a system crash.

Future prospects

The pilot projects in Geneva, Neuchâtel and Zurich have now been evaluated. The government and parliament will soon decide whether and how electronic voting should be made available in Switzerland as a supplementary form of voting.

---

[6] At: www.admin.ch/ch/e/rs/c161_1.html
[7] At: www.admin.ch/ch/d/sr/c161_11.html

Further information on e-voting:
www.admin.ch/e-gov

08 FACTSHEET
DIRECT DEMOCRACY IN THE CANTONS

OVERVIEW OF SELECTED TYPES OF CANTONAL INITIATIVES AND REFERENDUMS
[O]=OBLIGATORY / [F]= FACULTATIVE (CONSTITUTIONAL REFERENDUM IS OBLIGATORY FOR ALL CANTONS)

Canton	Subject of referendum	*Popular initiatives	Collection period	*Facultative referendums	Collection period
Aargau	Laws [O+F] Finances [F]	0.9	12 months	0.9	90 days
Appenzell Inner-Rhodes	Laws [O+F] Finances [F]	Popular assembly			
Appenzell Outer-Rhodes	Laws [O+F] Finances [O+F]	2		2	60 days
Basel Country	Laws [O+F] Finances [F] Admin. [O]	0.9		0.9	56 days
Basel City	Laws [F] Finances [F]	3.2		1.6	42 days
Bern	Laws [F] Finances [F] Admin. [F]	2.2	6 months	1.5	90 days
Fribourg	Laws [F] Finances [O+F]	3.9	3 months	3.9	90 days
Geneva	Laws [F] Finances [F] Admin. [F]	4.8	4 months	3.4	40 days

*Minimum number of signatures, as a percentage of the electorate

08 FACTSHEET
DIRECT DEMOCRACY IN THE CANTONS

OVERVIEW OF SELECTED TYPES OF CANTONAL INITIATIVES AND REFERENDUMS
[O]=OBLIGATORY / [F]= FACULTATIVE (CONSTITUTIONAL REFERENDUM IS OBLIGATORY FOR ALL CANTONS)

Canton	Subject of referendum	*Popular initiatives	Collection period	*Facultative referendums	Collection period
Glarus	Laws [O] Finances [O] Admin. [O]	Popular assembly			
Graubünden	Laws [O+F] Finances [O+F] Admin. [O]	4.0	12 months	2.4	90 days
Jura	Laws [F] Finances [O+F] Admin. [O]	3.9	12 months	3.9	60 days
Lucerne	Laws [F] Finances [O+F]	2.2	12 months	1.3	60 days
Neuchâtel	Laws [F] Finances [O] Admin. [O]	5.7	6 months	5.7	40 days
Nidwalden	Laws [F] Finances [O+F] Admin. [O]	1.9	2 months	1.0	30 days
Obwalden	Laws [O+F] Finances [O+F]	2.3		0.5	30 days

*Minimum number of signatures, as a percentage of the electorate

SOURCE: Vatter Adrian: Kantonale Demokratien im Vergleich (Opladen 2002), p. 226f.

08 FACTSHEET
Direct democracy in the cantons

Overview of selected types of cantonal initiatives and referendums
[O]=obligatory / [F]= facultative (Constitutional referendum is obligatory for all cantons)

Canton	Subject of referendum	*Popular initiatives	Collection period	*Facultative referendums	Collection period
St. Gallen	Laws [F] Finances [O+F]	2.8	3–6 months	1.4	30 days
Schaffhausen	Laws [O+F] Finances [O+F] Admin. [O]	2.1		2.1	90 days
Schwyz	Laws [O+F] Finances [O]	2.4		2.4	30 days
Solothurn	Laws [O+F] Finances [O+F] Admin. [O]	1.8	18 months	0.9	90 days
Thurgau	Laws [F] Finances [O+F]	2.9	6 months	1.4	90 days
Ticino	Laws [F] Finances [F]	5.3	2 months	3.7	30 days
Uri	Laws [O+F] Finances [O+F]	2.4		1.8	90 days
Valais	Laws [F] Finances [F] Admin. [O]	3.3	12 months	1.7	90 days

*Minimum number of signatures, as a percentage of the electorate

08 FACTSHEET
DIRECT DEMOCRACY IN THE CANTONS

OVERVIEW OF SELECTED TYPES OF CANTONAL INITIATIVES AND REFERENDUMS
[o]=obligatory / [f]= facultative (Constitutional referendum is obligatory for all cantons)

Canton	Subject of referendum	*Popular initiatives	Collection period	*Facultative referendums	Collection period
Vaud	Laws [f] Admin. [o]	3.3	3 months	1.7	40 days
Zug	Laws [f] Finances [o]	3.2		2.4	60 days
Zurich	Laws [o] Finances [o+f] Admin. [o]	1.3 Individual initiative	6 months	0.6	60 days

Source: Vatter, Adrian: Kantonale Demokratien im Vergleich (Opladen 2002), p. 226f.

FACTSHEET
Constitutional extracts from 1798, 1848, 1874 and 1999

The first Helvetic constitution of 12th April 1798
(Drafted by Peter Ochs and accepted without debate at Aarau on 12th April 1798, in part temporarily suspended by the decrees of 5th November 1798, 15th February 1799 and 18th May 1799, de facto annulled by the coup d'état of 7th January 1800).
Source: Hilty, Carl: Öffentliche Vorlesungen über die Helvetik (Bern 1878), p.731ff.

Title 1. Main principles.

Art 1   The Helvetic Republic constitutes a single, indivisible state. There are no longer any borders between the cantons and the subject territories, nor between one canton and another. The unity of the fatherland and the general interest will henceforth replace the weak bond which held together strange, dissimilar, unrelated, small-minded localities and areas subject to indigenous prejudices and led them without a clear sense of direction. For as long as all the separate parts were weak, the whole could not help but be weak also. The united strength of all will henceforth generate a common strength.

Art 2   The totality of the citizens is the sovereign or overlord. No part, nor any single right of overlordship can be detached from the whole to become the property of any individual. The form of government, even if it should be altered, shall always remain that of representative democracy.
(…)

Title 3. The political status of the citizens.

Art 19   All those who are currently genuine citizens of a governing town or municipality, of a subject or free village, become Swiss citizens by virtue of the present constitution. This applies equally to those who had the right of tenancy in perpetuity ("Hintersässrecht"), and to all tenants ("Hintersässen") born in Switzerland.

Art 20   A foreigner becomes a citizen after he has lived for 20 consecutive years in Switzerland, if he has made himself useful, and if he can show favourable testimonials to his behaviour and morals. He must, however – for himself and his descendants – renounce all other citizens' rights, he must swear the civic oath and his name will be inscribed in the register of Swiss citizens which is retained in the National Archive.
(…)

Title 4. On the primary and elective assemblies

Art 28   The primary assemblies consist of the citizens and the sons of citizens who have lived in the same commune for five years, reckoned from the date when they declared their intention of settling there. There are cases, however, where the legislative councils may accept only the place of birth – whether of the citizen himself, or of his father, if he was not born in Switzerland – as the place of residence. To be able to vote in a primary or elective assembly, one must have reached the age of 21.

09 FACTSHEET
CONSTITUTIONAL EXTRACTS FROM 1798, 1848, 1874 AND 1999

Art 29 Every village or place which can count 100 citizens entitled to vote constitutes a primary assembly.

Art 30 The citizens of every village or place which does not contain at least 100 citizens entitled to vote will join together with the citizens of the nearest place or village.

Art 31 The towns and cities have a primary assembly in each district. The legislative councils will determine the number of citizens.

Art 32 The primary assemblies take place:
1) in order to accept or reject the state constitution
2) in order to nominate every year the members of the elective assembly of the canton

Art 33 One elector is nominated for every 100 persons who possess the required qualification to be citizens.
(…)

TITLE 11. AMENDING THE CONSTITUTION

Art 106 The Senate proposes these amendments; however, the proposed changes do not acquire the force of a formal decision until they have twice been decreed, and a period of five years must elapse between the first and second decree. The decisions of the Senate must then be either rejected or accepted by the Great Council; in the latter case, they are then sent to the primary assemblies to be accepted or rejected.

Art 107 If the primary assemblies accept them, they then become new basic laws of the state constitution.

SWISS FEDERAL CONSTITUTION OF 1848
Source: Offizielle Sammlung der das schweizerische Staatsrecht betreffenden Aktenstücke, Bundesgesetze, Verträge und Verordnungen seit der Einführung der neuen Bundesverfassung vom 12. September 1848 bis 8. Mai 1850, 2. Aufl., Bern 1850, S. 3 ff.

PART I.

GENERAL PROVISIONS.
Art 1 The peoples of the 22 sovereign cantons joined together by the present alliance, to wit: Zurich, Bern, Lucerne, Ury, Schwyz, Unterwalden (ob and nid dem Wald), Glarus, Zug, Fribourg, Solothurn, Basel (City and Country), Schaffhausen, Appenzell (both Rhodens),

09 FACTSHEET
CONSTITUTIONAL EXTRACTS FROM 1798, 1848, 1874 AND 1999

St. Gallen, Graubünden, Aargau, Thurgau, Ticino, Vaud, Valais, Neuchâtel and Geneva, form in their totality the Swiss Confederation.

Art 2 The purpose of the alliance is: maintenance of the independence of the fatherland against external threat, the management of peace and order internally, the protection of the freedom and the rights of Swiss citizens and the promotion of their common welfare.

Art 3 The cantons are sovereign insofar as their sovereignty is not limited by the federal constitution; as such, they exercise all those rights which have not been transferred to the power of the Federation.

Art 4 All Swiss citizens are equal before the law. In Switzerland no-one is subject to any other and there are no privileges either of place, of birth, of family or of person.

Art 5 The Federation guarantees to the cantons their territory, their sovereignty within the limits of Article 3, the constitutions, freedom, rights of the people and the constitutional rights of the citizens, as well as the rights and powers which the people has transferred to the authorities.

Art 6 The cantons are obliged to formally request the Federation for guarantees for their constitutions. The Federation will issue such guarantees insofar as:
a. they contain nothing which runs counter to the rules of the federal constitution;
b. they ensure the exercise of political rights according to republican – representative or democratic – models;
c. they have been accepted by the people and can be revised if an absolute majority of the people demand it.

Art 42 Every citizen of a canton is a Swiss citizen. As such he can exercise his political rights on federal and cantonal matters in any canton in which he is established. However, he can only exercise these rights under the same conditions as the citizens of the canton and, in respect of cantonal matters, only after having lived in the canton for a longer period of time, the length of which will be determined by cantonal legislation, but which must not be longer than two years.

No-one may exercise political rights in more than one canton.

Section 3.
Revision of the federal constitution.

Art 111 The federal constitution can be revised at any time.
Art 112 The revision shall be carried out in accordance with the forms laid down for federal legislation.

09 FACTSHEET
Constitutional extracts from 1798, 1848, 1874 and 1999

Art 113 If one part of the federal assembly decides on a revision and the other part does not agree, or if fifty thousand Swiss citizens entitled to vote demand a revision of the constitution, the question as to whether a revision shall be carried out or not must in both cases be submitted to the Swiss people for decision in a vote.

If in either of these cases the majority of the Swiss citizens casting a vote give an affirmative answer, both Councils shall be elected anew in order to undertake the revision.

Art 114 The revised federal constitution enters into force if it is approved by a majority of the Swiss citizens casting a vote and a majority of the cantons.

Swiss federal constitution of 1874
Source: www.oefre.unibe.ch/law/verfassungsgeschichte/1874_bundesverfassung.html

Section 1. General provisions

Art 43 [Citizenship, Right to Vote]
(1) Every citizen of a canton is a Swiss citizen.
(2) In this capacity, he may take part in all federal elections and votes at his domicile after having duly proved his right to vote.
(3) No one may exercise political rights in more than one canton.
(4) The established Swiss citizen shall enjoy at his domicile all the rights of the citizens of that canton and, with these, all the rights of the citizens of that Commune. However, sharing in property belonging in common to local citizens or to corporations and the right to vote in matters exclusively regarding local citizens are excepted unless cantonal legislation should provide otherwise.
(5) He acquires voting rights on communal affairs within the canton after he has been resident for three months.
(6) The cantonal laws relating to residency and the voting rights of residents in the Communes are subject to the approval of the Federal Council.

Art 89 [Federal Assembly Legislation]
(1) Federal laws and federal decrees must be approved by both Councils.
(2) Federal laws and non-urgent generally binding federal decrees must besubmitted to the people for approval or rejection if 30,000 Swiss citizens entitled to vote or eight cantons so demand.

Art 90 [Federal Assembly Legislation Formalities]
Federal legislation shall lay down the necessary rules concerning the formalities and time-limits for popular votes.

09 FACTSHEET
CONSTITUTIONAL EXTRACTS FROM 1798, 1848, 1874 AND 1999

TITLE 3. REVISION OF THE CONSTITUTION

Art 118 [Constitutional Revision]
At any time, the Federal Constitution may be revised.

Art 119 [Constitutional Revision]
The revision shall be carried out in accordance with the forms laid down for federal legislation.

Art 120 [Constitutional Revision Procedures]
(1) If one chamber of the Federal Assembly decides on a revision of the Federal Constitution and the other does not consent or if 50,000 Swiss citizens entitled to vote demand the revision of the Federal Constitution, the question whether such a revision should take place or not must be submitted in both cases to the vote of the Swiss people.
(2) If in either of these cases the majority of the Swiss citizens casting a vote give an affirmative answer, both Councils shall be elected anew in order to undertake the revision.

Art 121 [Constitutional Revision Approval]
(1) The revised Federal Constitution shall enter into force if it has been approved by the majority of the Swiss citizens casting a vote and the majority of the cantons.
(2) In order to determine the majority of the cantons, the vote of each half-canton is counted as half a vote.
(3) The result of the popular vote in each canton is considered to be the vote of that canton.

SWISS FEDERAL CONSTITUTION OF 1999 (AS OF 18TH APRIL 1999)
SOURCE: Amtliche Sammlung 1999, S. 2556-2611 (AS 1999 2556)

TITLE 2 FUNDAMENTAL RIGHTS, CITIZENSHIP AND SOCIAL GOALS
CHAPTER 1 FUNDAMENTAL RIGHTS

Art 34 Political rights
(1) Political rights are guaranteed
(2) Guarantees of political rights protect the free formation of opinion by citizens and the true and certain expression of their will

09 FACTSHEET
Constitutional extracts from 1798, 1848, 1874 and 1999

Title 4 People and cantons
Chapter 1 General Provisions

Art 136 Political Rights
(1) All Swiss citizens who are 18 years or older, and are not under guardianship because of mental illness or weakness, shall have political rights in federal matters. All shall have the same political rights and obligations.
(2) They may participate in elections to the House of Representatives and in federal votes and may launch and sign popular initiatives and referenda in federal matters.

Art 137 Political Parties
The political parties shall contribute to the forming of the opinion and the will of the People.

Chapter 2 Initiative and referendum

Art 138 Popular Initiative for Total Revision of the Federal Constitution
(1) 100,000 citizens entitled to vote may propose a total revision of the Federal Constitution.
(2) This proposal has to be submitted to the people by referendum.

Art 139 Popular Initiative for Partial Revision of the Federal Constitution
(1) 100,000 citizens entitled to vote may propose a partial revision of the Federal Constitution.
(2) The popular initiative for a partial revision of the Federal Constitution may be in the form of a general suggestion or a formulated draft.
(3) If an initiative does not respect the principle of unity of form, the principle of unity of subject matter, or mandatory rules of international law, the Federal parliament shall declare the initiative invalid, in whole or in part.
(4) If the Federal parliament approves an initiative in the form of a general suggestion, it shall prepare a partial revision in the sense of the initiative, and submit it to the vote of the people and the cantons. If it rejects the initiative, it shall submit it to the vote of the People; the People shall decide whether the initiative should be followed. If the People approves the initiative, the Federal parliament shall formulate a corresponding draft.
(5) An initiative in the form of a formulated draft shall be submitted to the vote of the People and the cantons. The Federal Parliament shall recommend its approval or its rejection. If it recommends its rejection, it may submit its own counter-draft.
(6) The People and the cantons shall vote simultaneously on the initiative and the counter-draft. The voters may approve both drafts. They may indicate which draft they prefer, should both be approved; should one of the drafts obtain the majority of the People's votes and the other the majority of the votes of the cantons, neither of them shall come into force.

FACTSHEET
CONSTITUTIONAL EXTRACTS FROM 1798, 1848, 1874 AND 1999

Art 140 Mandatory Referendum
(1) The following shall be submitted to the vote of the People and the cantons:
a. Revisions of the Federal Constitution;
b. The entry into organizations for collective security or into supranational communities;
c. Federal Statutes declared urgent which have no constitutional basis and whose validity exceeds one year; such Federal Statutes must be submitted to the vote within one year after their adoption by the Federal Parliament.
(2) The following shall be submitted to the vote of the People:
a. Popular initiatives for total revision of the Federal Constitution;
b. Popular initiatives for partial revision of the Federal Constitution in the form of a general suggestion which were rejected by the Federal Parliament;
c. The question whether a total revision of the Constitution should be carried out if both Chambers disagree.

Art 141 Optional Referendum
(1) The following are submitted to the vote of the People at the request of 50,000 citizens entitled to vote, or of eight cantons:
a. Federal Statutes;
b. Federal Statutes declared urgent with a validity exceeding one year;
c. Federal decrees to the extent the Constitution or the statute foresee this;
d. International treaties which:
    1. are of unlimited duration and may not be terminated;
    2. provide for the entry into an international organization;
    3. involve a multilateral unification of law.
(2) The Federal Parliament may submit further international treaties to optional referendum.

Art 142 Required Majorities
(1) Proposals submitted to the vote of the People shall be accepted if the majority of those voting approves them.
(2) Proposals submitted to the vote of the People and the cantons shall be accepted if the majority of those voting and the majority of the cantons approve them.
(3) The result of a popular vote in a canton determines the vote of that canton.
(4) The cantons of Obwalden, Nidwalden, Basel City, Basel Country, Appenzell Outer-Rhodes and Appenzell Inner-Rhodes have each one half of a cantonal vote.

10

FACTSHEET
ON THE DEVELOPMENT OF DIRECT DEMOCRACY
AT THE LEVEL OF THE SWISS FEDERAL STATE

ORIGINS

1848	Federal constitution of 1848: the initiative for a total revision of the constitution and the obligatory constitutional referendum.
1872 and 1961	Introduction of the legislative initiative rejected.
1874	Completely revised federal constitution of 1874: Citizens' rights extended by addition of the facultative legislative referendum
1891	Introduction of the popular initiative for a partial revision of the constitution

DEVELOPMENT SINCE 1891

Once the popular initiative is introduced, direct democracy becomes a subject for itself – which may lead to it being developed and extended, or to being dismantled. Reforms can of course also be initiated by the authorities. Among the elements which were added after 1891 belong

a) the introduction and extension of the referendum on international treaties, which gives voters a direct say on foreign policy (1921, 1977, 2003);
b) the "double yes" option with a deciding question where there is an initiative and a counter-proposal (1987, 2003);
c) the introduction of the general popular initiative (2003).

The Swiss federal constitution provides that in the case of accession to "organisations for collective security or supranational communities", the people will have the final word. So Swiss voters first of all rejected accession to the UN (in 1986) and then voted in favour of it in a second referendum held in 2002. They also voted against joining the European Economic Area in 1992. If there had been no referendum on international treaties, the people would not have been asked and Switzerland might now be a member of the EU.

In February 2003, at the suggestion of the government and parliament, the referendum on international treaties was extended once more. The rationale was that voters must be able to be involved in deciding on important issues, and that international law and international treaties were raising such issues more and more frequently. The introduction of (in 1921), and the first extension to (in 1977), the referendum on international treaties had come about as a result of the pressure of popular movements and popular initiatives.

National democracies become less important when, as a result of globalisation and European integration, political decision-making more and more takes place outside the sphere of democracy. The appropriate response to this challenge would be to extend democracy beyond the national boundaries. For Switzerland, there is the added question as to whether accession to the EU would inevitably bring about the gradual dismantling of direct democracy. The threat could be diminished by introducing direct democracy into the European Union.

Attempts to expand direct democracy at the federal level have repeatedly been rejected. Thus, the finance referendum was rejected in 1956, the legislative initiative in 1961, the right to have a say on

10 FACTSHEET
ON THE DEVELOPMENT OF DIRECT DEMOCRACY AT THE LEVEL OF THE SWISS FEDERAL STATE

motorway building in 1978 and on the granting of licences for nuclear power stations in 1979, the referendum on armaments in 1987 and the constructive referendum in 2000.

There have also been attempts to dismantle direct democracy, all of them unsuccessful so far. In 1935, the new right-wing forces, which dreamed of replacing democracy with an authoritarian order, were sent packing. The "March 2000 initiative" which wanted the "speeding up of direct democracy" (by shortening the period of time allowed for processing a citizens' initiative presented as a detailed proposal) was decisively rejected, preventing even more radical attempts to weaken direct democracy under the pretext of making it more practical.

1918	introduction of proportional voting for elections to the National Council at the third attempt (after earlier attempts in 1900 and 1910).
1910 and 1942	direct popular election of the Federal Council rejected.
1956	attempt to introduce the finance referendum at the federal level fails.
1921	introduction of the facultative referendum on international treaties (initially restricted to open-ended international treaties; simple majority of the voters), which is supplemented in 1977 by the obligatory referendum on international treaties (with a "double majority" of the people and the cantons) for accession to international organisations.
2003	extension of the facultative referendum on international treaties.
1949	introduction of the obligatory referendum for urgent, general federal decrees which are not based on the constitution. Such decrees have to be submitted to popular referendum vote within a year after they have entered into force. If a majority of voters oppose them, they are annulled. If they are based on the constitution, the facultative referendum applies.
1971	introduction of voting rights (elections and referendums) for women (rejected in 1959).
1973	repeal of Articles 51 & 52 of the constitution concerning Jesuits and monasteries (the "confessional exceptional articles").
1977	increase of signature quorums for initiative and referendum.
1978	rejection of the popular initiative "Enhancing parliamentary and popular participation in decision-making on matters of highway construction".
1981	incorporation into the constitution of an article: "Equal rights for men and women".
1987	initiative aimed at giving voters a say on military expenditure fails to win a majority in the referendum.
1987	the "double Yes" for popular referendum votes where there is an initiative and a counter-proposal is accepted.

FACTSHEET
ON THE DEVELOPMENT OF DIRECT DEMOCRACY AT THE LEVEL OF THE SWISS FEDERAL STATE

2003	"double Yes" refined.
1991	voting age reduced to 18 (rejected in 1976).
1999	on 18th April, the federal decree on a completely revised federal constitution was accepted in a popular vote. The new constitution came into force on 1st Januray 2000.
12.3.2000	rejection of the popular initiative "For speeding up direct democracy (processing times for popular initiatives in the form of a specific draft)", which wanted to reduce the period of time between the handing in of the initiative and the referendum vote to 12 months.
24.9.2000	rejection of the popular initiative "Increased citizens' rights through referendums with counter-proposals (Constructive referendum)".
12.3.2000	rejection of the popular initiative "For a fair representation of women in the federal authorities (3rd March initiative)", which demanded a proper representation of women in all the federal authorities – in the national council, in the council of states, in the Federal Council and in the federal court.
9.2.2003	introduction of the general popular initiative, the extension of the facultative referendum on international treaties and a refined version of the "double Yes".

FACTSHEET
VOTING BEHAVIOUR IN INITIATIVES & REFERENDUMS

Swiss voters generally vote the way the authorities – the government (Federal Council) and parliament (National Council and Council of States) – wish. Exceptions such as the three referendum ballots of 8th February 2004, which all went against what the authorities had wanted, only confirm the rule.

Evolution

The evolution of voting behaviour is especially interesting. Up to the mid-1900's, popular referendum votes which went the authorities' way were still the exception: only one in five results matched the authorities' recommendations. But since then, the majority opinion of Swiss voters has more and more approached that of the Federal Council and parliament: the percentage of ballots which support the authorities' wishes has risen from less than 20% to more than 80%. This trend parallels the growth in the number of popular referendum votes in the second half of the 20th century. In other words, it seems that the authorities were more than able to meet the increased challenge of direct democracy.

Institutional differences

If we look at the success of the authorities in relation to the three main institutions – the obligatory referendum, the facultative (optional) referendum and the initiative – we find big differences: while the authorities' success rate in the obligatory referendum has steadily grown, their experience of the facultative referendum has been something of a roller-coaster ride. In the 19th century, the facultative referendum was a big problem for the authorities: two out of three proposals were rejected by the people. But in the first twenty years of the 20th century, there was a turnaround in the authorities' fortunes: during this period they could count on getting the citizens' support on two out of three occasions. During the 1920's and 1930's, the Federal Council and parliament lost four out of five referendum ballots. Since the 1970's, the authorities' chances of getting the result they want in a facultative referendum have once again risen to over 50%. Nonetheless, from the point of view of the authorities, the facultative referendum remains "the most dangerous" popular right.

Non-threatening initiatives?

Popular initiatives present much less of a threat to government and parliament than facultative referendums. In nine out of ten cases, initiative results go the way the authorities wanted. Popular initiatives almost always demand something which goes further than the elected institutions are prepared to go. So the authorities recommend the rejection of the initiative, but have the option of presenting either a direct or an indirect (in the form of a law) counter-proposal. Since the reform of popular rights on 9th February 2003, parliament can also suggest a counter-proposal which takes a wider view of the issue . Historically, there was only a short period (between 1910 and 1920) when an equal number of initiatives succeeded and were rejected (2 each) at the final hurdle of the popular vote. Since 1940, nine out of every ten initiatives have been rejected by the voters, although in retrospect most initiative groups reckon they have scored an indirect success, because their intentions were introduced in part or in a watered-down form in the legislation.

FACTSHEET
Voting behaviour in initiatives & referendums

Why are the authorities so successful?

The primary reasons for the relative success of the authorities are probably the government's principle of concordance and parliament's aim of achieving maximum consensus. In other words, the more closely the major political forces have to work together in government and the greater the consensus in parliament for a particular proposal, the better are the Federal Council's and parliament's chances of winning a popular referendum vote. But if the Federal Council fails to convince on a particular issue and parliament cannot find a large majority in favour, things can become very tricky for the authorities at the ballot box. That's what happened on 8th February 2004, when 63% of those who voted rejected the proposed extension of the road network (the "Avanti counter-proposal"), 56% of voters accepted a citizens' initiative for "lifelong detention for the perpetrators of sexual or violent crimes who are judged to be highly dangerous and untreatable" which the authorities had opposed, and 64% rejected a proposed new right for tenants.

Source: Trechsel, Alexander: Feuerwerk der Volksrechte (Basel 2000)

12 FACTSHEET
POPULAR INITIATIVES, ACCEPTED BY PEOPLE AND CANTONS

DATE OF POPULAR VOTE	TITLE	PEOPLE YES (NO)	CANTONS ACCEPT (REJECT)	REMARKS
20.08.1893	1 "Prohibition of ritual slaughter without prior anaesthetisation" (Federal constitution (FC) Art. 25bis)	191,527 (127,101)	10 3/2 (9 3/2)	BBl 1893 IV 399–403, AS NF XIII 1020; formally in force legislatively
05.07.1908	2 "Ban on absinthe" (FC Art. 31b and Art. 32ter)	241,078 (138,669)	17 6/2 (2)	BBl 1908 IV 572, AS XXIV 879; formally repealed
13.10.1918	3 "Proportional election of the National Council" (FC Art. 73)	299,550 (149,035)	17 5/2 (2 1/2)	BBl 1918 V 100, AS 34 1219; formally in force
21.03.1920	4 "Prohibition on the setting up of casinos" (FC Art. 35)	271,947 (241,441)	11 2/2 (8 4/2)	BBl 1921 II 302f, AS 37 301; cf. No. 6: formally repealed
30.01.1921	5 "For the introduction of a referendum on treaties with unlimited duration or with a duration of more than 15 years (Referendum on international treaties)" (FC Art. 89)	398,538 (160,004)	17 6/2 (2)	BBl 1921 I 424, AS 37 303; formally repealed
02.12.1928	6 "Casinos" (FC Art. 35)	296,395 (274,528)	13 3/2 (6 3/2)	BBl 1929 I 94, AS 45 68; modified version, formally in force
11.09.1949	7 "Return to direct democracy" (abrogation of war law) (FC Art. 89bis)	280,755 (272,599)	11 3/2 (8 3/2)	BBl 1949 II 582, AS 1949 511; formally in force
28.11.1982	8 "Prevention of false pricing" (FC Art. 31septies)	730,938 (530,498)	16 2/2 (4 4/2)	BBl 1983 I 928, AS 1983 240; formally in force

SOURCE: Swiss Federal Chancellery, political rights section (www.admin.ch/ch/e/pore/index.html)

FACTSHEET
Popular initiatives, accepted by people and cantons

Date of popular vote	Title	People YES (NO)	Cantons ACCEPT (REJECT)	Remarks
06.12.1987	9 "Rothenthurm" initiative for the protection of moorland (FC Art. 24sexies Abs. 5 and transitional provisions)	1,153,448 (843,555)	17 6/2 (3)	BBl 1988 I 572, AS 1988 352; formally in force
23.09.1990	10 "Moratorium on nuclear power station construction" (FC transitional provisions Art. 19)	946,077 (789,209)	17 5/2 (3 1/2)	BBl 1991 I 309, AS 1991 247; formally expired, no longer in force
26.09.1993	11 "For a federal work-free holiday on 1 August (1st August Initiative)" (FC Art. 116bis and transitional provisions Art. 20)	1,492,285 (289,122)	20 6/2 (0)	BBl 1993 IV 266 and 269, AS 1993 3041; formally in force
20.02.1994	12 "To protect the Alpine region from transit traffic" (FC Art. 36sexies and transitional provisions Art. 22)	954,491 (884,362)	13 6/2 (7)	BBl 1994 II 701, AS 1994 1101; formally in force
03.03.2002	13 "For Switzerland's membership of the United Nations (UN)" (FC Art. 197 Ziff. 1)	1,489,110 (1,237,629)	11 2/2 (9 4/2)	BBl 2002 3690[1]; AS 2002 885[2]; formally in force
08.02.2004	14 "Lifelong detention for perpetrators of sexual or violent crimes who are judged to be highly dangerous and untreatable" (FC Art. 123a)	1,198,751 (934,576)	19 5/2 (1 1/2)	BBl 2004 2199[3]
27.11.2005	15 "For food grown without genetic modification" (FC Art. 197 Ziff. 7)	1,125,835 (896,482)	20 6/2 (0)	BBl 2006 1061

[1] www.admin.ch/ch/d/ff/2002/3690.pdf
[2] www.admin.ch/ch/d/as/2002/885.pdf
[3] www.admin.ch/ch/d/ff/2004/2199.pdf

FACTSHEET 13
Bandwidths of indirect and direct democracy

	Purely representative democracy	Well developed direct democracy
Image of the human being	Politically "immature" citizens, "mature" politicians	"Mature" citizens as politicians
Relationship between citizens and politicians	Established-outsiders relationship, institutionalised categorical inequality	More even distribution of power: no categorical inequality; citizens enjoy independent possibilities of controlling the political process and of making proposals
Distribution of the resources of political power	Politicians monopolise: 1) the right to make substantive political decisions 2) the right to determine the political agenda 3) access to important information	Politicians have no monopoly on substantive political decisions or agenda setting
Political rights of citizens	Voting in elections	Voting in elections and referendums
Participatory procedures	Elections, plebiscites, possibly obligatory constitutional referendums	Elections, popular initiatives, popular referendums, obligatory constitutional referendums and obligatory referendums on issues which are defined in the constitution (for example, accession to international organisations and supranational communities)
Citizen's role	Voter, passive citizen, outsider, elects people and parties, makes no substantive decisions, offers opinions to politicians, political external regulation	Voter, occasional politician, active citizen, makes the important decisions, elects the political office-holders, political self-regulation
Politician's role	Decision-maker, governs for citizens, receives citizens' opinion, active citizen, member of the established group	Decision-maker, governs together with other citizens, advises citizens, active citizen
Freedom	Negative freedom, renunciation of freedom as autonomy	Positive freedom, freedom as autonomy

14 FACTSHEET
RESULTS OF POPULAR CONSULTATIONS IN THE JURA REGION

1950   In the referendum vote in the canton Bern on 29th October 1950 the Jura Statute was accepted by 69,089 "Yes"-votes to 7,289 "No"-votes on a turnout of around 31%. The proposal was accepted in all districts, even more clearly in the Jura districts than in the old part of the canton.

1959   On 5th July 1959, the initiative of the Rassemblement Jurassien was rejected across the canton by 80,141 "No"-votes to 23,130 "Yes"-votes, and in the seven Jura districts by 16,352 "No"-votes to 15,159 "Yes"-votes. However, the Jura region was divided: Franches-Montagnes, Delémont and Porrentruy approved the proposal with "Yes"-votes of between 66% and 76%. Courtelary, Laufen, Moutier and Neuenstadt rejected the proposal with "No"-votes of between 65% and 75%. Turnout was 85% for the Jura and 31% for the old part of the canton.

1970   The "Supplement to the constitution of the canton Bern in respect of the Jura region", which conceded the right of self-determination to the Jura districts, was accepted in the referendum vote on 1st March 1970 by 90,358 "Yes"-votes to 14,133 "No"-votes. Turnout was around 60% in the Jura and 38% across the whole canton. The constitutional amendment was approved in all districts, especially clearly in those of the Jura.

1974   23rd June 1974: Consultative referendum of eligible voters in the Jura region: "Do you wish to form a new canton?"

District	Yes	No	Invalid/blank	Turnout (%)
Courtelary	3,123	10,260	288	90.03
Delémont	11,070	2,948	509	92.50
Franches-Montagnes	3,573	1,058	76	93.48
Laufen	1,433	4,119	51	73.16
Moutier	7,069	9,330	383	91.48
Neuenstadt	931	1,776	41	86.47
Porrentruy	9,603	4,566	404	93.62
Jura	36,802	34,057	1,752	88.67

14 FACTSHEET
RESULTS OF POPULAR CONSULTATIONS IN THE JURA REGION

1975 16th March 1975: Consultative referendums in three districts: "Do you wish to continue to belong to the canton Bern?"

District	Yes	No	Invalid/blank	Turnout (%)
Courtelary	10,802	3,268	115	92.13
Moutier	9,947	7,740	113	96.02
Neuenstadt	1,927	997	28	91.48

1978 24th September 1978: Federal popular referendum vote on recognition of the new, 26th Swiss canton. The proposal was accepted by all the cantons and by a majority of the people, with 1,309,841 "Yes"-votes to 281,873 "No"-votes. Voter turnout was 42%.

FACTSHEET
Chronology of the Jura conflict (1815–2004)

1815   At the Congress of Vienna, the canton Bern receives the former principality of Basel, now known as the Jura region, in compensation for the loss of Vaud and the Aargau.

1815–1945   5 protest movements in the Jura: 1826–31, 1834–36, 1838–39, 1867–69, 1913–19. They are all of short duration and fail to mobilize the people. Other lines of conflict, which divide the Jura rather than uniting it, take precedence.

1947   The Moeckli affair. Georges Moeckli, government member from the Jura, is denied the ministry of public works by the parliament in Bern on the grounds of his supposed "defective knowledge of German". Two thousand demonstrators protest in Delémont. The Comité de Moutier is formed. Its goal: autonomy within the canton Bern. The Mouvement séparatiste jurassien (MSJ) is founded. In its newspaper "Jura libre", it demands the separation of the Jura from Bern.

1948   The Comité de Moutier addresses a 21-point memorandum to the cantonal government in Bern; it demands autonomy for the Jura und the federalisation of the canton Bern. The government in Bern is prepared to make only some less wide-ranging concessions.

1949   The cantonal government in Bern approves the first report on the Jura drawn up by Markus Feldmann.

29.10.1950   A referendum vote endorses a change to the Bern cantonal constitution – the Jura Statute – by a clear majority. In the new constitution, the existence of a "people of the Jura" – separate from the people of the old part of the canton – is explicitly recognized.

1951   The cantonal government in Bern recognizes the Jura coat of arms. The MSJ renames itself the Rassemblement Jurassien (RJ)

1952   The Comité de Moutier is wound up. The anti-separatists form the Union des Patriotes Jurassiens (UPJ).

1957   The RJ launches an initiative aimed at determining what the people of the Jura think about founding a new canton Jura.

5.7.1959   Referendum vote – the RJ initiative is rejected.

1961   The separatists submit 4 popular initiative proposals. The referendum ballot takes place on 27.5.1962.

1962   The "Béliers" youth wing of the RJ is founded. The "Berberat" case: first lieutenant Romain Berberat is punished for declaring – at a separatist carnival at which he is wearing civilian clothes – Bern to be "an autocratic dictatorship of politicians who have never understood us".

1963   The "Front de libération jurassien" (FLJ – Jura Liberation Front) admits carrying out arson and bomb attacks. It consists of three men who acted independently of the RJ.

FACTSHEET
Chronology of the Jura conflict (1815–2004)

1964	The "Les Rangiers" affair: separatist demonstrators interrupt a service of commemoration for the Swiss Army.
1967	The Bern government appoints the "Commission of the 24" to study the Jura issue. Its report outlines three options for the people of the Jura: status quo, autonomy, separation.
1968	At the suggestion of the Federal Council, Bern appoints the "Good Services Commission"; it is meant to mediate between the different parties and produces its "First Report" on 13.5.1969.
1.3.1970	Popular referendum vote on the "Supplement to the constitution of the canton Bern in respect of the Jura region", which grants the right of self-determination to the Jura districts. Efforts to formulate an autonomous status fail.
23.6.1974	Popular consultation among Jura electorate: "Do you wish to form a new canton?". A slim majority votes "Yes".
16.3.1975	Popular consultations in the districts of Courtelary, Moutier and Neuenstadt: "Do you want to continue to belong to the canton Bern?". A majority in all the districts votes to remain with Bern.
7 and 14.9.1975	Popular consultations in border communes about which canton they want to belong to. Moutier, Grandval, Perrefitte, Rebévelier and Schelten – all communities with a Protestant majority – vote to remain with Bern. Châtillon, Corban, Courchapoix, Courrendlin, Lajoux, Les Genevez, Mervelier and Rossemaison (all with a Catholic majority) decide to join the canton Jura.
14.9.1975	Popular consultation: Laufental rejects accession to Bern. A law passed in November 1975 permits the Laufental to seek accession to a different, neighbouring canton. A treaty of accession to Basel Country is made, but this is rejected in 1983 by the voters of Laufental. This decision is later declared invalid, and on 12.11.1989 Laufental decides to join Basel Country.
19.10.1975	The community of Roggenburg (Catholic, German-speaking) decides to remain with the district of Laufen.
21.3.1976	Election of a constitutional assembly in the Jura.
20.3.1977	Approval of the constitution of the new canton Jura in a popular referendum vote.
24.9.1978	The Swiss electorate agrees to the canton Jura being accepted into the Federation (popular referendum on an appropriate change to the constitution).
1.1.1979	The "République et canton du Jura" (the Republic and the canton Jura) is proclaimed. This raises the number of Swiss cantons to 26.
1980	A convention of the RJ in the community of Cortébert (in the Bernese Jura) is violently disrupted. Subsequently, violence gradually diminishes.

FACTSHEET
CHRONOLOGY OF THE JURA CONFLICT (1815–2004)

1990   The canton Bern applies to the federal court for the annulment of a popular initiative "Unite" launched by the RJ to create a law on the unity of the Jura. Two years later, the court decides in favour of Bern. In 1994, the canton Jura formally repeals the "Unite" law passed by the cantonal parliament.

8.3.1993   Dominique Haenni presents to the cantonal government his report on "The French speakers in the canton Bern", which he drew up as a result of the Pétermann proposal of 7.9.1989. Haenni recommended a process of increasing autonomy for the French-speaking ("Jura") areas of the canton Bern, as a means of improving the relationship between them and the canton. As a result (see following)

19.1.1994   On the 19th January 1994 the Bernese parliament passes the "Law on the strengthening of political participation of the Bernese Jura and of the French-speaking population of the municipality of Biel", which continues to govern the position of the French-speaking minority in the canton Bern.

6.6.1993   The new Bernese cantonal constitution is approved in a referendum ballot. It enters into force on 1.1.1995. Uniquely, the Bernese Jura is granted special regional status (cf. Art. 5) within the canton. The three districts of the Bernese Jura are French-speaking and the roughly 51,000 inhabitants (5.4% of the total cantonal population) form a relatively small minority.
Art. 5 (of the Bernese cantonal constitution) The Bernese Jura
1) Special status is accorded to the Bernese Jura, consisting of the districts of Courtelary, Moutier and La Neuveville. This should enable it to preserve its identity and its special linguistic and cultural character and to take an active part in cantonal politics.
2) The canton will adopt measures to strengthen the links between the Bernese Jura and the rest of the canton.

25.3.1994   An agreement between the federation and the cantons of Jura and Bern formalises dialogue between the Jura proper and the Bernese Jura and creates the Assemblée interjurassienne (AIJ) – the Inter-Jura Assembly. The Federal Council maintains regular contact with the governments of Bern and the Jura. The basic idea of the agreement is that the Jura region should produce its own proposals for solving its problems.

1.1.1994   Laufental joins the canton Basel Country.

10.3.1996   Federal popular referendum vote: the community of Vellerat joins the canton Jura.

27.9.2000   Report of the regional council (conseil régional Jura bernois et Bienne romande) on how increased autonomy for the Bernese Jura can be implemented.

15
FACTSHEET
CHRONOLOGY OF THE JURA CONFLICT (1815–2004)

20.12.2000   Resolution No. 44 of the Inter-Jura Assembly (AIJ) on how the Jura issue is to be addressed politically. It provides for a two-stage process: during the first two to three years, ways and means of creating cooperation between the canton Jura and the Bernese Jura are to be put in place. In the second, four-year, phase the practical results of the cooperation should be seen. There is a plan for a regional parliament with its own executive.

2003   The "Mouvement autonomiste jurassien" (Movement for the Autonomy of the Jura) (MAJ) launches the initiative "Un seul Jura" (One Jura). Their goal is a form of re-unification of the Jura: the three districts of the Bernese Jura are to be offered shared sovereignty across the whole territory of the six French-speaking districts of the Jura. The Force démocratique (FD) sees the MAJ initiative as provocation.

2003–2004   Draft of the law on the special statute for the Bernese Jura and the French-speaking minority in the district of Biel (Special Statute Law, SStG). The law came into force in 2006. It is designed to enable the population of the Bernese Jura "to retain their identity within the canton, to maintain their linguistic and cultural individuality and to play an active part in the political life of the canton". The regional council will be dissolved and replaced by the Bernese Jurassic Council. A new "regional initiative" is introduced: a citizens' initiative "whose subject matter must be related to the identity and the linguistic or cultural individuality of the Bernese Jura". For the initiative to proceed, a minimum 2000 signatures must be collected within a period of six months.

SOURCES:
- Historisches Lexikon der Schweiz (www.dhs.ch)
- Junker, Beat: Geschichte des Kantons Bern seit 1798: Band III Tradition und Aufbruch 1881–1995 (Bern 1996). Herausgegeben vom Historischen Verein des Kantons Bern (www.stub.unibe.ch/extern/hv/gkb/iii/)
- Neue Zürcher Zeitung, 26.4.2004, Sonderstatut für den Berner Jura
- Schwander, Marcel: Jura. Konfliktstoff für Jahrzehnte (Zurich/Köln 1977)
- Vortrag der Staatskanzlei an den Regierungsrat zum Entwurf des Gesetzes über das Sonderstatut des Berner Juras und die französischprachige Minderheit des Amtsbezirks Biel (Sonderstatutgesetz, SStG). Entwürfe vom 7. Mai bzw. 19. Juni 2003 sowie Gesetzesentwurf: www.be.ch/aktuell/sonderstatut/sonderstatut.asp [German and French]
- Website of the Interjurassischen Versammlung (IJV)/Assemblée interjurassienne (AIJ): www.assemblee-interjura.ch/ [in French]
- Website of the canton Jura: www.ju.ch [in French]
- Website of the Conseil régional Jura bernois et Bienne romande (www.conseilregional-jb.ch/)

FACTSHEET
The Army XXI referendum on 18 May, 2003

Federal law on the army and military administration ("Militärgesetz: MG"), amendment.
The proposal was accepted

Electorate	Total eligible voters:		4,764,888
	Of which Swiss living or staying abroad:		84,216
Turnout	Voting slips received:		2,361,382
	Turnout:		50%
Voting slips disregarded	Blank slips:		90,232
	Invalid slips:		11,121
Voting slips taken into account	Valid slips:		2,260,029
	"Yes" votes:	(76.0%)	1,718,452
	"No" votes:	(24.0%)	541,577

Sources:
- Referendum vote of 18.05.2003: BBl 2003 5164
  (www.admin.ch/ch/d/ff/2003/5164.pdf)
- Amendment to MG of 04.10.2002: AS 2003 3957
  (www.admin.ch/ch/d/as/2003/3957.pdf)
- Parliamentary decision of 04.10.2002: BBl 2002 6543
  (www.admin.ch/ch/d/ff/2002/6543.pdf)
- Statement by Federal Council of 24.10.2001: BBl 2002 858
  (www.admin.ch/ch/d/ff/2002/858.pdf)

FACTSHEET
The popular initiative "Equal rights for the disabled"

The text of the popular initiative reads:

"The federal constitution shall be amended as follows:

Art. 4bis (new)

1 No-one shall be discriminated against on grounds either of country of origin, race, gender, language, age, position in society, way of life, religious, philosophical or political conviction, or because they are subject to any physical, mental or psychological disablement.

2 The law guarantees equality of rights for disabled people. It provides for measures to remove and compensate for existing discrimination.

3 Access to public buildings and facilities, and the right to make use of utilities and services intended for public use, shall be guaranteed as long as this does not incur unreasonable expense."

Stages in the popular initiative:

	Chronology	Source
18.05.2003	Referendum vote *The proposal was rejected*	BBl 2003 5164 (www.admin.ch/ch/d/ff/2003/5164.pdf)
13.12.2002	Decision of parliament *Recommendation: rejection*	BBl 2002 8152 (www.admin.ch/ch/d/ff/2002/8152.pdf)
11.12.2000	Statement by the Federal Council	BBl 2001 1715 (www.admin.ch/ch/d/ff/2001/1715.pdf)
04.02.2000	End of signature collection period	
04.08.1999	Officially validated	BBl 1999 7312 (www.admin.ch/ch/d/ff/1999/7312.pdf)
14.06.1999	Signatures handed in	
04.08.1998	Start of signature collection period	
21.07.1998	Preliminary check	BBl 1998 3964

17 FACTSHEET
THE POPULAR INITIATIVE "EQUAL RIGHTS FOR THE DISABLED"

REFERENDUM BALLOT OF 18.5.2003
ON THE CITIZENS' INITIATIVE "EQUAL RIGHTS FOR THE DISABLED"
THE INITIATIVE WAS REJECTED BY THE PEOPLE AND THE CANTONS.

ELECTORATE	Total eligible voters:	4,764,888
	Of which Swiss living or staying abroad:	84,216
TURNOUT	Voting slips received:	2,367,883
	Turnout:	50%
VOTING SLIPS DISREGARDED	Blank slips:	47,178
	Invalid slips:	10,563
VOTING SLIPS TAKEN INTO ACCOUNT	Valid slips:	1,738,070
	"Yes" votes:	(37.7%) 870,249
	"No" votes:	(62.3%) 1,439,893
CANTONS	Number of cantons supporting the proposal	3
	Number of cantons rejecting the proposal	17 6/2

18 FACTSHEET
Citizens' rights at the federal level in Switzerland

Probably no other country in the world has such extensive rights of political co-determination as Switzerland. Swiss citizens enjoy the following political rights at the federal (national) level:

1) Voting in elections

Active voting right	Passive voting right
Elections to the National Council	Eligibility to be elected to the National Council, the Federal Council and the Federal Court
All adult Swiss citizens who have reached the age of 18 are entitled to elect representatives to the National Council	All adult Swiss citizens who have reached the age of 18 are entitled to put themselves up for election.

2) Voting in referendum votes (general voting rights)

All Swiss citizens, whether living in Switzerland or abroad, who have reached the age of 18 and who are not disqualified on grounds of mental illness or mental handicap are entitled to vote. The term "Stimmrecht" ("the right to vote") means the right to take part – literally to "have a say" – in citizens' referendum votes. However, the term is also understood more widely to mean the right to take up one's political rights or to exercise one's citizens' rights. The right to vote includes the right to take part in elections and referendum votes, to sign referendum demands and popular initiatives and to exercise other democratic rights.

3) The right of initiative

At the federal level, Swiss citizens can demand a referendum vote on a change which they wish to have made to the constitution. Before an initiative can be officially validated, the signatures of 100,000 citizens who are entitled to vote have to be gathered within 18 months. An initiative can be formulated as a general proposal or be presented as a fully worked-out text.

4) The right to referendum

'The people' (i.e. all those with the right to vote) has the right to decide in retrospect on decisions made by parliament. Federal laws, federal decrees, open-ended international treaties and treaties which provide for accession to international organisations are subject to the facultative i.e. optional referendum. This means that if 50,000 citizens request it (by giving their signatures), the matter must be referred to a referendum vote. The signatures must be handed in to the authorities within 100 days of the official publication of the parliamentary decision. (All amendments to the constitution and accession to certain international organisations are subject to the obligatory referendum i.e. a referendum vote must take place).

FACTSHEET
CITIZENS' RIGHTS AT THE FEDERAL LEVEL IN SWITZERLAND

5) THE RIGHT OF PETITION

All persons of sound mind – not only those who have the right to vote – are entitled to direct written requests, proposals and complaints to the authorities. The latter must take note of such petitions. The authorities are not bound to respond, but in practice, all petitions are dealt with and responses given. Any activity of the state can be the subject of a petition.

SOURCE: Swiss Federal Chancellery, political rights section (www.admin.ch/ch/e/pore/index.html)

19 FACTSHEET
THE RESULT OF THE PARLIAMENTARY ELECTIONS IN 2003

Distribution of seats in the National Council

Party	Seats	% of total seats	Women	%	Men	%
SVP	55	26.7	3	5.5	52	94.5
SPS	52	23.3	24	46.2	28	53.8
FDP	36	17.3	7	19.4	29	80.6
CVP	28	14.4	9	32.1	19	67.9
GPS	13	7.4	7	53.8	6	46.2
LPS	4	2.2	1	25.0	3	75.0
EVP	3	2.3			3	100.0
PdA	2	0.7	1	50.0	1	50.0
EDU	2	1.3			2	100.0
CSP	1	0.4			1	100.0
FGA	1	0.5			1	100.0
SD	1	1.0			1	100.0
Lega	1	0.4			1	100.0
Sol	1	0.5			1	100.0

Distribution of seats in the Council of States

Party	Seats	Women	%	Men	%
FDP	14	5	35.7	9	64.3
CVP	15	2	13.3	13	86.7
SPS	9	4	44.4	5	55.6
SVP	8			8	100.0

FACTSHEET
The result of the parliamentary elections in 2003

Election turnout

Canton	%
Zurich	45.1
Bern	42.1
Lucerne	50.9
Uri	44.4
Schwyz	48.2
Obwalden	45.7
Nidwalden	39.4
Glarus	25.3
Zug	52.6
Fribourg	45.4
Solothurn	47.4
Basel City	49.6
Geneva	45.9
Basel Country	44.2
Schaffhausen	63.2
Appenzell Outer-Rhodes	49.3
Appenzell Inner-Rhodes	35.1
St. Gallen	42.8
Graubünden	39.1
Aargau	42.3
Thurgau	42.9
Ticino	48.6
Vaud	42.7
Valais	53.3
Neuchâtel	50.3
Jura	46.6

Source: Swiss Federal Chancellery, political rights section (www.admin.ch/ch/e/pore/index.html)

20 FACTSHEET
THE MAJOR INITIATORS OF POPULAR INITIATIVES & REFERENDUMSS

THE MAJOR INITIATORS OF "POPULAR DEMANDS" (POPULAR INITIATIVES AND FACULTATIVE REFERENDUMS) IN THE CANTONS BETWEEN 1979–2000

1. Political parties initiate 37% of all popular demands
   - Share: 60% Green/Left camp, 40% "bourgeois" camp
   - Major subjects: system of state organisation, finances/taxation, social welfare/health
2. Ad-hoc initiative committees initiate 30% of all popular demands
   - Emphasis on transport policies, democracy
3. Combined sponsorship
4. Interest groups initiate 10% of all popular demands
   - The most active groups: environmental, trade unions, tenants, employers, house owners
   - Emphasis on financial, environmental and educational issues
5. New social movements and individuals initiate 7% of all popular demands
   - Emphasis on the system of government, energy and the environment.

THE MAJOR TRENDS IN THE SPONSORSHIP OF POPULAR DEMANDS

1. At the beginning of the 21st century, the most successful initiatives do not originate in either left-wing or right-wing political circles, but in the political centre-ground, which has always done badly in parliamentary elections in recent years.
2. An increasing number of popular demands (initiatives and referendums) are launched by established groups. The citizens' movements which stood behind many popular initiatives during the 1990's have been less prominent of late.
3. The maxim that people from the Left and Green camps primarily turn to the popular initiative (the "gas pedal"), while bourgeois and right-wing circles tend to use the facultative referendum (the "brake"), is no longer true.

Source: Gross, Andreas: Trendwende bei den Volksrechten? (NZZ, 12.01.2004)

FACTSHEET
THE MAIN ISSUES OF INITIATIVES AND REFERENDUMS AT THE FEDERAL LEVEL AND IN THE CANTONS

The 3 major subject areas covered by national popular initiatives since 1951

	1	2	3
1951–1960	Social welfare	The economy	Peace
1961–1970	Social welfare	The economy	Peace
1971–1980	Social welfare	The economy	The environment
1981–1990	The environment	The economy	Social welfare
1991–2000	The environment	Social welfare	Peace
2001–2003	Social welfare	The environment	Social integration policies

The three major subject areas for popular initiatives and facultative referendums in the cantons since 1979

Governance: the state & democracy	Distribution: finances & social welfare	The Environment: energy & transport
Fribourg	Basel Country	Aargau
Graubünden	Basel City	Basel Country
Jura	Geneva	Bern
Obwalden	Lucerne	Jura
Schwyz	Neuchâtel	Lucerne
Uri	St. Gallen	Solothurn
	Schaffhausen	Zug
	Thurgau	
	Ticino	
	Valais	
	Vaud	
	Zurich	

Sources:
- Swiss Federal Chancellery, political rights section (www.admin.ch/ch/e/pore/index.html)
- Vatter, Adrian: Kantonale Demokratien im Vergleich (Opladen, 2002)

FACTSHEET
Referendum votes on issues relating to foreigners in the federation

Naturalization, residence, citizens' rights, law on foreigners, asylum law

Date	Subject	Outcome [people] / [cantons]
14.01.1866	Equal domiciliary rights for Jews and naturalized citizens	ACCEPTED [P] / [C]
14.01.1866	Permanent residents' right to vote on community matters	REJECTED [P] / [C]
14.01.1866	Tax and civil rights in relation to permanent residents	REJECTED [P] / [C]
14.01.1866	Permanent residents' right to vote on cantonal matters	REJECTED [P] / [C]
21.10.1877	Federal law on the political rights of permanent and temporary residents and the loss of political rights of Swiss citizens	REJECTED
11.06.1922	Popular initiative "Naturalization"	REJECTED [P] / [C]
11.06.1922	Popular initiative "Expulsion of foreigners"	REJECTED [P] / [C]
25.10.1925	Federal decree concerning temporary and permanent residence of foreigners	ACCEPTED [P] / [C]
20.05.1928	Federal decree on revision of Art. 44 of the federal constitution (measures to limit number of foreigners)	ACCEPTED [P] / [C]
07.06.1970	Popular initiative "Foreigners, reduction of number"	REJECTED [P] / [C]
20.10.1974	Popular initiative "Foreigners, reduction of number"	REJECTED [P] / [C]
13.03.1977	Popular initiative "Foreigners, reduction of number (N° 4)"	REJECTED [P] / [C]
13.03.1977	Popular initiative "Restriction on naturalization of foreigners"	REJECTED [P] / [C]
05.04.1981	Popular initiative "New, friendlier policy towards foreign residents"	REJECTED [P] / [C]
06.06.1982	Law on foreigners (AuG)	REJECTED
04.12.1983	Federal decree on changes to citizenship rules in the constitution	ACCEPTED [P] / [C]
04.12.1983	Federal decree on making naturalization easier in certain cases	REJECTED [P] / [C]

22 FACTSHEET
REFERENDUM VOTES ON ISSUES RELATING TO FOREIGNERS IN THE FEDERATION

NATURALIZATION, RESIDENCE, CITIZENS' RIGHTS, LAW ON FOREIGNERS, ASYLUM LAW

DATE	SUBJECT	OUTCOME [PEOPLE] / [CANTONS]
05.04.1987	Asylum law, amendment of 20th June 1986	ACCEPTED
05.04.1987	Federal law on rights of stay and domicile of foreigners, revision of 20.6.1986	ACCEPTED
04.12.1988	Popular initiative "On restriction of immigration"	REJECTED [P] / [C]
12.06.1994	Federal decree on the revision of the rules on citizens' rights in the federal constitution (easier acquisition of citizenship for young foreigners)	FAILED TO WIN A MAJORITY OF CANTONS
04.12.1994	Federal law on compulsory measures in the law on foreigners	ACCEPTED
01.12.1996	Federal decree on the popular initiative "against illegal immigration" (counter-proposal)	REJECTED [P] / [C]
13.06.1999	Asylum law (AsylG)	ACCEPTED
13.06.1999	Federal decree on urgent measures in the area of asylum and foreigners (BMA)	ACCEPTED
24.09.2000	Popular initiative "for regulation of immigration"	REJECTED [P] / [C]
24.11.2002	Popular initiative "against the abuse of asylum rights"	FAILED TO WIN A MAJORITY OF POPULAR VOTES
26.09.2004	Federal decree of 3rd October 2003 on the proper handling of naturalisations, as well as easier naturalisation for young, second-generation foreigners	REJECTED [P] / [C]
26.09.2004	Federal decree of 3rd October 2003 on the acquisition of citizenship by third-generation foreigners	REJECTED [P] / [C]
24.09.2006	Federal decree of 16nd December 2005 on foreigners	
24.09.2006	Federal decree of 16nd December 2005 on the asylum law	

SOURCE: Swiss Federal Chancellery, political rights section (www.admin.ch/ch/e/pore/index.html)

23 FACTSHEET
THE LAW ON THE PROTECTION OF WATER RESOURCES (1983–92)

FEDERAL LAW OF 24.1.1991
ON THE PROTECTION OF LAKES AND RIVERS (GEWÄSSERSCHUTZGESETZ, GSchG)

	CHRONOLOGY	SOURCE
1 NOV 1992	Entry into force	AS 1992 1860
17 MAY 1992	Referendum vote	BBl 1992 V 455
14 JUN 1991	Referendum officially validated	BBl 1991 II 1575
24 JAN 1991	Decision of parliament	BBl 1991 I 250
29 APR 1987	Statement by the Federal Council	BBl 1987 II 1061

THE PROPOSAL WAS ACCEPTED AT THE REFERENDUM VOTE OF 17.5.1992
ON THE FEDERAL LAW ON THE PROTECTION OF LAKES AND RIVERS (GEWÄSSERSCHUTZGESETZ, GSchG)

ELECTORATE	Total eligible voters:		4,516,994
	Of which Swiss living or staying abroad:		14,361
TURNOUT	Voting slips received:		1,771,843
	Turnout:		39,22%
VOTING SLIPS DISREGARDED	Blank slips:		26,233
	Invalid slips:		2,664
VOTING SLIPS TAKEN INTO ACCOUNT	Valid slips:		1,742,946
	"Yes" votes:	(66.1%)	1,151,706
	"No" votes:	(33.9%)	591,240

FACTSHEET
THE LAW ON THE PROTECTION OF WATER RESOURCES (1983–92)

FEDERAL POPULAR INITIATIVE: "SAVE OUR LAKES AND RIVERS"
The text of the citizens' initiative is as follows:

The federal constitution shall be amended as follows:

Art. 24octies (new)
1 Natural water courses and sections of such which are still largely in an original state, together with the adjacent riverbanks, are to be subject to comprehensive protection.

2 Interventions to parts of water courses which are close to a natural state, which despite existing pressures have largely retained their original appearance and ecological functions, are to be locally restricted. Intervention for purposes of exploitation which either directly or indirectly alters the ecological or scenic character of sections of water courses which are close to a natural state or of larger sections which are subject to considerable environmental pressure.

3 Water courses or sections thereof which are same term as above. are to be rehabilitated along with their riparian borders, taking into account also their tributaries and feeder channels, wherever restoration to a natural state is justified for ecological or scenic reasons. The free movement of fishes and the natural reproductive activity of animals are to be ensured.

4 Any work carried out on water courses and the adjacent riverbanks is to be done with care and limited to what is absolutely essential.

5 The intervention of the hydraulic engineering police is only to be permitted if it is imperative to protect human life and health or sizeable material assets.

6 In the case of new and existing damming measures and extraction of water, a sufficient flow is to be ensured continually and along the entire length of the watercourse. The flow is deemed to be sufficient when, in particular, it ensures the continued existence of the local animal and plant communities; does not seriously damage countryside worthy of protection or valuable elements of the countryside or the quantity and quality of groundwater; ensures that effluent is adequately diluted and the fertility of the ground is maintained

7 Any diminution of legitimate rights will be compensated for in line with Article 22ter. The Federation will establish a fund, paid for by the owners of hydro-electric stations, to provide compensation for restrictions to property rights which have a legitimate claim to such compensation.

8 Organisations involved in the protection of nature, the countryside and the environment shall be accorded the status of a party that is entitled to launch a complaint.

23 FACTSHEET
THE LAW ON THE PROTECTION OF WATER RESOURCES (1983–92)

9 Where objections and complaints are directed against actions aimed at the exploitation of water courses, such actions will be deferred.

Transitional arrangements

1 Plans for which valid concessions or approvals already exist are to count as new interventions, if essential building work has not yet begun at the point when Art. 24octies is approved.

2 Until such time as the legal provisions are created, the government shall issue the necessary rules and in particular manage the process of issuing permits and arranging restoration work. If these rules have not been issued within two years after acceptance of Article 24octies, no work is to be permitted other than by the hydraulic engineering police.

3 Article 24octies and the aforementioned provisions enter into force when they have been approved by the people and the cantons."

STAGES OF THE CITIZENS' INITIATIVE:

	CHRONOLOGY	SOURCE
17.05.1992	Referendum vote. *The proposal was rejected*	BBl 1992 V 459
06.10.1989	Decision of the parliament *Recommendation: rejection of the initiative, indirect counter-proposal*	BBl 1989 III 900
29.04.1987	Statement by the Federal Council	BBl 1987 II 1061
08.11.1984	Officially validated	BBl 1984 III 994
01.12.1984	End of signature collection period	
09.10.1984	Signatures handed in	
31.05.1983	Start of signature collection period	
17.05.1983	Preliminary check	BBl 1983 II 354

23 FACTSHEET
THE LAW ON THE PROTECTION OF WATER RESOURCES (1983–92)

REFERENDUM BALLOT OF 17.5.1992
ON THE FEDERAL POPULAR INITIATIVE "SAVE OUR LAKES AND RIVERS"
THE PROPOSAL WAS REJECTED BY THE PEOPLE AND THE CANTONS

ELECTORATE	Total eligible voters:		4,516,994
	Of which Swiss living or staying abroad:		14,361
TURNOUT	Voting slips received:		1,771,722
	Turnout:		39%
VOTING SLIPS DISREGARDED	Blank slips:		31,086
	Invalid slips:		2,566
VOTING SLIPS TAKEN INTO ACCOUNT	Valid slips:		1,738,070
	"Yes" votes:	(37.1%)	644,083
	"No" votes:	(62.9%)	1,093,987
CANTONS	Number of cantons supporting the proposal		0
	Number of cantons rejecting the proposal		20 6/2

FACTSHEET
RESTRICTIONS ON THE CONSTITUTIONAL INITIATIVE IN SWITZERLAND

Article 192, § 1 of the federal constitution states that the constitution may be subjected to a total or partial revision at any time. In the case of a total revision, the proposers (the initiative committee) are only allowed to demand that a referendum vote be held to decide whether the constitution should be revised or not (Art. 138 federal constitution (FC)). In the case of an initiative for a partial revision of the federal constitution, on the other hand, the initiative committee can propose a specific change in content. However, the proposers do not have an entirely free hand: they must bear in mind certain restrictions on what can be proposed arising from national and international law.

Article 139 § 3 of the federal constitution states that in the case of a popular initiative for a partial revision of that constitution: "If an initiative does not respect the principle of unity of form, the principle of unity of subject matter, or mandatory rules of international law, the Federal Parliament shall declare the initiative invalid, in whole or in part." If an initiative is declared invalid, no referendum vote is held.

VIOLATION OF THE PRINCIPLE OF UNITY OF FORM
Initiatives for a partial revision of the federal constitution can be presented in the form either of a general proposal, or of a detailed, precisely worded draft. It is only permitted to choose one or the other form. If the proposal contains a mixture of forms, the initiative will violate the principle of unity of form.

VIOLATION OF THE PRINCIPLE OF UNITY OF SUBJECT MATTER
In order that the voters can vote freely on the issue, the proposal for a partial revision of the federal constitution must restrict itself to a specific subject matter. There must therefore be a material connection between the various parts of the initiative proposal (Art. 75 § 2 Federal Law on Political Rights). If the proposers wish to present materially distinct proposals, they must present these as separate initiatives. There is no provision for an initiative to be split up into different components, because it would not be possible to ascertain whether the various individual parts had secured the required number of signatures.

VIOLATION OF MANDATORY RULES OF INTERNATIONAL LAW
In the case of a popular initiative proposal which violates the mandatory rules of international law, the federal constitution specifies that it – or that part of it which violates ius cogens – must be declared invalid (Art. 139 § 2 for the current popular initiative; Art. 139a § 2 FC for the "general initiative" which is being introduced). However, the mandatory rules of international law are binding not only on the proposers of popular initiatives, but equally on the members of the federal parliament (Art. 193 § 4 and Art. 194 § 2 FC).

Switzerland bound itself to the mandatory rules of international law by ratifying the Vienna Convention on the Law of Treaties (SR 0.111 = AS 1990 1112), which standardized the relevant principle (Art. 53). The Convention was signed on 23.5.1969 and ratified by Switzerland on 7.5.1990 (AS 1990 1111 and 1144). It was as a result of this ratification that the federal popular initiative "For a sensible asylum policy" – which violated the principle of non-refoulement i.e. non-expulsion of refugees (BBI 1994 III 1492–1500) – had to be declared invalid (BBI 1996 I 1355).

FACTSHEET
Restrictions on the constitutional initiative in Switzerland

The Federal Council, in its statement of 20th November 1996 on the reform of the constitution (BBl 1997 I 362), defined what was covered by the mandatory rules of international law. In the same way that the essence of fundamental human rights must be inviolable (Art. 36 § 4 FC), the international community protects certain minimal rules of behaviour between states; any state which "legitimises" crimes against humanity places itself outside the community of nations. Genocide, slavery and torture, the compulsory return of refugees to the country persecuting them on grounds of race or religious or philosophical beliefs, the violation of the most basic internationally agreed humanitarian rules for the conduct of war, or of the ban on the use of violence and aggression, or the absolute guarantees of the European Convention on Human Rights – all these violate such fundamental rules, according to the current widespread view of justice in the European community of nations. The mandatory norms of international law include:

- the European Convention on the Protection of Human Rights and Fundamental Freedoms of 4th November 1950 (entry into force in Switzerland 28th November 1974, SR 0.101 = AS 1974 2151, Art. 2,3,4 § 1,7,and 15 § 2);
- the UN Pact of 16th December 1966 on Civil and Political Rights (entry into force in Switzerland on 18th September 1992, SR 0.103.2 = AS 1993 750; BBl 1991 I 1189–1247; Art. 4 § 2,6,7,8 § 1 and 2,11,15,16 and 18; cf. also in a preliminary form the UN General Declaration of Human Rights of 10th December 1948 [reproduced in BBl 1982 II 791–797] Arts. 4,5,6,9 and 28);
- the UN Convention of 10th December 1984 against Torture and Other Cruel, Inhuman or Degrading Treatment or Punishment (entry into force in Switzerland 26th June 1987, SR 0.105 = AS 1987 1307; BBl 1985 III 301–314, Art. 2 § 2 and 3 and Art. 3);
- the Geneva Convention of 28th July 1951 on the Status of Refugees (entry into force in Switzerland on 21st April 1955, SR 0.142.30 = AS 1955 443, Art. 33).

It is not unlikely that the international community will elaborate further such basic rules and that these will become universally accepted norms.

Unwritten material restrictions on constitutional revision
What happens when the content of an initiative violates law or is impermissible? The specific consequences in such an instance are regulated neither in the constitution nor in legislation – with the exception of the case in which the proposal violates non-mandatory international law: in such cases, an initiative may not be declared invalid. There has been a controversy lasting decades over whether Swiss constitutional law contains any further limits to constitutional revision. For example, some maintain that certain fundamental principles of the Swiss form of state (federalism, the separation of powers etc.) may not be altered. In practice, the only unwritten material restriction which has so far been accepted is one relating to the temporal impossibility of executing the initiative proposal, viz. the case of the popular initiative "Temporary reduction of military expenditure (moratorium on new acquisitions of arms)", which demanded the cutting of expenditure for years which would already have elapsed when the ruling came into force (BBl 1955 II 325).

FACTSHEET
Restrictions on the constitutional initiative in Switzerland

Four cases of invalidity
To date, the Federal Assembly has declared a popular initiative invalid on four occasions:

1. Federal popular initiative:
   Temporary reduction of military expenditure (moratorium on new acquisitions of arms)".
   Declared invalid by parliament on 15.12.1955 (BBI 1955 II 1463).
   Reason: Temporal inexecutability.
   Statement by the Federal Council: BBI 1955 I 527, II 325

2. Federal popular initiative:
   "Against rising prices and inflation".
   Declared invalid by parliament on 16.12.1977 (BBI 1977 III 919).
   Reason: violation of unity of subject matter.
   Statement by the Federal Council: BBI 1977 II 501

3. Federal popular initiative:
   "For less military expenditure and more investment in policies for peace".
   Declared invalid by parliament on 20.06.1995 (BBI 1995 III 570).
   Reason: violation of unity of subject matter.
   Statement by the Federal Council: BBI 1994 III 1201

4. Federal popular initiative:
   "For a sensible asylum policy".
   Declared invalid by parliament on 14.03.1996 (BBI 1996 I 1355).
   Reason: violation of mandatory rules of international law.
   Statement by the Federal Council: BBI 1994 III 1486

FACTSHEET
THE EXPECTATIONS OF THE SWISS DIRECT DEMOCRACY MOVEMENT IN THE 19TH CENTURY

The introduction of citizens' direct law-making was accompanied by the following claims and expectations:

- "The decisive control and use of political power should be transferred from the hands of the few onto the broad shoulders of the many"
- "Republican life depends on the continuous steady balancing of opposing tendencies"
- "The people should acquire wider political knowledge and opinions"
- "The authorities, statesmen and representatives will try much harder to acquaint ordinary people with their thoughts and convictions"
- "The people will approach them with the clear and genuine expression of their needs and preferences"
- "The moral-spiritual-intellectual life of the people" should be stimulated by "being deeply involved with the great issues of the common public weal"
- "We are taking into our own hands the decisions which affect the destiny of our country; in some way or other we wish to have the final word on these matters"
- "The will of the people and the spirit of the times, the understanding of the common man and the great thoughts of the statesmen should be peacefully negotiated and reconciled";
- "The creation of popular rule in happy union with representation"

The spokesmen of what was in effect a democratic revolution and which between 1867 and 1869 put a system of direct democracy in place of the former liberal rule in the canton Zurich identified two fundamental elements of "the heart of the democratic movement":

"In our view [the heart of the movement] consists in the people being able by constitutional means to win respect for its own faculty of judgment, which the elected representatives have arrogantly and bluntly denied it on all too many occasions"

"We protest against the debasement and belittlement of the people of Zurich, which consists in their being declared incompetent to recognize true progress and to make the necessary sacrifices [to achieve it]. We see in this false evaluation of the people the main seeds of the present movement"

Source: Der Landbote (Winterthur), Der Grütlianer (Bern) quoted and translated in Gross, Andreas/Kaufmann, Bruno: IRI Europe Country Index on Citizenlawmaking (Amsterdam 2002)

FACTSHEET
KEY POINTS FOR FREE AND FAIR REFERENDUMS IN EUROPE

BEFORE VOTING DAY
- Be aware of the plebiscite trap!
  The origin of a popular vote is important. An exclusively presidentially or governmentally triggered process (a plebiscite) tends to be much more "unfree" and unfair than a constitutionally or citizen-triggered referendum vote.
- The democratic debate needs time!
  The gap between the announcement of the popular vote and voting day itself is critical and should be at least six months in duration.
- Money matters!
  Without complete financial transparency during the campaign, unequal opportunities and unfair practices may prevail. Disclosure rules are extremely important; spending limits and state contributions can also be useful.
- The campaign needs guidance!
  Equal access to media sources (principally public and electronic) as well as the balanced dissemination of information (e.g. a general referendum pamphlet to all voters) are vital aspects of fair referendum campaigns. These may be supervised by an independent body.

ON VOTING DAY
- Avoid referendum votes on election day!
  Having a referendum on the same day as a general election tends to mix up party-politics and issue-politics. This should definitely be avoided, especially if a country is not used to referendums.
- Expand the voting "day" to a "period"!
  Since a referendum is a process with various phases, the voting phase should be longer than just a single day. In order to make participation as easy as possible, citizens should be able to vote by ballot box or postal mail over a two weeks period.
- Keep it secret!
  During the voting period, everybody has the right to express his / her will freely. This means in absolute secrecy and without briefings on events as they develop.

AFTER VOTING DAY
- Avoid unnecessary and special majority requirements!
  A democratic decision is based on a simple majority of the votes cast. Turnout thresholds exceeding 25% of the electorate tend to provoke boycott strategies.
- Non-binding decisions are non-decisions!
  In many countries a popular vote result is non-binding. This is a democratic contradiction in terms and creates an uncertain and unfair process. The role of parliament and government in the implementation of the result must be limited. A referendum decision can only be changed by another referendum decision.
- Guarantee a free and fair post-referendum period!
  It is vital to have judicial safeguards in place. For example, each citizen could have the opportunity to appeal against a referendum decision in a court.

Source: Kaufmann, Bruno (Ed.): Initiative & Referendum Monitor 2004/2005, the IRI Europe Toolkit for Free and Fair Referendums and Citizens Initiatives (Amsterdam 2004)

FACTSHEET
THE ECONOMIC EFFECTS OF THE USE OF DIRECT DEMOCRACY

In order to study whether direct democracy makes a difference to the outcomes of the political process, a natural starting point is to look at public expenditure and revenues. Fiscal decisions are the central activities of most governments and policy priorities are to a large extent formed in the budgeting process. In a sample of 132 large Swiss towns carried out in 1990, the authors replicated their examination of the mandatory referendum on budget deficits. In cities where a budget deficit has to be approved by the citizenry, expenditure and revenue, on average, are lower by about 20%, while public debt is reduced by about 30%.

PURELY REPRESENTATIVE DEMOCRACIES ARE LESS EFFICIENT

The cost-efficient use of public money under different institutional settings can be directly studied for single publicly provided goods. In a careful study of refuse collection (Pommerehne 1990) finds that this service is provided at the lowest cost in Swiss towns which have extended direct-democratic rights of participation and choose a private company to provide the service. If the service is provided by the municipality instead of by a private company, costs are about 10% higher. Efficiency losses are about 20% in municipalities with purely representative democracy (compared to direct democratic ones). The average cost of refuse collection is highest in municipalities which rely on representative democratic decision-making only, as well as on publicly organized collection (about 30% higher than in the most efficient case).

A hint as to the efficiency of public services comes from a study that relates fiscal referendums to economic performance in Swiss cantons (Feld and Savioz 1997). For the years 1984 to 1993, a neo-classical production function is estimated which includes the number of employees in all sectors, cantonal government expenditure for education, including grants, as well as a proxy for capital based on investments in building and construction. The production function is then extended by a dummy variable that identifies cantons with extended direct-democratic participation rights in financial issues at the local level. Total productivity – as measured by the cantonal GDP per capital – is estimated to be 5% higher in cantons with extended direct democracy, compared to cantons where these instruments are not available.

Based on an aggregate growth equation, Blomberg et al. (2004) analyze to what extent public capital (utilities, roads, education, etc.) is productively provided and whether there is a difference between initiative and non-initiative states in the US. The data on gross state product, private and public capital, employment and population are for 48 US states between 1969 and 1986. They find that non-initiative states are only about 82% as effective as states with the initiative right in providing productive capital services, i.e. approximately 20% more government expenditure is wasted where citizens have no possibility to launch initiatives, compared to states where this institution is installed.

INITIATIVE RIGHT REDUCES CORRUPTION

The misuse of public office for private gains is measured based on a survey of reporters' perception of public corruption. It is found that, in addition to a number of control variables, there is a statistically significant effect of voter initiatives on perceived corruption. In initiative states, corruption is lower than in non-initiative states, and this effect is the larger, the lower the signature requirement to launch an initiative.

FACTSHEET
THE ECONOMIC EFFECTS OF THE USE OF DIRECT DEMOCRACY

In a study for Switzerland in the early '90s, the effect of direct-democratic participation rights on people's reported satisfaction with life is empirically analyzed (Frey and Stutzer 2002). Survey answers are from more than 6,000 interviews. The proxy measure for individual utility is based on the following question: "How satisfied are you with your life as a whole these days?" People answered on a scale from one (=completely dissatisfied) to ten (=completely satisfied).

The institutionalized rights of individual political participation are measured at the cantonal level, where there is considerable variation. A broad index is used that measures the different barriers preventing the citizens from entering the political process via initiatives and referendums across cantons. The main result is a sizeable positive correlation between the extent of direct-democratic rights and people's reported subjective well-being.

Source: Stutzer, Alois/Frey, Bruno S.: Direct democracy: designing a living constitution (Zurich 2003)

Selected further reading:
- Pommerehne, Werner W.: The Empirical Relevance of Comparative Institutional Analysis. European Economic Review 1990, 34 (2–3): 458–469
- Feld, Lars P. / Savioz, Marcel R.: Direct democracy Matters for Economic Performance: An Empirical Investigation. Kyklos 1997, 50 (4): 507–538
- Blomberg, S. Brock/Hess, Gregory D./Weerapana, Akila: The Impact of Voter Initiatives on Economic Activity. European Journal of Political Economy 2004
- Frey, Bruno S./Stutzer, Alois: Happiness and Economics. How the Economy and Institutions Affect Human Well-Being (Princeton 2002)

FACTSHEET
IMPORTANT FACTORS IN THE SHAPING OF DIRECT-DEMOCRATIC PROCEDURES

Democratic procedures are very demanding. They can only function to the extent that the basic conditions for democracy are met. These conditions include:

- a functioning media and public space
- a state operating under the rule of law, protection of the constitution and fundamental human rights
- education for democracy in addition to people and organisations which have internalised the democratic principle
- institutionalised self-criticism of democracy
- research and development of democracy

Democratic procedures are only useful if they have been well designed and implemented and if they are sensibly matched. The same conditions and standards apply also to direct democracy, on the shaping of which this factsheet focuses.

The usefulness of direct-democratic instruments depends on their design. But the presence of well-designed direct-democratic procedures does not in itself ensure that they will be frequently used. The frequency of use of direct-democratic instruments depends also on other factors – such as the make-up of society (more or less complex, more or less conflict-ridden) – as well as on the way problems and conflicts are handled in a particular society. A comparison of direct democracy in the cantons of Switzerland shows that well-designed direct-democratic procedures are used more often in societies which are complex and conflict-ridden, than in smaller and simpler societies.
(cf. Vatter, Adrian: Kantonale Demokratien im Vergleich (Opladen 2002)

IMPORTANT ASPECTS IN THE SHAPING OF DIRECT-DEMOCRATIC PROCEDURES

1 Number of signatures

Question	How many signatures of eligible voters are required in order to hold a referendum vote?
Experience	International experience shows that large signature quorums (more than 5% of eligible voters) deter the majority of individuals and organisations from using the instruments of the popular initiative and the popular referendum, while very high hurdles (10% or more) make these instruments unusable.
Recommendation	Depending on the particular instrument (e.g. constitutional initiative, facultative referendum) and level of the polity (local, regional, national, transnational), the entry quorums should not be higher than 5% of the total eligible electorate.

28 FACTSHEET
IMPORTANT FACTORS IN THE SHAPING OF DIRECT-DEMOCRATIC PROCEDURES

2 Time allowed for collection of signatures

Question	How much time is allowed for signatures to be collected?
Experience	Communication – informing, discussing, learning – is the heart of direct democracy. It cannot happen without sufficient time. So the time allowances for collecting signatures must reflect this. If the periods are too short e.g. only 3 months for nationwide signature collection, this blocks the crucially important processes of communication
Recommendation	For launching a nationwide initiative, there should be at least 12 months – and preferably 18. For a facultative referendum, 2–4 months should be sufficient, as the referendum issue is already on the political agenda

3 How the signatures are collected

Question	Is there free (uncontrolled) collection of signatures with subsequent official verification – or does the signature-giving have to take place at designated official centres and/or be officially monitored?
Experience	Uncontrolled signature collection is controversial. In many countries the authorities want to restrict the options for signature collection or check the eligibility of the signatories before they sign. In Austria, signatures for popular initiatives can only be given in official centres. In the USA, collecting signatures in public places, such as at the post office, is actually forbidden.
Recommendation	A well-developed direct democracy does not require any special restrictions on signature collection: it is sufficient to check the legitimacy of the signatures. Signature collection ought to be organised in a way that encourages debate and makes it easy for people who wish to sign to do so.

4 How the popular initiative is worded

Questions	Does the wording of the initiative proposal presuppose special legal know-ledge, or can the proposal be submitted in clear and ordinary language?
Experience	In Switzerland, a specific initiative proposal can be formulated in normal language, requiring no knowledge of legalese. Any title can be chosen as long as it is not misleading, does not cause confusion or contain commercial or personal advertising. The appropriate authorities assist the initiative sponsors with the formal questions, but have no input into the content.
Recommendation	The authorities should advise the sponsors in the launching of an initiative with the aim of ensuring that the latter are enabled to express their political will freely and clearly and in a way which everyone can understand. Two things are required: that the authorities do not interfere with the content; and that the text is clear, comprehensible, unambiguous and consistent. Any kind of specialist jargon would be unsuitable.

FACTSHEET
IMPORTANT FACTORS IN THE SHAPING OF DIRECT-DEMOCRATIC PROCEDURES

5 How the referendum question is worded	
Questions	Who decides how the referendum question is worded? Is the title of the initiative or of the law repeated in the question?
Experience	In Switzerland, the referendum question contains the title of the initiative or law which is being subjected to ballot.
Recommendation	The title of the proposal should be included in the referendum question, so that the voters know precisely what they are voting on. The question should also be formulated in such a way that it is clear whether a "yes" vote means approval or rejection of the proposal. The referendum question may not be misleading, as this makes it impossible to ascertain how the voters actually intended to vote.
6 Content and formal legal requirements	
Questions	What procedure exists for checking that the initiative satisfies the formal legal requirements and the rules regarding content?
Experience	The validity of the content of the initiative text can be checked by one of the organs of state (parliament, authorities, courts). There is disagreement over which procedure is preferable – whether it should be parliament or the constitutional court which decides on the validity of an initiative. In Switzerland, it is parliament which checks that the content of the initiative satisfies the rules: it does so only after the required 100,000 signatures have been collected. In the U.S., this happens before the signature collection starts. Procedures vary: in Florida, it is the State Supreme Court which checks validity, whereas in Oregon it is the Attorney General.
Recommendation	The validity rules (e.g. that the initiative must not contravene binding international law; that it may not include several different issues; that it must be unambiguous in form) must be clear and transparent; they can, for example, be laid down in the constitution. The check on content may be carried out as soon as the initiative is launched, or only once the signature collection is completed. It can be performed by a constitutional court or by one of the political organs of state – by parliament, or by one of the authorities. How great a risk exists that the body charged with checking the initiative might fail to be impartial is more a question of the political culture and cannot be entirely "designed out".
7 Interaction with government and parliament	
Questions	Is parliament able to debate the subject-matter of a popular initiative and make its own recommendation? Does parliament have the right to present a counter-proposal? Does the interaction between the sponsors of the initiative and either parliament or the government allow space for negotiation and compromise? Is there a withdrawal clause?

FACTSHEET 28
Important factors in the shaping of direct-democratic procedures

Experience	In California, initiatives bypass parliament and are put directly to the voters. There is no such "direct initiative" in Switzerland, only an "indirect" one, which includes the government and parliament in the initiative process; they express a view on every referendum issue, take part in the public debate, and parliament can make a counter-proposal. The indirect initiative thus produces greater public discussion and it is possible to create a space in which government and parliament are able to negotiate with the promoters of the initiative and reach a possible compromise solution. In order to facilitate this negotiating space, a withdrawal clause was introduced in Switzerland. The sponsors can withdraw the initiative if, for example, they have been able to reach a satisfactory compromise with the government and parliament.
Recommendation	Direct and indirect democracy should be linked in a way which strengthens both. This can be achieved, for example, by making it obligatory for parliament to consider popular initiative proposals and express an opinion, and by giving parliament the right to make counter-proposals. Where there is both an original initiative proposal and a counter-proposal to be voted on, the voters should be able to vote "yes" to both proposals and, in addition, indicate which of the two they prefer if both are approved (the so-called "double Yes"). A withdrawal clause gives the initiative sponsors the chance of withdrawing the initiative if, for example, they have managed to reach an acceptable compromise with the government and parliament. This creates a manoeuvring space for negotiations and compromise which both sponsors and the authorities can take advantage of.

8 Time periods allowed for government and parliament to express an opinion, and for the referendum campaign

Questions	How much time is allowed to the government, the parliament and the voters to debate and reach a considered opinion on an initiative or referendum proposal? How much time should be allowed for the referendum campaign?
Experience	Involving all the parties to a referendum vote in an exchange of views, in dialogue, negotiations and a collective learning process takes time. This must be taken into account in setting the statutory time periods.
Recommendation	The basic rule is: there must be adequate time allowed for all the stages of an initiative or referendum process – for the initiative committee to collect the required signatures, for the government to express a view on the proposal, for parliament to debate the issue and possibly work out a counter-proposal, for all the individuals and groups involved to carry out a proper referendum campaign. A simple rule of thumb is that a period of 6 months should be allowed for each of these stages.

FACTSHEET 28
IMPORTANT FACTORS IN THE SHAPING OF DIRECT-DEMOCRATIC PROCEDURES

9 Validating the referendum ballot: majority approval requirements and minimum turnout quorums

Questions	Does approval require a qualified majority and/or a minimum turnout quorum, or is a simple majority of the voters sufficient?
Experience	The satisfaction of special turnout or approval quorums is often demanded to validate referendum votes, whereas there is no minimum turnout requirement for parliamentary elections. In practice, turnout quorums of 40% or more often leads to the result of a referendum being annulled. This can give direct democracy a bad name. High approval quorums can make it very difficult to secure approval for any proposal.
Recommendation	Turnout quorums, at least the ones higher than 25%, should be avoided. Such quorums mean that the proposal can be rejected by a combination of "no"-votes and non-votes; they assist those groups which refuse to get involved in a public democratic debate and instead call for the ballot to be boycotted. This promotes undemocratic behaviour. The same applies to approval quorums which require a qualified majority of the eligible voters.

10 Issues which can be voted on/exclusion of issues

Questions	What issues may – or may not – be decided direct-democratically?
Experience	In many countries, important issues are withheld from direct-democratic decision-making. This weakens the foundations of direct democracy. The exclusion of certain subjects is often based on specific historical experiences. In Switzerland, no subject is in principle excluded from direct-democratic procedures. However, initiatives which contravene binding international law must be declared invalid. In actual practice, the following three subject areas are the main focus of direct-democratic activity: 1. The form of state and democracy; 2. Financial and tax policy; 3. Welfare and health provision.
Recommendation	Citizens should be able to decide on the same range of issues as their elected representatives. Creating special exclusion lists for initiatives and referendums contradicts the democratic principle of equal participation in politics. The limits imposed on democratic decisions by fundamental human rights and international law apply equally to parliamentary and direct-democratic decisions.

FACTSHEET
IMPORTANT FACTORS IN THE SHAPING OF DIRECT-DEMOCRATIC PROCEDURES

11 Supervision and advice/consultation

Questions	Is there provision for supervision of initiative and referendum processes? Is there an independent authority which has this specific task?
Experience	In order to guarantee the fairness and correct handling of popular referendum procedures, some countries (e.g. Ireland and Great Britain) have instituted referendum commissions. The duties and powers of these commissions vary. In Switzerland, the federal referendum procedures are looked after by the Federal Chancellery. The "Political Rights" section of the Chancellery "advises initiative and referendum committees, checks submitted signature lists and popular initiatives, organises the federal referendums and the elections to the National Council, and deals with complaints about elections and referendums". It is also responsible for testing electronic voting.
Recommendation	A referendum authority or commission can have a variety of duties, such as advising initiative committees, making a preliminary examination of the initiative proposal, authenticating signatures, supervising the referendum campaign (including checking for fairness and equality), as well as the monitoring and evaluation of referendums. It can also be charged with the task of informing the voters; the minimum should be a referendum pamphlet or booklet for each eligible voter.

12 Financing and transparency

Questions	Do parties and groups have to reveal how much money they spend on a referendum campaign, and where the money comes from? Do groups without access to significant financial resources receive any support funding to make the referendum process more equal?
Experience	The important role of money in referendums is generally recognised: money can be one of the decisive factors.
Recommendation	Transparency (e.g. information on the source of funding) and fairness (e.g. equality of financial resources and equality of access to the public through the media and advertising) are important to ensure the genuinely democratic formation of the political will. The sponsors of initiatives and referendums can be supported, for example by having a portion of their expenses refunded once the required number of signatures has been collected and the referendum date set.

FACTSHEET
Voting rights of Swiss citizens living or staying abroad

The principle

Swiss citizens living or staying abroad who are eligible to vote are able to take part at the national level in referendum votes and elections, as well as giving their signatures to initiatives and referendums (Art. 3, § 1 of BPRAS – the federal law on the political rights of Swiss citizens living or staying abroad[1]). They have the right not only to take part in the elections for the National Council (active voting right), but to be elected themselves to either the National Council, the Federal Council or the federal court (passive voting right). However, they may only take part in elections for the Council of States if the law of the canton to which they are attached provides for the right to vote for Swiss citizens living or staying abroad. In the Swiss federal system, those Swiss living or staying abroad do not constitute a distinct voting area or constituency[2]; they choose one commune as their "voting commune" (this could be the commune in which they were born, or one in which they have been previously resident; Art. 5, § 1 BPRAS). Eligible expatriate Swiss voters who wish to exercise their political rights must notify the Swiss office of their chosen voting commune of their intention. The notification must be renewed every four years (Art. 5a BPRAS). Eligible Swiss voters living or staying abroad can submit their vote for proposals at the federal level either personally in the voting commune in Switzerland, or by post (Art. 1 BPRAS).

Some figures

At the end of 2005 there were some 634,200 Swiss citizens living abroad[3], of whom about 485,100 were potentially eligible to vote i.e. they were 18 or over and were not disqualified by reason of mental illness or feeble-mindedness. At the end of December 2005, around 102,000 persons were actually entered in the voting register of a Swiss commune and were therefore eligible to vote. The figure represents 2.1% of all eligible Swiss voters (4.86 million[4]).

Voting behaviour of Swiss living or staying abroad

A survey carried out in 2003 by ASO (Organisation of the Swiss Abroad) and swissinfo/Swiss Radio International revealed that Swiss living or staying abroad have a very distinctive profile, which is formed far less by their political opinions than by such values as modernity of outlook, cosmopolitanism, openness to change, tolerance towards foreigners and belief in the free market.[5]

---

[1] Federal law of 19.12.1975 (SR 161.5) on the political rights of Swiss citizens living or staying abroad, available online at: www.admin.ch/ch/d/sr/c161_5.html
[2] The cantons form the constituencies; cf. Art. 149, § 3 of the federal constitution (SR 101); available online at: www.admin.ch/ch/itl/rs/1/c101ENG.pdf
[3] Source: Federal Department of Foreign Affairs. Status as of end-December 2005
[4] Source: Federal Chancellery. Status as of end-December 2005
[5] The final report of the study carried out by the GfS research institute can be downloaded from the Internet at: www.aso.ch/pdf/ASO-Bericht%20berdef.pdf

FACTSHEET
VOTING RIGHTS OF SWISS CITIZENS LIVING OR STAYING ABROAD

Representation of Swiss abroad in the parliament
In the National Council elections of 19th October 2003, the Swiss People's Party (SVP) in the canton Zurich came up with a list of candidates for Swiss abroad ("List 31: SVP-Union of Swiss Abroad"). To date, however, no overseas candidate has ever been elected to the federal parliament. One reason for this may lie in the fact that the electoral potential of the Swiss abroad is diffused. Since they do not form their own constituency, their votes are distributed among the 26 cantons. The election in Spring 2004 of Beat Eberle from Bad Ragaz, at that time military attaché in Stockholm, to the Great Council (parliament) in St. Gallen showed, however, that it is possible for Swiss citizens living abroad to be elected.

SURVEY 1
ALL POPULAR VOTES IN SWITZERLAND SINCE 1848

NATIONAL REFERENDUM VOTES

DATE		SUBJECT	APPROVED				REJECTED			
			OR	PI	CP	FR	OR	PI	CP	FR
06.06.1848	1	Total revision of 12th September 1848	1							
14.01.1866	2	Fixing weights and measures					1			
14.01.1866	3	Equal domiciliary rights for Jews and naturalized citizens	2							
14.01.1866	4	Settlers' right to vote on community matters					2			
14.01.1866	5	Tax and civil rights in relation to settlers					3			
14.01.1866	6	Settlers' right to vote on cantonal matters					4			
14.01.1866	7	Freedom of belief and religious practice					5			
14.01.1866	8	Exclusion of certain punishable offences					6			
14.01.1866	9	Protection of intellectual property rights					7			
14.01.1866	10	Ban on lotteries and games of chance					8			
12.05.1872	11	Total revision					9			
19.04.1874	12	Total revision	3							
23.05.1875	13	Federal law regarding determination and recording of civil status and of marriage				1				
23.05.1875	14	Federal law on voting rights for Swiss citizens								1
23.04.1876	15	Federal law on issue and cashing of bank notes								2
09.07.1876	16	Federal law on tax substitute for military service								3
21.10.1877	17	Federal law on factory work				2				
21.10.1877	18	Federal law on tax substitute for military service								4

FR = Facultative Referendum, CP = Counter-proposal, OR = Obligatory Referendum, PI = Popular Initiative, Art. = article, § = paragraph

SURVEY 1
ALL POPULAR VOTES IN SWITZERLAND SINCE 1848

NATIONAL REFERENDUM VOTES

DATE		SUBJECT	APPROVED				REJECTED			
			OR	PI	CP	FR	OR	PI	CP	FR
21.10.1877	19	Federal law on the political rights of settlers and the temporarily resident and the loss of political rights of Swiss citizens								5
19.01.1879	20	Federal law on granting of subsidies for Alpine railways				3				
18.05.1879	21	Federal decree on amending Art. 65 of the federal constitution (death penalty)	4							
31.10.1880	22	Federal decree regarding the proposal made in the Popular Initiative of 3rd August 1880 for revision of the federal constitution						10		
30.07.1882	23	Federal decree on protection of inventions						11		
30.07.1882	24	Federal law on measures to combat dangerous epidemics								6
26.11.1882	25	Federal decree on the execution of Art. 27 of the federal constitution								7
11.05.1884	26	Federal law on organisation of the federal department of justice and police								8
11.05.1884	27	Federal decree on patent taxes for commercial travellers								9
11.05.1884	28	Federal law on supplementing the federal criminal code of 4th February 1853								10
11.05.1884	29	Federal decree concerning granting of the sum of 10,000 Franks towards the running costs of the Swiss embassy in Washington								11
25.10.1885	30	Federal decree concerning the partial revision of the federal constitution	5							
15.05.1887	31	Federal law on spirits				4				

FR = Facultative Referendum, CP = Counter-proposal, OR = Obligatory Referendum, PI = Popular Initiative, Art. = article, § = paragraph

SURVEY 1
ALL POPULAR VOTES IN SWITZERLAND SINCE 1848

NATIONAL REFERENDUM VOTES

DATE		SUBJECT	APPROVED				REJECTED			
			OR	PI	CP	FR	OR	PI	CP	FR
10.07.1887	32	Federal decree on supplementing Art. 64 of the federal constitution of 29th May 1874	6							
17.11.1889	33	Federal law on prosecution of debt and bankruptcy				5				
26.10.1890	34	Federal decree on supplementing 29th May 1874 constitution by adding a clause relating to the right to legislate on accident and health insurance	7							
15.03.1891	35	Federal law on federal officials and employees who have become unable to work								12
05.07.1891	36	Federal decree on revision of the federal constitution	8							
18.10.1891	37	Federal decree on revision of Art. 39 of the federal constitution	9							
18.10.1891	38	Federal law on Swiss customs duty				6				
06.12.1891	39	Federal decree on purchasing of the Swiss central railway								13
20.08.1893	40	Popular Initiative "Prohibition of ritual slaughter without prior anaesthetisation"		1						
04.03.1894	41	Federal decree of 20th December 1893 on addition to the federal constitution of a clause relating to the right to legislate on trade/business					12			
03.06.1894	42	Popular Initiative "Guarantee of the right to work"						1		
04.11.1894	43	Popular Initiative "Sharing of a portion of customs revenue among the cantons"						2		
03.02.1895	44	Federal law on foreign representation for Switzerland								14

FR = Facultative Referendum, CP = Counter-proposal, OR = Obligatory Referendum, PI = Popular Initiative, Art. = article, § = paragraph

SURVEY 1
ALL POPULAR VOTES IN SWITZERLAND SINCE 1848

NATIONAL REFERENDUM VOTES

			APPROVED				REJECTED			
DATE		SUBJECT	OR	PI	CP	FR	OR	PI	CP	FR
29.09.1895	45	Federal decree on addition to the federal constitution of a clause on introduction of a monopoly on matches					13			
03.11.1895	46	Federal decree on revision of the constitutional articles relating to the military					14			
04.10.1896	47	Federal law on guarantees in buying and selling of cattle								15
04.10.1896	48	Federal law on railway company accounts				7				
04.10.1896	49	Federal law on disciplinary code for the Swiss army								16
28.02.1897	50	Federal law on setting up the Swiss National Bank								17
11.07.1897	51	Federal decree on revision of Art. 24 of the federal constitution	10							
11.07.1897	52	Federal decree concerning federal legislation on trade of foodstuffs and semi-luxury goods and of commodities which may endanger life or health	11							
20.02.1898	53	Federal law on acquisition and operation of railways at federal expense and the administrative organisation of the Swiss national railways				8				
13.11.1898	54	Federal decree concerning revision of Art. 64 of the federal constitution	12							
13.11.1898	55	Federal decree concerning introduction of Art. 64bis into the federal constitution	13							
20.05.1900	56	Federal law on health and accident insurance, including military insurance								18
04.11.1900	57	Popular Initiative "Popular election of the Federal Council and an increase in the number of its members"						3		

FR = Facultative Referendum, CP = Counter-proposal, OR = Obligatory Referendum, PI = Popular Initiative, Art. = article, § = paragraph

SURVEY 1
ALL POPULAR VOTES IN SWITZERLAND SINCE 1848

NATIONAL REFERENDUM VOTES

DATE		SUBJECT	APPROVED				REJECTED			
			OR	PI	CP	FR	OR	PI	CP	FR
04.11.1900	58	Popular Initiative "Proportional election of the National Council"						4		
23.11.1902	59	Federal decree concerning federal support for public primary schools	14							
15.03.1903	60	Federal law on Swiss customs duty				9				
25.10.1903	61	Federal law on supplementing federal criminal law of 4th February 1853								19
25.10.1903	62	Popular Initiative "Election of the National Council on the basis of the Swiss residential population"						5		
25.10.1903	63	Federal decree concerning amendment to Art. 32bis of the federal constitution					15			
19.03.1905	64	Federal decree on revision of Art. 64 of the federal constitution (extension of patent rights)	15							
10.06.1906	65	Federal law on trading of foodstuffs and commodities				10				
03.11.1907	66	Military organisation of the Swiss Confederation				11				
05.07.1908	67	Federal decree on extension to the federal constitution in respect of the right to legislate on trade	16							
05.07.1908	68	Popular Initiative "Ban on absinthe"		2						
25.10.1908	69	Federal decree on adopting supplementary Art. 24bis into the federal constitution relating to federal legislation on exploiting water power and the transmission and use of electrical energy		1						
23.10.1910	70	Popular Initiative "Proportional election of the National Council"						6		

FR = Facultative Referendum, CP = Counter-proposal, OR = Obligatory Referendum, PI = Popular Initiative, Art. = article, § = paragraph

SURVEY 1
ALL POPULAR VOTES IN SWITZERLAND SINCE 1848

NATIONAL REFERENDUM VOTES

			APPROVED				REJECTED			
DATE		SUBJECT	OR	PI	CP	FR	OR	PI	CP	FR
04.02.1912	71	Federal law on health and accident insurance				12				
04.05.1913	72	Federal decree concerning revision of arts. 69 and 31 (§ 2, letter d) of the federal constitution (combatting human and animal diseases)	17							
25.10.1914	73	Federal decree concerning revision of Art. 103 of the federal constitution and insertion of an Art. 114bis	18							
06.06.1915	74	Federal decree concerning enactment of a constitutional article relating to raising of a non-recurring war tax	19							
13.05.1917	75	Federal decree concerning insertion of arts. 41bis and 42, letter g into the federal constitution (stamp duty)	20							
02.06.1918	76	Popular Initiative "Introduction of a direct federal tax"						7		
13.10.1918	77	Popular Initiative "Proportional election of the National Council"		3						
04.05.1919	78	Federal decree concerning adoption of an Art. 24ter into the federal constitution (shipping)	21							
04.05.1919	79	Federal decree concerning enactment of a constitutional provision for the raising of a new extraordinary war tax	22							
10.08.1919	80	Federal decree concerning adoption of transitional rules on Art. 73 of the federal constitution	23							
21.03.1920	81	Federal law on regulating working conditions								20
21.03.1920	82	Popular Initiative "Prohibition on the setting up of casinos"		4						

FR = Facultative Referendum, CP = Counter-proposal, OR = Obligatory Referendum, PI = Popular Initiative, Art. = article, § = paragraph

SURVEY 1
ALL POPULAR VOTES IN SWITZERLAND SINCE 1848

NATIONAL REFERENDUM VOTES

			Approved				Rejected			
DATE		SUBJECT	OR	PI	CP	FR	OR	PI	CP	FR
21.03.1920	83	Counter-proposal							1	
16.05.1920	84	Federal decree on accession of Switzerland to the League of Nations	24[1]							
31.10.1920	85	Federal law concerning working hours on railways and other forms of public transport				13				
30.01.1921	86	Popular Initiative "For the introduction of a referendum on treaties with unlimited duration or with a duration of more than 15 years (Referendum on international treaties)"		5						
30.01.1921	87	Popular Initiative "Abolition of military courts"						8		
22.05.1921	88	Federal decree concerning adoption of new arts. 37bis and 37ter into the federal constitution (automobile and cycle traffic, aeronautics)	25							
22.05.1921	89	Federal decree concerning adoption of new Art. 37ter into the federal constitution (aeronautics)	26							
11.06.1922	90	Popular Initiative part 1 "Naturalisation"						9		
11.06.1922	91	Popular Initiative part 2 "Expulsion of foreigners"						10		
11.06.1922	92	Popular Initiative "Eligibility of civil servants for the National Council"						11		
24.09.1922	93	Federal law concerning amendment to federal criminal code of 4th February 1853 in respect of breaches of constitutional order and internal security and the introduction of conditional execution of the sentence								21

[1] This referendum vote was initiated by the government and declared as an „obligatory referendum". It was de facto a plebiscite.

FR = Facultative Referendum, CP = Counter-proposal, OR = Obligatory Referendum, PI = Popular Initiative, Art. = article, § = paragraph

SURVEY 1
ALL POPULAR VOTES IN SWITZERLAND SINCE 1848

NATIONAL REFERENDUM VOTES

			APPROVED				REJECTED			
DATE		SUBJECT	OR	PI	CP	FR	OR	PI	CP	FR
03.12.1922	94	Popular Initiative "For a one-off capital tax"						12		
18.02.1923	95	Popular Initiative "Preventive detention (for Swiss citizens endangering internal security)"						13		
18.02.1923	96	Federal decree concerning ratification of the treaty signed in Paris on 7th August 1921 between Switzerland and France concerning trade relations and border traffic between the previous free trade zones of Hochsavoyen, the county of Gex and the Swiss neighbor cantons.								22
15.04.1923	97	Popular Initiative "Maintaining and protecting the people's rights in customs matters"						14		
03.06.1923	98	Federal decree concerning revision of arts. 31 and 32bis (alcoholic beverages) of the federal constitution					16			
17.02.1924	99	Federal law concerning amendment to Art. 41 of factory law of 18th June 1914/27th June 1919								23
24.05.1925	100	Popular Initiative "Disability, old age-, widows- and orphans insurance"						15		
25.10.1925	101	Federal decree concerning temporary and permanent residence of foreigners	27							
06.12.1925	102	Federal decree on disability, old age-, widows- and orphans insurance	28							
05.12.1926	103	Federal decree on adopting a new Art. 23bis into the federal constitution relating to national provision of grain					17			
15.05.1927	104	Federal decree concerning amendment to Art. 30 of the federal constitution	29							

FR = Facultative Referendum, CP = Counter-proposal, OR = Obligatory Referendum, PI = Popular Initiative, Art. = article, § = paragraph

SURVEY 1
ALL POPULAR VOTES IN SWITZERLAND SINCE 1848

NATIONAL REFERENDUM VOTES

			APPROVED				REJECTED			
DATE		SUBJECT	OR	PI	CP	FR	OR	PI	CP	FR
15.05.1927	105	Federal law on automobile and cycle traffic								24
20.05.1928	106	Federal decree on revision of Art. 44 of the federal constitution (Foreigners, reduction of number)	30							
02.12.1928	107	Popular Initiative "Casinos"		6						
03.03.1929	108	Popular Initiative "Supply of cereals"						16		
03.03.1929	109	Counter-proposal			2					
03.03.1929	110	Federal law on amendment to Art. 14 of the federal constitution of 10th October 1902 on Swiss customs duty				14				
12.05.1929	111	Popular Initiative "Legislative authority in the area of road traffic"						17		
12.05.1929	112	Popular Initiative "Prohibition of spirits"						18		
06.04.1930	113	Federal decree on revision of arts. 31 and 32bis of the federal constitution and adoption of a new Art. 32quater (alcoholic beverages)	31							
08.02.1931	114	Federal decree on the Popular Initiative for revision of Art. 12 of the federal constitution (ban on religious orders) (counter-proposal)			3					
15.03.1931	115	Federal decree on revision of Art. 72 of the federal constitution (election of National Council)	32							
15.03.1931	116	Federal decree on revision of arts. 76, 96 § 1 and 105 § 2 (period of office of National Council, Federal Council and Federal Chancellor)	33							
06.12.1931	117	Federal law on old age-, widows- and orphans insurance								25
06.12.1931	118	Federal law on taxation of tobacco								26

FR = Facultative Referendum, CP = Counter-proposal, OR = Obligatory Referendum, PI = Popular Initiative, Art. = article, § = paragraph

SURVEY 1
ALL POPULAR VOTES IN SWITZERLAND SINCE 1848

NATIONAL REFERENDUM VOTES

			Approved				Rejected			
DATE		SUBJECT	OR	PI	CP	FR	OR	PI	CP	FR
28.05.1933	119	Federal law on temporary lowering of salaries of federal employees								27
11.03.1934	120	Federal law on the defence of public order								28
24.02.1935	121	Federal law on amendment to federal law of 12th April 1907 on organisation of the army (reorganising training)				15				
05.05.1935	122	Federal law on regulating the transport of goods and animals in motor vehicles on public roads								29
02.06.1935	123	Popular Initiative "Measures against the economic crisis"						19		
08.09.1935	124	Popular Initiative "Total revision of the constitution"						20		
28.11.1937	125	Popular Initiative "Prohibition of freemasonry"						21		
20.02.1938	126	Federal decree on revision of arts. 107 and 116 of the federal constitution (recognition of Rhaeto-Romanic as a national language)	34							
20.02.1938	127	Popular Initiative "Emergency law and maintenance and protection of people's rights" (Submission of emergency law to the optional referendum)						22		
20.02.1938	128	Popular Initiative "Private armaments industry"						23		
20.02.1938	129	Counter proposal			4					
03.07.1938	130	Swiss penal code				16				
27.11.1938	131	Federal decree on transitional ordering of the budget	35							

FR = Facultative Referendum, CP = Counter-proposal, OR = Obligatory Referendum, PI = Popular Initiative, Art. = article, § = paragraph

SURVEY 1
All popular votes in Switzerland since 1848

National referendum votes

Date		Subject	Approved				Rejected			
			OR	PI	CP	FR	OR	PI	CP	FR
22.01.1939	132	Popular Initiative "Maintaining and protecting the constitutional rights of citizens (Extension of constitutional jurisdiction)"						24		
22.01.1939	133	Federal decree on the popular inititative to restrict the application of the emergency clause (Counter-proposal).			5					
04.06.1939	134	Federal decree on addition to the federal constitution for setting up and partial guarantee for credits to increase national defence and counter unemployment	36							
03.12.1939	135	Federal law on changing conditions of service and insurance of federal employees								30
01.12.1940	136	Federal law on amendment to arts. 103 and 104 of federal law of 12th May 1907 on military organisation (introduction of compulsory military pre-training)								31
09.03.1941	137	Popular Initiative "Reform of legislation on liquor"						25		
25.01.1942	138	Popular Initiative "Popular election of the Federal Council and increase in the number of its members"						26		
03.05.1942	139	Popular Initiative "Reorganisation of the National Council"						27		
29.10.1944	140	Federal law on unfair competition				17				
21.01.1945	141	Federal law on Swiss Railways				18				
25.11.1945	142	Federal decree on Popular Initiative "for the family" (Counter proposal)			6					
10.02.1946	143	Federal decree on Popular Initiative concerning regulation of goods traffic							2	
08.12.1946	144	Popular Initiative "Right to work"						28		

FR = Facultative Referendum, CP = Counter-proposal, OR = Obligatory Referendum, PI = Popular Initiative, Art. = article, § = paragraph

SURVEY 1
ALL POPULAR VOTES IN SWITZERLAND SINCE 1848

NATIONAL REFERENDUM VOTES

DATE		SUBJECT	APPROVED				REJECTED			
			OR	PI	CP	FR	OR	PI	CP	FR
18.05.1947	145	Popular Initiative "Economic reform and employment legislation"						29		
06.07.1947	146	Federal decree on revision of economic articles of the federal constitution	37							
06.07.1947	147	Federal decree on old age-, widows- and orphans insurance			19					
14.03.1948	148	Federal decree on regulation of Swiss sugar industry								32
22.05.1949	149	Federal decree on revision of Art. 39 of the federal constitution concerning the Swiss National Bank					18			
22.05.1949	150	Federal law on supplementing federal law of 13th June 1928 on measures against T.B.								33
11.09.1949	151	Popular Initiative "Return to direct democracy" (regulation on urgent affairs)		7						
11.12.1949	152	Federal law concerning change to federal law of 30th June 1927 on employment conditions of federal employees				20				
29.01.1950	153	Federal decree on extending the period of applicability and changes to the decree on measures to promote house building								34
04.06.1950	154	Federal decree on constitutional revision of federal budget					19			
01.10.1950	155	Popular Initiative "Protecting the land and work by preventing speculation"						30		
03.12.1950	156	Federal decree on change to Art. 72 of the federal constitution (election of National Council)	38							
03.12.1950	157	Federal decree on budget for 1951–1954	39							

FR = Facultative Referendum, CP = Counter-proposal, OR = Obligatory Referendum, PI = Popular Initiative, Art. = article, § = paragraph

SURVEY 1
ALL POPULAR VOTES IN SWITZERLAND SINCE 1848

NATIONAL REFERENDUM VOTES

			Approved				Rejected			
DATE		SUBJECT	OR	PI	CP	FR	OR	PI	CP	FR
25.02.1951	158	Federal decree on motorised transport of persons and goods on public roads								35
15.04.1951	159	Popular Initiative "Guarantee of purchasing power and full employment"						31		
15.04.1951	160	Counter proposal			7					
08.07.1951	161	Popular Initiative "Taxation of public enterprises for the benefit of national defence"						32		
02.03.1952	162	Federal decree on extending period of applicability of federal decree on requirement to gain approval to open or extend inns								36
30.03.1952	163	Federal law on promoting agriculture and supporting farmers (agriculture law)				21				
20.04.1952	164	Popular Initiative "Federal sales tax"						33		
18.05.1952	165	Popular Initiative "Financing of armaments and protection of social progress"						34		
06.07.1952	166	Federal decree on covering expenditure on arms					20			
05.10.1952	167	Federal law on changing rules on taxing tobacco in the federal law on old age-, widows- and orphans insurance				22				
05.10.1952	168	Federal decree on creation of air-raid shelters in existing houses								37
23.11.1952	169	Federal decree on temporary continuation of limited price control	40							
23.11.1952	170	Federal decree on national provision of bread-making cereals	41							
19.04.1953	171	Federal law on revision of federal law on postal services								38

FR = Facultative Referendum, CP = Counter-proposal, OR = Obligatory Referendum, PI = Popular Initiative, Art. = article, § = paragraph

SURVEY 1
ALL POPULAR VOTES IN SWITZERLAND SINCE 1848

NATIONAL REFERENDUM VOTES

			Approved				Rejected			
DATE		SUBJECT	OR	PI	CP	FR	OR	PI	CP	FR
06.12.1953	172	Federal decree on constitutional reorganisation of federal budget					21			
06.12.1953	173	Federal decree on supplementing the federal constitution by an Art. 24quater concerning protection of waters against pollution	42							
20.06.1954	174	Federal decree on certification for shoemakers, hairdressers, saddlers and coachbuilders								39
20.06.1954	175	Federal decree on special aid for expatriate Swiss injured in the war								40
24.10.1954	176	Federal decree on budget for 1955–1958	43							
05.12.1954	177	Popular Initiative "Protection of river sites and of the Rheinau bequest"						35		
13.03.1955	178	Popular Initiative "Protection of consumers and tenants (continuation of price control)"						36		
13.03.1955	179	Counter proposal							3	
04.03.1956	180	Federal decree on temporary continuation of limited price control (extension to supplement to the federal constitution of 26th September 1952)	44							
13.05.1956	181	Popular Initiative "Distribution of concessions for the use of hydro-power"						37		
13.05.1956	182	Federal decree on measures to strengthen the economy of the canton Graubünden by means of a grant to the local timber processing factory								41
30.09.1956	183	Federal decree on revision of national bread-making cereals supply regulation					22			
30.09.1956	184	Federal decree on Popular Initiative on decisions on expenses by National Assembly (Counter-proposal)							4	

FR = Facultative Referendum, CP = Counter-proposal, OR = Obligatory Referendum, PI = Popular Initiative, Art. = article, § = paragraph

SURVEY 1
ALL POPULAR VOTES IN SWITZERLAND SINCE 1848

NATIONAL REFERENDUM VOTES

			APPROVED				REJECTED			
DATE		SUBJECT	OR	PI	CP	FR	OR	PI	CP	FR
03.03.1957	185	Federal decree on supplementing the federal constitution by Art. 22bis on civil protection					23			
03.03.1957	186	Federal decree on supplementing the federal constitution by Art. 36bis on radio and TV					24			
24.11.1957	187	Federal decree on supplementing the federal constitution by Art. 24quinquies on nuclear power and radiological protection	45							
24.11.1957	188	Federal decree on temporary extension of period of validity of transitional ruling on national supply of bread-making cereals	46							
26.01.1958	189	Popular Initiative "Against the misuse of economic power"						38		
11.05.1958	190	Federal decree on constitutional reorganisation of federal finances	47							
06.07.1958	191	Federal decree on supplementing the federal constitution by Art. 27ter on cinemas	48							
06.07.1958	192	Federal decree on Popular Initiative for improvement of the road network (counter-proposal)			8					
26.10.1958	193	Popular Initiative "Forty-four hour working week"						39		
07.12.1958	194	Federal decree on change to the federal constitution (gambling in spas and casinos)	49							
07.12.1958	195	Federal decree on ratification of the agreement reached between the Swiss Confederation and the Republic of Italy on harnessing the energy of the river Spoel			23					

FR = Facultative Referendum, CP = Counter-proposal, OR = Obligatory Referendum, PI = Popular Initiative, Art. = article, § = paragraph

SURVEY 1
ALL POPULAR VOTES IN SWITZERLAND SINCE 1848

NATIONAL REFERENDUM VOTES

DATE		SUBJECT	APPROVED				REJECTED			
			OR	PI	CP	FR	OR	PI	CP	FR
01.02.1959	196	Federal decree on introduction of women's suffrage at national level					25			
24.05.1959	197	Federal decree on supplementing the federal constitution by Art. 22bis on civil protection	50							
29.05.1960	198	Federal decree on continuation of temporary price control measures	51							
04.12.1960	199	Federal decree on amending the federal decree on additional economic and financial measures in milk production			24					
05.03.1961	200	Federal decree on supplementing the federal constitution by an Art. 26bis on pipelines for liquid and gaseous fuels	52							
05.03.1961	201	Federal decree on increasing fuel duty to finance motorways								42
22.10.1961	202	Popular Initiative "Introduction of the legislative initiative at the federal level"						40		
03.12.1961	203	Federal decree on Swiss watch industry			25					
01.04.1962	204	Popular Initiative "Ban on nuclear weapons"						41		
27.05.1962	205	Federal decree on supplementing the federal constitution by an Art. 24sexies on nature conservation	53							
27.05.1962	206	Federal law on amendment to federal law on per diems and travel expenses for members of the National Council and of the Commission of the Federal Assembly								43
04.11.1962	207	Federal decree on amending the federal constitution by Art. 72 (election of National Council)	54							
26.05.1963	208	Popular Initiative "Right of Swiss citizens to decide whether the Swiss army should have nuclear weapons"						42		

FR = Facultative Referendum, CP = Counter-proposal, OR = Obligatory Referendum, PI = Popular Initiative, Art. = article, § = paragraph

SURVEY 1
ALL POPULAR VOTES IN SWITZERLAND SINCE 1848

NATIONAL REFERENDUM VOTES

DATE		SUBJECT	APPROVED				REJECTED			
			OR	PI	CP	FR	OR	PI	CP	FR
08.12.1963	209	Federal decree on continuing federal finance arrangements (extension of period of validity of Art. 41ter of the federal constitution and lowering of army tax)	55							
08.12.1963	210	Federal decree on supplementing the federal constitution by an Art. 27quater on grants and other forms of support for education	56							
02.02.1964	211	Federal decree on issuing of a general tax amnesty as of 1st January 1965					26			
24.05.1964	212	Federal law on professional education							26	
06.12.1964	213	Federal decree on continuation of temporary price control measures	57							
28.02.1965	214	Federal decree on control of inflation through measures affecting the money and capital markets and banking	58							
28.02.1965	215	Federal decree on control of inflation through measures affecting the building sector	59							
16.05.1965	216	Federal law concerning amendment to a decree of the Federal Assembly on milk, milk products and edible fats				27				
16.10.1966	217	Federal decree on supplementing the federal constitution by an Art. 45bis concerning the Swiss living or staying abroad	60							
16.10.1966	218	Popular Initiative "Fight against alcoholism"						43		
02.07.1967	219	Popular Initiative "Against land speculation"						44		
18.02.1968	220	Federal decree on issuing a general tax amnesty	61							

FR = Facultative Referendum, CP = Counter-proposal, OR = Obligatory Referendum, PI = Popular Initiative, Art. = article, § = paragraph

SURVEY 1
ALL POPULAR VOTES IN SWITZERLAND SINCE 1848

NATIONAL REFERENDUM VOTES

DATE		SUBJECT	APPROVED				REJECTED			
			OR	PI	CP	FR	OR	PI	CP	FR
19.05.1968	221	Federal law on tobacco tax								44
01.06.1969	222	Federal law on federal Technical Universities								45
14.09.1969	223	Federal decree on supplementing the federal constitution by arts. 22ter and 22quater (property laws)	62							
01.02.1970	224	Federal decree on national sugar production				28				
07.06.1970	225	Popular Initiative "Foreigners, reduction of number"						45		
27.09.1970	226	Federal decree on supplementing the federal constitution by an Art. 27quinquies on support for gymnastics and sport	63							
27.09.1970	227	Popular Initiative "For the right to housing and better protection of the family"						46		
15.11.1970	228	Federal decree on amendment to federal budget					27			
07.02.1971	229	Federal decree on introduction of women's suffrage at federal level	64							
06.06.1971	230	Federal decree on supplementing the federal constitution by an Art. 24septies on protecting people and the natural environment from harmful or annoying impacts	65							
06.06.1971	231	Federal decree on extension of federal budget	66							
05.03.1972	232	Popular Initiative "Promotion of construction of housing"						47		
05.03.1972	233	Counter-proposal			9					

FR = Facultative Referendum, CP = Counter-proposal, OR = Obligatory Referendum, PI = Popular Initiative, Art. = article, § = paragraph

SURVEY 1
ALL POPULAR VOTES IN SWITZERLAND SINCE 1848

NATIONAL REFERENDUM VOTES

DATE		SUBJECT	APPROVED				REJECTED			
			OR	PI	CP	FR	OR	PI	CP	FR
05.03.1972	234	Federal decree on supplementing the federal constitution by an Art. 34septies on declaration of general bindingness of leasing contracts and measures to protect tenants	67							
04.06.1972	235	Federal decree on measures to stabilise the construction market	68							
04.06.1972	236	Federal decree on protection of Swiss currency	69							
24.09.1972	237	Popular Initiative "Greater control of arms and ban on exports of arms"						48		
03.12.1972	238	Popular Initiative "For a real old age and sickness pension" and amendment to the federal constitution in the field of disability, old age-, widows- and orphans insurance						49		
03.12.1972	239	Counter-proposal			10					
03.12.1972	240	Federal decree on the agreement between the Swiss Confederation and the EEC and the member states of the EC on coal and steel	70[1]							
04.03.1973	241	Federal decree on amendment to the federal constitution concerning education					28			
04.03.1973	242	Federal decree on supplement to the federal constitution on support for scientific research	71							
20.05.1973	243	Federal decree on repeal of constitutional arts. 51 and 52 concerning Jesuits and monasteries	72							

[1] This referendum vote was initiated by the government and declared as an „obligatory referendum". It was de facto a plebiscite.

FR = Facultative Referendum, CP = Counter-proposal, OR = Obligatory Referendum, PI = Popular Initiative, Art. = article, § = paragraph

SURVEY 1
ALL POPULAR VOTES IN SWITZERLAND SINCE 1848

NATIONAL REFERENDUM VOTES

DATE		SUBJECT	APPROVED				REJECTED			
			OR	PI	CP	FR	OR	PI	CP	FR
02.12.1973	244	Federal decree on measures to monitor prices	73							
02.12.1973	245	Federal decree on measures in the banking sector (credit control)	74							
02.12.1973	246	Federal decree on measures to stabilise the construction market	75							
02.12.1973	247	Federal decree on limitation to tax depreciation on federal, cantonal and communal income tax	76							
02.12.1973	248	Federal decree on replacement of Art. 25bis of the federal constitution by an article on animal protection	77							
20.10.1974	249	Popular Initiative "Foreigners, reduction of number"						50		
08.12.1974	250	Federal decree on improvement to the federal economy					29			
08.12.1974	251	Federal decree on aggravation of decisions on expenditure	78							
08.12.1974	252	Popular Initiative "Social health insurance"						51		
08.12.1974	253	Counter-proposal							5	
02.03.1975	254	Federal decree on constitutional article on the economy					30			
08.06.1975	255	Federal decree on protection of the currency (amendment of 28th June 1974)	79							
08.06.1975	256	Federal decree on financing of national highways (amendment of 4th October 1974)			29					
08.06.1975	257	Federal law on change of general customs duty								46
08.06.1975	258	Federal decree on raising income from taxes from 1976	80							

FR = Facultative Referendum, CP = Counter-proposal, OR = Obligatory Referendum, PI = Popular Initiative, Art. = article, § = paragraph

SURVEY 1
ALL POPULAR VOTES IN SWITZERLAND SINCE 1848

NATIONAL REFERENDUM VOTES

			APPROVED				REJECTED			
DATE		SUBJECT	OR	PI	CP	FR	OR	PI	CP	FR
08.06.1975	259	Federal decree on aggravation of decisions on expenditure	81							
07.12.1975	260	Federal decree on amending the federal constitution (freedom of domicile and social assistance)	82							
07.12.1975	261	Federal decree on amending the federal constitution (water resources)	83							
07.12.1975	262	Federal law on import and export of agricultural products				30				
21.03.1976	263	Popular Initiative "For workers' participation in decision-making"						52		
21.03.1976	264	Counter-proposal							6	
21.03.1976	265	Popular Initiative "Reform of taxes (fairer taxes and abolition of tax privileges)"						53		
13.06.1976	266	Federal law on spatial planning								47
13.06.1976	267	Federal decree relating to an agreement between Switzerland and the International Development Agency on a loan of 200 million francs								48
13.06.1976	268	Federal decree on a revision of unemployment insurance	84							
26.09.1976	269	Federal decree on an article of the federal constitution concerning radio and TV					31			
26.09.1976	270	Popular Initiative "Federal third-party insurance for motor vehicles and bicycles"						54		
05.12.1976	271	Federal decree on monetary and credit policy	85							
05.12.1976	272	Federal decree on price monitoring	86							

FR = Facultative Referendum, CP = Counter-proposal, OR = Obligatory Referendum, PI = Popular Initiative, Art. = article, § = paragraph

SURVEY 1
ALL POPULAR VOTES IN SWITZERLAND SINCE 1848

NATIONAL REFERENDUM VOTES

			Approved				Rejected			
DATE		SUBJECT	OR	PI	CP	FR	OR	PI	CP	FR
05.12.1976	273	Popular Initiative "Reduction of the workweek to forty hours"						55		
13.03.1977	274	Popular Initiative "Foreigners, reduction of number (N° 4)"						56		
13.03.1977	275	Popular Initiative "Restriction of naturalisation of foreigners"						57		
13.03.1977	276	Popular Initiative "Reorganisation of the referendum on international treaties"						58		
13.03.1977	277	Counter-proposal			11					
12.06.1977	278	Federal decree on revision of VAT and direct federal taxation					32			
12.06.1977	279	Federal decree on tax harmonisation	87							
25.09.1977	280	Popular Initiative "For an effective protection of tenants"						59		
25.09.1977	281	Counter-proposal							7	
25.09.1977	282	Popular Initiative "Against air pollution from motor vehicles (Albatross Initiative)"						60		
25.09.1977	283	Federal decree on raising the signature threshold for referendums (arts. 89 and 89bis of the federal constitution).	88							
25.09.1977	284	Federal decree on raising the signature threshold for the constitutional initiative (arts.120 and 121 of the federal constitution)	89							
25.09.1977	285	Popular Initiative "Decriminalisation of abortion"						61		
04.12.1977	286	Popular Initiative "Higher taxes on big incomes"						62		
04.12.1977	287	Federal law on political rights				31				

FR = Facultative Referendum, CP = Counter-proposal, OR = Obligatory Referendum, PI = Popular Initiative, Art. = article, § = paragraph

SURVEY 1
ALL POPULAR VOTES IN SWITZERLAND SINCE 1848

NATIONAL REFERENDUM VOTES

			APPROVED				REJECTED			
DATE		SUBJECT	OR	PI	CP	FR	OR	PI	CP	FR
04.12.1977	288	Federal decree on introduction of civil service as alternative to military service					33			
04.12.1977	289	Federal law on measures to balance the national budget				32				
26.02.1978	290	Popular Initiative "Enhancing parliamentary and popular participation in decision-making on matters of highway construction"						63		
26.02.1978	291	Federal law on old age-, widows- and orphans insurance, amendment of 24th June 1977 (9th revision)				33				
26.02.1978	292	Popular Initiative "On lowering retirement age"						64		
26.02.1978	293	Federal decree on the federal constitutional article on economic policy	90							
28.05.1978	294	Law on summer time								49
28.05.1978	295	Law on customs duties, amendment of 7th October 1977				34				
28.05.1978	296	Federal law on protection of pregnancy and abortion as a punishable offence								50
28.05.1978	297	Federal law on funding for higher education and research								51
28.05.1978	298	Popular Initiative "Twelve Sundays a year without motor traffic"						65		
24.09.1978	299	Federal decree on creation of the canton Jura (arts.1 and 80 of the federal constitution)	91							
03.12.1978	300	1977 milk supply decree				35				
03.12.1978	301	Federal law on protection of animals				36				
03.12.1978	302	Federal law on federal obligation to provide security police								52
03.12.1978	303	Federal law on professional education				37				

FR = Facultative Referendum, CP = Counter-proposal, OR = Obligatory Referendum, PI = Popular Initiative, Art. = article, § = paragraph

SURVEY 1
ALL POPULAR VOTES IN SWITZERLAND SINCE 1848

NATIONAL REFERENDUM VOTES

			Approved				Rejected			
DATE		SUBJECT	OR	PI	CP	FR	OR	PI	CP	FR
18.02.1979	304	Federal decree on lowering voting age to 18					34			
18.02.1979	305	Federal decree on the Popular Initiative "promotion of footpaths and trails" (Counter proposal)			12					
18.02.1979	306	Popular Initiative "Ban liquor and tobacco advertising"						66		
18.02.1979	307	Popular Initiative "Maintaining and protecting the people's rights and security when building and operating nuclear plants"						67		
20.05.1979	308	Federal decree on revision of VAT and direct federal taxes					35			
20.05.1979	309	Federal decree on the federal law on atomic energy				38				
02.03.1980	310	Popular Initiative "Complete separation of church and state"						68		
02.03.1980	311	Federal decree on revision of arrangements for national supplies	92							
30.11.1980	312	Federal traffic law, amendment of 21st March 1980 (compulsory seatbelts and helmets)				39				
30.11.1980	313	Federal decree on withdrawing the cantonal share of revenues from banking "stamp duty".	93							
30.11.1980	314	Federal decree on redistribution of revenues of the federal alcohol ministry from the duty on spirits	94							
30.11.1980	315	Federal decree on revision of national regulations on bread-making cereals	95							
05.04.1981	316	Popular Initiative "New, friendlier policy towards foreign residents"						69		

FR = Facultative Referendum, CP = Counter-proposal, OR = Obligatory Referendum, PI = Popular Initiative, Art. = article, § = paragraph

SURVEY 1
ALL POPULAR VOTES IN SWITZERLAND SINCE 1848

NATIONAL REFERENDUM VOTES

DATE		SUBJECT	APPROVED				REJECTED			
			OR	PI	CP	FR	OR	PI	CP	FR
14.06.1981	317	Federal decree on Popular Initiative "Equal rights for men and women" (Counter-proposal)			13					
14.06.1981	318	Federal decree on Popular Initiative "Protection of consumer rights" (Counter-proposal)			14					
29.11.1981	319	Federal decree on continuation of budget and improvement in federal finances	96							
06.06.1982	320	Law on foreigners								53
06.06.1982	321	Swiss penal code, amendment of 9th October 1981				40				
28.11.1982	322	Popular Initiative "Prevention of false pricing"		8						
28.11.1982	323	Counter-proposal							8	
27.02.1983	324	Federal decree on revision of fuel duty	97							
27.02.1983	325	Federal decree on energy policy article in the federal constitution					36			
04.12.1983	326	Federal decree on changes to nationality rules in the federal constitution	98							
04.12.1983	327	Federal decree on easing naturalization in certain cases					37			
26.02.1984	328	Federal decree on raising a heavy goods vehicle tax	99							
26.02.1984	329	Federal decree on a motorway toll	100							
26.02.1984	330	Popular Initiative "For a genuine community service based on actual evidence of social engagement"						70		
20.05.1984	331	Popular Initiative "Against abuse of banking secrecy and banking power"						71		
20.05.1984	332	Popular Initiative "Against selling of land to foreigners"						72		

FR = Facultative Referendum, CP = Counter-proposal, OR = Obligatory Referendum, PI = Popular Initiative, Art. = article, § = paragraph

SURVEY 1
ALL POPULAR VOTES IN SWITZERLAND SINCE 1848

NATIONAL REFERENDUM VOTES

			Approved				Rejected			
DATE		SUBJECT	OR	PI	CP	FR	OR	PI	CP	FR
23.09.1984	333	Popular Initiative "For a future without new nuclear plants"						73		
23.09.1984	334	Popular Initiative "for a safe, economic and environmentally friendly energy policy"						74		
02.12.1984	335	Popular Initiative "Effective protection of motherhood"						75		
02.12.1984	336	Federal decree on a constitutional article on radio and TV	101							
02.12.1984	337	Federal decree on the Popular Initiative "Compensation for victims of violent offences" (Counter-proposal)			15					
10.03.1985	338	Federal decree on ending federal primary school subsidies	102							
10.03.1985	339	Federal decree on ending federal public health subsidies	103							
10.03.1985	340	Federal decree on education subsidies					38			
10.03.1985	341	Popular Initiative "Lengthening paid holidays"						76		
09.06.1985	342	Popular Initiative "Right to life"						77		
09.06.1985	343	Federal decree on suspending cantonal share of revenues from banking stamp duty	104							
09.06.1985	344	Federal decree on redistribution of income from tax on spirits	105							
09.06.1985	345	Federal decree on withdrawal of subsidies for self-sufficient supply with bread-making cereals	106							
22.09.1985	346	Federal decree on Popular Initiative "Standardised beginning of school year in all cantons" (Counter-proposal)			16					

FR = Facultative Referendum, CP = Counter-proposal, OR = Obligatory Referendum, PI = Popular Initiative, Art. = article, § = paragraph

SURVEY 1
ALL POPULAR VOTES IN SWITZERLAND SINCE 1848

NATIONAL REFERENDUM VOTES

			Approved				Rejected			
DATE		SUBJECT	OR	PI	CP	FR	OR	PI	CP	FR
22.09.1985	347	Federal decree on insurance against innovation-related risk for small and medium-sized companies								54
22.09.1985	348	Swiss civil law, amendment of 5th October 1984 (marriage and inheritance law)				41				
01.12.1985	349	Popular Initiative "Abolition of vivisection"						78		
16.03.1986	350	Federal decree on accession of Switzerland to the UN					39			
28.09.1986	351	Popular Initiative "Culture initiative"						79		
28.09.1986	352	Counter-proposal							9	
28.09.1986	353	Popular Initiative "For guaranteed vocational training and retraining"						80		
28.09.1986	354	Federal decree on home sugar production, amendment of 21st June 1985								55
07.12.1986	355	Federal decree on the Popular Initiative "Tenants' protection" (Counter-proposal)			17					
07.12.1986	356	Popular Initiative "Fair taxation of heavy trucks"						81		
05.04.1987	357	Asylum law, amendment of 20th June 1986				42				
05.04.1987	358	Federal law on rights of stay and domicile of foreigners, revision of 20th June 1986				43				
05.04.1987	359	Popular Initiative "Right to referendum on all military expenditure (arms referendum)"						82		
05.04.1987	360	Federal decree on the referendum procedure for Popular Initiatives where there is a counter-proposal ("double yes")	107							

FR = Facultative Referendum, CP = Counter-proposal, OR = Obligatory Referendum, PI = Popular Initiative, Art. = article, § = paragraph

SURVEY 1
ALL POPULAR VOTES IN SWITZERLAND SINCE 1848

NATIONAL REFERENDUM VOTES

			APPROVED				REJECTED			
DATE		SUBJECT	OR	PI	CP	FR	OR	PI	CP	FR
06.12.1987	361	Federal decree on "Rail 2000" project				44				
06.12.1987	362	Popular Initiative "Rothenthurm" initiative for the protection of moorland		9						
06.12.1987	363	Federal law on health insurance, amendment of 20th March 1987								56
12.06.1988	364	Federal decree on the constitutional basis for a coordinated traffic policy					40			
12.06.1988	365	Popular Initiative "On lowering retirement age to 62 years for men and 60 years for women"						83		
04.12.1988	366	Popular Initiative "Town and country initiative against land speculation"						84		
04.12.1988	367	Popular Initiative "Reduction of working hours"						85		
04.12.1988	368	Popular Initiative "On restriction of immigration"						86		
04.06.1989	369	Popular Initiative "For ecological farming – against animal factories (Small farmers initiative)"						87		
26.11.1989	370	Popular Initiative "For abolition of the Swiss army and a comprehensive policy for peace"						88		
26.11.1989	371	Popular Initiative "For speed limits of 130 and 100 kph"						89		
01.04.1990	372	Popular Initiative "No more concrete – restriction on new road building!"						90		
01.04.1990	373	Popular Initiative "For a motorway-free zone between Murten and Yverdon"						91		
01.04.1990	374	Popular Initiative "For a motorway-free district of Knonau"						92		

FR = Facultative Referendum, CP = Counter-proposal, OR = Obligatory Referendum, PI = Popular Initiative, Art. = article, § = paragraph

SURVEY 1
ALL POPULAR VOTES IN SWITZERLAND SINCE 1848

NATIONAL REFERENDUM VOTES

			APPROVED				REJECTED			
DATE		SUBJECT	OR	PI	CP	FR	OR	PI	CP	FR
01.04.1990	375	Popular Initiative "For a motorway-free zone between Biel and Solothurn/Zuchwil"						93		
01.04.1990	376	Federal decree on wine growing								57
01.04.1990	377	Federal law on judicial organization, amendment of 23rd June 1989								58
23.09.1990	378	Popular Initiative "Stop using nuclear power"						94		
23.09.1990	379	Popular Initiative "Moratorium on nuclear power station construction"		10						
23.09.1990	380	Federal decree on the constitutional article on energy policy	108							
23.09.1990	381	Federal law on road traffic, amendment of 6th October 1989				45				
03.03.1991	382	Federal decree on lowering the voting age to 18	109							
03.03.1991	383	Popular Initiative "On promotion of public transport"						95		
02.06.1991	384	Federal decree on revision of federal finances					41			
02.06.1991	385	Amendment to military penal code of 5th October 1990				46				
16.02.1992	386	Popular Initiative "For an affordable health insurance"						96		
16.02.1992	387	Popular Initiative "for a gradual but drastic reduction in animal experiments (an end to animal experimentation!)"						97		
17.05.1992	388	Federal decree on Swiss accession to the Bretton Woods institutions (IMF and World Bank)				47				

FR = Facultative Referendum, CP = Counter-proposal, OR = Obligatory Referendum, PI = Popular Initiative, Art. = article, § = paragraph

SURVEY 1
ALL POPULAR VOTES IN SWITZERLAND SINCE 1848

NATIONAL REFERENDUM VOTES

DATE		SUBJECT	APPROVED				REJECTED			
			OR	PI	CP	FR	OR	PI	CP	FR
17.05.1992	389	Federal law governing Swiss involvement with the Bretton Woods institutions				48				
17.05.1992	390	Federal law on protection of waters				49				
17.05.1992	391	Federal decree on the Popular Initiative "Against misuses of reproductive and genetic technology in humans" (Counter proposal)			18					
17.05.1992	392	Federal decree on the introduction of civil service for conscientious objectors	110							
17.05.1992	393	Swiss penal code and military penal code, amendment of 21st June 1991 (punishable offences against sexual integrity)				50				
17.05.1992	394	Popular Initiative "Save our lakes and rivers"						98		
27.09.1992	395	Federal decree on building of Swiss transalpine railway				51				
27.09.1992	396	Federal law on procedures within the Federal Assembly and on the form, publication and entering into force of its laws, amendment of 4th October 1991				52				
27.09.1992	397	Federal law on stamp duty, amendment of 4th October 1991				53				
27.09.1992	398	Federal law on farmers' soil law				54				
27.09.1992	399	Federal law on MP's per diems and contributions to parliamentary groups, amendment of 4th October 1991								59
27.09.1992	400	Federal law on contributions to infrastructure costs for MPs and parliamentary groups								60
06.12.1992	401	Federal decree on European Economic Area					42			

FR = Facultative Referendum, CP = Counter-proposal, OR = Obligatory Referendum, PI = Popular Initiative, Art. = article, § = paragraph

SURVEY 1
ALL POPULAR VOTES IN SWITZERLAND SINCE 1848

NATIONAL REFERENDUM VOTES

			APPROVED				REJECTED			
DATE		SUBJECT	OR	PI	CP	FR	OR	PI	CP	FR
07.03.1993	402	Federal law on raising fuel duty of 9th October 1992				55				
07.03.1993	403	Federal decree on repealing the ban on casino gambling	111							
07.03.1993	404	Popular Initiative "To abolish experiments on animals"						99		
06.06.1993	405	Popular Initiative "40 army training camps are enough – protection of the environment within the military as well"						100		
06.06.1993	406	Popular Initiative "For a Switzerland without new fighter planes"						101		
26.09.1993	407	Federal decree against the misuse of weapons	112							
26.09.1993	408	Federal decree on the transfer of the district of Laufen from the canton Bern to the canton Basel Country	113							
26.09.1993	409	Popular Initiative "For a federal work-free holiday on 1st August (1st August Initiative)"		11						
26.09.1993	410	Federal decree on temporary measures against rising costs in health insurance				56				
26.09.1993	411	Federal decree on measures for unemployment insurance				57				
28.11.1993	412	Federal decree on organization of federal finances	114							
28.11.1993	413	Federal decree on increased contribution to federal revenues	115							
28.11.1993	414	Federal decree on measures to preserve social insurance	116							
28.11.1993	415	Federal decree on certain consumption taxes	117							

FR = Facultative Referendum, CP = Counter-proposal, OR = Obligatory Referendum, PI = Popular Initiative, Art. = article, § = paragraph

SURVEY 1
ALL POPULAR VOTES IN SWITZERLAND SINCE 1848

NATIONAL REFERENDUM VOTES

DATE		SUBJECT	APPROVED				REJECTED			
			OR	PI	CP	FR	OR	PI	CP	FR
28.11.1993	416	Popular Initiative "To reduce the problems of alcohol"						102		
28.11.1993	417	Popular Initiative "To reduce the problems of tobacco"						103		
20.02.1994	418	Federal decree on continuation of the motorway tax	118							
20.02.1994	419	Federal decree on continuation of the heavy goods vehicle tax	119							
20.02.1994	420	Federal decree on introduction of a heavy goods vehicle tax based on engine size or fuel consumption	120							
20.02.1994	421	Popular Initiative "To protect the Alpine region from transit traffic"		12						
20.02.1994	422	Federal air traffic law, amendment of 18th June 1993				58				
12.06.1994	423	Federal decree on Art. 27septies of the federal constitution relating to support for culture					43			
12.06.1994	424	Federal decree on revision of the naturalization rules in the federal constitution (making naturalization easier for young foreigners)					44			
12.06.1994	425	Federal law on use of Swiss troops in peace-keeping operations								61
25.09.1994	426	Federal decree on ending subsidy for home bread-making cereals	121							
25.09.1994	427	Swiss penal code, military penal code, amendment of 18th June 1993				59				
04.12.1994	428	Federal law on health insurance				60				
04.12.1994	429	Popular Initiative "For sound health insurance"						104		

FR = Facultative Referendum, CP = Counter-proposal, OR = Obligatory Referendum, PI = Popular Initiative, Art. = article, § = paragraph

SURVEY 1
ALL POPULAR VOTES IN SWITZERLAND SINCE 1848

NATIONAL REFERENDUM VOTES

			APPROVED				REJECTED			
DATE		SUBJECT	OR	PI	CP	FR	OR	PI	CP	FR
04.12.1994	430	Federal law on compulsory measures in the law relating to foreigners				61				
12.03.1995	431	Federal decree on the Popular Initiative "for an environmentally just and efficient agriculture"						10		
12.03.1995	432	Milk production decree 1988, amendment of 18th March 1994								62
12.03.1995	433	Agriculture law, amendment of 8th October 1993								63
12.03.1995	434	Federal decree on brake on expenditure	122							
25.06.1995	435	Federal law on old age-, widows- and orphans insurance, amendment of 7th October 1994				62				
25.06.1995	436	Popular Initiative "To expand the state old age-, widows-, orphans- and disability insurance"						105		
25.06.1995	437	Federal law on acquisition of real estate by persons living abroad, amendment of 7th October 1994								64
10.03.1996	438	Federal decree on revision of the language article in the federal constitution (Art. 116)	123							
10.03.1996	439	Federal decree on the transfer of the Bernese community of Vellerat to the canton Jura	124							
10.03.1996	440	Federal decree on the withdrawal of cantonal competence in respect of the personal equipment of military personnel					45			
10.03.1996	441	Federal decree on remission of the obligation to purchase distilling equipment and take over distilled products	125							

FR = Facultative Referendum, CP = Counter-proposal, OR = Obligatory Referendum, PI = Popular Initiative, Art. = article, § = paragraph

SURVEY 1
ALL POPULAR VOTES IN SWITZERLAND SINCE 1848

NATIONAL REFERENDUM VOTES

			APPROVED				REJECTED			
DATE		SUBJECT	OR	PI	CP	FR	OR	PI	CP	FR
10.03.1996	442	Federal decree on cessation of federal funding for station car parks	126							
09.06.1996	443	Counter-proposal of National Assembly of 21st December 1995 to the Popular Initiative "Farmers and consumers – for an agriculture in harmony with nature"			19					
09.06.1996	444	Law on organization of government and administration of 6th October 1995								65
01.12.1996	445	Federal decree on the Popular Initiative "against illegal immigration"						106		
01.12.1996	446	Federal law on labor in industry, trade and commerce, amendment of 22nd March 1996								66
08.06.1997	447	Popular Initiative "Negotiations on joining the EU: let the people decide!"						107		
08.06.1997	448	Popular Initiative "For a prohibition on the export of materials of war"						108		
08.06.1997	449	Federal decree on cessation of federal monopoly on the manufacture and sale of gunpowder	127							
28.09.1997	450	Federal decree of 13th December 1996 on financing of unemployment insurance								67
28.09.1997	451	Federal decree on the Popular Initiative "youth without drugs"						109		
07.06.1998	452	Federal decree on measures to balance the budget	128							
07.06.1998	453	Popular Initiative "To protect life and the environment from gene manipulation (Gene protection Initiative)"						110		
07.06.1998	454	Popular Initiative "Switzerland without police snooping"						111		

FR = Facultative Referendum, CP = Counter-proposal, OR = Obligatory Referendum, PI = Popular Initiative, Art. = article, § = paragraph

SURVEY 1
ALL POPULAR VOTES IN SWITZERLAND SINCE 1848

NATIONAL REFERENDUM VOTES

DATE		SUBJECT	APPROVED				REJECTED			
			OR	PI	CP	FR	OR	PI	CP	FR
27.09.1998	455	Federal law on engine size related heavy goods vehicle tax				63				
27.09.1998	456	Popular Initiative "For inexpensive foodstuffs and ecological farming"						112		
27.09.1998	457	Popular Initiative "For the 10th revision of old age insurance without raising the retirement age"						113		
29.11.1998	458	Federal decree on construction and financing of public transport infrastructure plans	129							
29.11.1998	459	Federal decree on a temporary new constitutional article on cereals	130							
29.11.1998	460	Popular Initiative "For a sensible drugs policy"						114		
29.11.1998	461	Federal law on employment in industry, trade and commerce				64				
07.02.1999	462	Federal decree on changing the eligibility conditions for election to the National Council	131							
07.02.1999	463	Federal decree on constitutional article on medical transplantation	132							
07.02.1999	464	Popular Initiative "Home-ownership for all"						115		
07.02.1999	465	Federal law on spatial planning, amendment of 20th March 1998				65				
18.04.1999	466	Federal decree on a new federal constitution	133							
13.06.1999	467	Asylum law				66				
13.06.1999	468	Federal decree on urgent measures in relation to asylum and foreigners				67				
13.06.1999	469	Federal decree on prescription of heroin by doctors				68				

FR = Facultative Referendum, CP = Counter-proposal, OR = Obligatory Referendum, PI = Popular Initiative, Art. = article, § = paragraph

SURVEY 1
ALL POPULAR VOTES IN SWITZERLAND SINCE 1848

NATIONAL REFERENDUM VOTES

DATE		SUBJECT	APPROVED				REJECTED			
			OR	PI	CP	FR	OR	PI	CP	FR
13.06.1999	470	Federal law on disability insurance								68
13.06.1999	471	Federal law on insurance for motherhood								69
12.03.2000	472	Federal decree on reform of judiciary	134							
12.03.2000	473	Popular Initiative "For speeding up direct democracy (processing times for Popular Initiatives in the form of a specific draft)"						116		
12.03.2000	474	Popular Initiative "For a fair representation of women in the federal authorities (3rd March initiative)"						117		
12.03.2000	475	Popular Initiative "For the protection of humans against manipulations in reproductive technology (Initiative for humane reproduction)"						118		
12.03.2000	476	Popular Initiative "To halve motorised road traffic for the preservation and improvement of living space (Traffic halving Initiative)"						119		
21.05.2000	477	Federal decree on approval of sectoral agreements between Switzerland and the EC and/or its member states, or Euratom				69				
24.09.2000	478	Popular Initiative "For a solar penny (Solar Initiative)"						120		
24.09.2000	479	Counter-proposal (article in the federal constitution on a levy to promote renewable energy)							11	
24.09.2000	480	Constitutional article on an environmental energy tax (counter-proposal to the withdrawn "Energy environment initiative")							12	
24.09.2000	481	Popular Initiative "For regulation of immigration"						121		

FR = Facultative Referendum, CP = Counter-proposal, OR = Obligatory Referendum, PI = Popular Initiative, Art. = article, § = paragraph

SURVEY 1
ALL POPULAR VOTES IN SWITZERLAND SINCE 1848

NATIONAL REFERENDUM VOTES

			APPROVED				REJECTED			
DATE		SUBJECT	OR	PI	CP	FR	OR	PI	CP	FR
24.09.2000	482	Popular Initiative "Increased citizens' rights through referendums with counter-proposals (Constructive referendum)"						122		
26.11.2000	483	Popular Initiative "For a more flexible old age-, widows- and orphans insurance – against raising the retirement age for women"						123		
26.11.2000	484	Popular Initiative "For a flexible retirement age from 62 upwards for women and men"						124		
26.11.2000	485	Popular Initiative "Saving on army and defence spending – for more peace and forward-looking jobs (Redistribution Initiative)"						125		
26.11.2000	486	Popular Initiative "For lower hospital costs"						126		
26.11.2000	487	Law on federal employees				70				
04.03.2001	488	Popular Initiative "Yes to Europe"						127		
04.03.2001	489	Popular Initiative "For lower-priced medicines"						128		
04.03.2001	490	Popular Initiative "For greater traffic safety based on a speed limit of 30 kph for built-up areas with exceptions (Roads for everyone)"						129		
10.06.2001	491	Amendment of 6th October 2000 to federal law on army and military authorities (weapons)				71				
10.06.2001	492	Amendment of 6th October 2000 to federal law on army and military authorities (training)				72				

FR = Facultative Referendum, CP = Counter-proposal, OR = Obligatory Referendum, PI = Popular Initiative, Art. = article, § = paragraph

SURVEY 1
ALL POPULAR VOTES IN SWITZERLAND SINCE 1848

NATIONAL REFERENDUM VOTES

DATE		SUBJECT	APPROVED				REJECTED			
			OR	PI	CP	FR	OR	PI	CP	FR
10.06.2001	493	Federal decree of 15th December 2000 on withdrawal of duty to have permission to create new bishoprics	135							
02.12.2001	494	Federal decree on reducing debts	136							
02.12.2001	495	Popular Initiative "For a guaranteed old age-, widows- and orphans insurance – tax energy instead of work!"						130		
02.12.2001	496	Popular Initiative "For a credible security policy and a Switzerland without an army"						131		
02.12.2001	497	Popular Initiative "Solidarity creates security: For a voluntary civilian peace service (CPS)"						132		
02.12.2001	498	Popular Initiative "For a capital gains tax"						133		
03.03.2002	499	Popular Initiative "For Switzerland's membership of the United Nations (UN)"		13						
03.03.2002	500	Popular Initiative "For a shorter working week"						134		
02.06.2002	501	Amendment to Swiss criminal code (termination of pregnancy)				73				
02.06.2002	502	Popular Initiative "For mother and child – for the protection of the unborn child and assistance for mothers in need"						135		
22.09.2002	503	Federal decree on the Popular Initiative "Surplus gold reserves for the old age-, widows- and orphans insurance fund (Gold Initiative)" and the counter-proposal "Gold for pension funds, cantons and foundations"							13	
22.09.2002	504	Counter-proposal (Gold for pension funds, cantons and foundations)							136	

FR = Facultative Referendum, CP = Counter-proposal, OR = Obligatory Referendum, PI = Popular Initiative, Art. = article, § = paragraph

SURVEY 1
ALL POPULAR VOTES IN SWITZERLAND SINCE 1848

NATIONAL REFERENDUM VOTES

			APPROVED				REJECTED			
DATE		SUBJECT	OR	PI	CP	FR	OR	PI	CP	FR
22.09.2002	505	Federal law on the electricity market								70
24.11.2002	506	Popular Initiative "Against the abuse of asylum rights"						137		
24.11.2002	507	Amendment to federal law on compulsory unemployment insurance and compensation for insolvency				74				
09.02.2003	508	Federal decree on amendment to citizens' rights	137							
09.02.2003	509	Federal law on adjusting canton's contributions to hospital costs				75				
18.05.2003	510	Amendment to federal law on the army and military administration				76				
18.05.2003	511	Federal law on civil protection				77				
18.05.2003	512	Popular Initiative "Yes to fair rents for tenants"						138		
18.05.2003	513	Popular Initiative "For one car-free Sunday per season – a 4-year trial (Sunday Initiative)"						139		
18.05.2003	514	Popular Initiative "Healthcare must be affordable (Health Initiative)"						140		
18.05.2003	515	Popular Initiative "Equal rights for the disabled"						141		
18.05.2003	516	Popular Initiative "Non-nuclear energy – for a change in energy policy and the gradual decommissioning of nuclear power plants (Non-nuclear energy)"						142		
18.05.2003	517	Popular Initiative "Moratorium Plus – for an extension of the moratorium on nuclear power plant construction and a limitation of the nuclear risk (MoratoriumPlus)"						143		

FR = Facultative Referendum, CP = Counter-proposal, OR = Obligatory Referendum, PI = Popular Initiative, Art. = article, § = paragraph

SURVEY 1
ALL POPULAR VOTES IN SWITZERLAND SINCE 1848

NATIONAL REFERENDUM VOTES

DATE		SUBJECT	APPROVED				REJECTED			
			OR	PI	CP	FR	OR	PI	CP	FR
18.05.2003	518	Popular Initiative "For adequate vocational training (Apprenticeship Initiative)"						144		
08.02.2004	519	Counter-proposal of Federal Assembly of 3rd October 2003 to the Popular Initiative "Avanti – for safe, efficient motorways"							14	
08.02.2004	520	Amendment of 13th December 2002 to the law on obligations (rents)									71
08.02.2004	521	Popular Initiative "Lifelong detention for perpetrators of sexual or violent crimes who are judged to be highly dangerous and untreatable"		14						
16.05.2004	522	Amendment of 3rd October 2003 to federal law on old age-, widows- and orphans insurance (11th revision)									72
16.05.2004	523	Federal decree of 3rd October 2003 on financing old age-, widows-, orphans- and disability insurance by raising level of VAT					46			
16.05.2004	524	Federal law of 20th June 2003 on amendments to regulations affecting taxation for married couples and families, on private housing and on stamp duty									73
26.09.2004	525	Federal decree of 3rd October 2003 on the proper conduct of naturalisation and on easier naturalisation for young, second-generation foreigners					47			
26.09.2004	526	Federal decree of 3rd October 2003 on acquisition of citizenship rights by third-generation foreigners					48			
26.09.2004	527	Popular Initiative "Postal services for all"						145		

FR = Facultative Referendum, CP = Counter-proposal, OR = Obligatory Referendum, PI = Popular Initiative, Art. = article, § = paragraph

SURVEY 1
ALL POPULAR VOTES IN SWITZERLAND SINCE 1848

NATIONAL REFERENDUM VOTES

			Approved				Rejected			
DATE		SUBJECT	OR	PI	CP	FR	OR	PI	CP	FR
26.09.2004	528	Amendment of 3rd October 2003 to federal law on financial compensation for loss of earnings for those serving in the armed forces, or performing the community service alternative, or in civil protection				78				
28.11.2004	529	Federal decree of 3rd October 2003 on revision of financial compensation and distribution of charges between the Confederation and the cantons	138							
28.11.2004	530	Federal decree of 19th March 2004 on new organization of federal finances	139							
28.11.2004	531	Federal law of 19th December 2003 on research on embryonic stem cells				79				
05.06.2005	532	Federal decree of 17.12.2004 on the approval and implementation of the bilateral agreements between Switzerland and the EU on the Schengen and Dublin accords				80				
05.06.2005	533	Federal law of 18.06.2004 on the registered partnership of same-sex couples (Partnership law)				81				
25.09.2005	534	Federal decree on approval and implementation of the protocol on the extension of the agreement on the free movement of persons to the new EU member states between the Swiss Confederation on the one hand and the European Union and its members states on the other, as well as on approval of the revision of the accompanying measures on the free movement of persons				82				

FR = Facultative Referendum, CP = Counter-proposal, OR = Obligatory Referendum, PI = Popular Initiative, Art. = article, § = paragraph

SURVEY 1
ALL POPULAR VOTES IN SWITZERLAND SINCE 1848

NATIONAL REFERENDUM VOTES

			Approved				Rejected			
DATE		SUBJECT	OR	PI	CP	FR	OR	PI	CP	FR
27.11.2005	535	Federal decree of 17.06.2005 on the citizens' initiative "For food grown without genetic modification"		15						
27.11.2005	536	Amendment of 08.10.2004 to the Federal Law on Employment in Industry, Trade and Commerce (Labour Law)				83				
21.05.2006	537	Federal decree of 16.12.2005 on a revision of the articles dealing with education in the federal constitution	140							
24.09.2006	538	Popular Initiative "Profits from the National Bank for the old age-, widows- and orphans insurance fund"								
24.09.2006	539	Federal decree of 16.12.2005 on foreigners								
24.09.2006	540	Federal decree of 16.12.2005 on the asylum law								

FR = Facultative Referendum, CP = Counter-proposal, OR = Obligatory Referendum, PI = Popular Initiative, Art. = article, § = paragraph

SURVEY 2
DIRECT-DEMOCRATIC PROCEDURES AND PLEBISCITES IN THE CONSTITUTIONS OF 32 EUROPEAN STATES

The following tables list the direct-democratic procedures and plebiscites which exist in individual countries (cf. list of countries), whether inscribed in the constitution or (where available) set out in specific referendum legislation. One table summarises the range of provisions in the 32 countries.

The tables give an impression of the current range of possibilities for direct democracy in Europe, but give no indication of the actual use made of the various instruments in practice.

What use is made of direct-democratic procedures depends on a number of factors – not least on the way in which political conflicts are normally resolved in a specific society i.e. on the political culture and on the number of conflicts there are to be resolved – which reflects the make-up (complexity) of the society and the present political configuration.

How well direct democracy can function depends, on the one hand, on the extent to which the basic conditions for the exercise of democracy are fulfilled and, on the other hand, on whether the tools of direct democracy have been so designed that they are genuinely usable. Democracy cannot function properly where violence is used as a means of resolving conflict. Poorly designed and implemented direct-democratic procedures are of little use, and may even be counter-productive.

In this respect, some caution is necessary in interpreting the information given in the tables. The institutional shaping and the precise design of the procedures of direct democracy cannot always be gleaned from the constitutions alone: there are often additional laws and statutory provisions. Laws, statutes and directives can restrict – or even nullify – what the constitution defines as an option. In short: "With popular rights, it's important to look at the small print" (Hans-Urs Wili).

Looked at from a different angle, we have to say: direct democracy is and remains controversial, both as an idea and in practice, and this struggle for and against direct democracy is expressed in how both indirect and direct-democratic procedures and rights are institutionalized in each democratic country through the constitution, laws and regulations. A brief glance at the table is sufficient to show that only relatively few countries have direct-democratic rights (the important ones being the popular referendum and the popular initiative) – with the necessary caution that this says nothing about the quality of the design of those rights.

The concept of direct democracy has more than one possible interpretation. It is therefore necessary to explain the concept of direct democracy which underlies the tables.

Modern direct democracy is not the same as classical assembly democracy. Direct democracy means today that citizens have the right to directly decide on substantive political issues by means of popular votes i.e. independently of the wishes of the government or parliament, on their own initiative or prescribed as mandatory by the constitution.

That definition already specifies the first criterion of direct democracy: direct democracy decides on substantive issues, not on people. So rights of recall and the direct election of representatives (e.g. direct elections for mayors or the president) do not belong to direct democracy.

SURVEY 2
DIRECT-DEMOCRATIC PROCEDURES AND PLEBISCITES IN THE CONSTITUTIONS OF 32 EUROPEAN STATES

A second criterion, which must also be fulfilled, can be expressed as follows: direct democracy empowers citizens; direct-democratic procedures are procedures for power sharing. Power sharing normally means that a legislatively prescribed number of citizens can launch a direct-democratic procedure, independently of the wishes of the government or parliament. This criterion means that plebiscites, i.e. popular vote procedures which citizens cannot initiate, but whose use lies exclusively within the control of the authorities, must equally be classified as not belonging to direct democracy. In terms of the point of view set out here, this distinction between plebiscites and referendums is fundamental to a proper understanding of direct democracy. The distinction is frequently not made, leading to considerable confusion in the debate about direct democracy.

Using the two criteria, direct-democratic and non-direct-democratic procedures of political participation can be distinguished from each other. Presented in table form:

DECISION ON / INTENDED FUNCTION	(SUBSTANTIVE) ISSUES	PEOPLE
EMPOWERING CITIZENS: power sharing	The constitution regulates the use of the procedure: • **OBLIGATORY REFERENDUM** A specified number of citizens have the right to initiate the procedure: • **FACULTATIVE REFERENDUM** • **INITIATIVE** • **ALTERNATIVE PROPOSAL** **DIRECT-DEMOCRATIC PROCEDURES**	Recall (removal of representatives from office before the end of their term)
EMPOWERING REPRESENTATIVES: normally strengthens the power of government (authority plebiscite – AP) and sometimes a minority within an authority (authority minority plebiscite – AMP)	The authorities have the exclusive right to decide on the use of the procedure: • **PLEBISCITE**	Direct and indirect election of representatives

As the table above shows, direct democracy comprises three types of procedure: **referendum**, **initiative** and **alternative proposal**. For each procedural type, various forms of procedure can be distinguished, and these, in turn, can be institutionalized in a variety of ways.

SURVEY 2
DIRECT-DEMOCRATIC PROCEDURES AND PLEBISCITES IN THE CONSTITUTIONS OF 32 EUROPEAN STATES

The following tables provide short explanations of the major types of procedure and the forms they take. It includes only those forms of procedure which are used in the table of countries; the list is not exhaustive, there exist other forms of procedure.

REFERENDUM

The right of citizens to either accept or reject a decision by an authority by means of a popular vote. A popular vote procedure whose use lies exclusively within the control of the authorities, is not a referendum but a plebiscite.

OBLR Obligatory referendum (initiated by Constitution)	In a representative democracy, restores the right of voters to have the final say: it means that important, or the most important, political decisions are made by the citizens themselves.
PopR Popular referendum (initiated by Citizens)	The right of a specified number of citizens to demand a popular vote on a decision made by an authority. The popular vote either accepts or rejects the decision. This procedure acts as a corrective to parliamentary decision-making in representative democracies and as a check on parliament and the government.
AR Authorities' referendum (initiated by majority in an authority)	The right of an authority to submit certain of its decisions to popular vote. This only applies to decisions which can be the subject of a popular referendum. This procedure may generate greater legitimacy for major decisions.
AMR Authorities' minority referendum (initiated by minority in an authority)	The right of a minority in an authority to submit to a popular vote a decision made by majority in the same authority. This applies only to decisions which may be the subject of a popular referendum. This procedure acts as a veto right of an authority, in which the whole electorate is called upon to judge the issue.
PopRP Popular referendum proposal	The right of a specified number of citizens to propose the calling of a popular referendum.

SURVEY 2
DIRECT-DEMOCRATIC PROCEDURES AND PLEBISCITES IN THE CONSTITUTIONS OF 32 EUROPEAN STATES

INITIATIVE

The right of a specified number of citizens to propose to the entire electorate the introduction of a new or renewed law. The decision on the proposal is made by means of a popular vote.

PopI Popular initiative	The sponsors of a popular initiative can force a referendum vote on their proposal (assuming that their initiative is formally adopted); they may also withdraw their initiative (where there is a withdrawal clause).
PopIP Popular proposal (Agenda Initiative)	The popular proposal is the right of one or more citizens to propose to a competent authority the adoption of a law; in contrast to the popular initiative, here it is the authority which decides what happens to the law proposal.

ALTERNATIVE PROPOSAL

The right of an authority or of a specified number of citizens to make an alternative proposal within the context of an initiative or referendum procedure; the proposal is decided on by a popular vote.

PopCP Popular counter-proposal	A specified number of citizens formulate an alternative proposal, for example within the framework of an initiative or referendum process, which is then decided on, at the same time as the original proposal, by popular vote.
ACP Authorities' counter-proposal	The alternative proposal is formulated by an authority. For example, within the framework of a popular initiative process, parliament can present a counter-proposal to the one put forward by the initiative sponsors. Both proposals are then decided on at the same time by popular vote. If both proposals are accepted, the decision on whether the original proposal or the parliament's counter-proposal should be implemented can be made by means of a special deciding question.

SURVEY 2
DIRECT-DEMOCRATIC PROCEDURES AND PLEBISCITES IN THE CONSTITUTIONS OF 32 EUROPEAN STATES

Country	OBLR	PopR	AR	AMR	PopRP	PopI	PopIP	ACP	PopCP	APL	AMPL
Austria	•[10]						•			•	•
Belgium		[•][1]								•	
Bulgaria										•[2]	
Cyprus										•	
Czech Rep.	•[11]										
Denmark	•		•								•
Estonia	•[3]									•	
Finland										•[4]	
France										•[5]	
Germany	[•]						[•]				
Great Britain										•	
Greece										•	
Hungary		•	•		•	•	•				
Iceland	[•][6]		•							•	
Ireland	•										•
Italy	•[7]	•[8]		•			•				
Latvia	•		•			•					
Liechtenstein		•	•			•				•	
Lithuania	•	•	•			•	•				
Luxembourg										•	
Malta	•[9]										
Netherlands							•				
Norway										•	
Poland							•			•	
Portugal					•		•			•	
Romania		•					•				
Sweden										•	•
Switzerland	•	•	•			•		•			
Slovakia	•	•	•			•					
Slovenia		•	•	•			•			•	•
Spain	•						•			•	•
Turkey										•	

SURVEY 2
DIRECT-DEMOCRATIC PROCEDURES AND PLEBISCITES IN THE CONSTITUTIONS OF 32 EUROPEAN STATES

[1] Draft 2002 law includes consultative popular referendum
[2] Blanket norms for authorities' plebiscite
[3] Obligatory constitutional referendum for revision of Chapters I and XV
[4] Consultative popular referendum
[5] Presidial plebiscite at the suggestion of the government or parliament (known as the "référendum legislatif") as well as the presidial plebiscite on changes to the constitution (known as the "référendum constituant")
[6] Amendment to Article 62 of the constitution ≈ state church
[7] Creation or amalgamation of regions
[8] "referendum abrogativo" (abrogative referendum)
[9] General extension of the legislature
[10] Total revision of the federal constitution
[11] Accession to EU. The question arises, whether this kind of referendum should not be classified as a plebiscite.

Sources:
This survey is based on the Finnish publication "Kohti osallistavaa demokratiaa" (Helsinki: LIKE, 2006) written by Rolf Büchi. In addition to the sources quoted for the individual countries, the following sources have been consulted:
· Wili, Hans-Urs: Volksrechte in den Verfassungen souveräner Staaten der Welt (Table)
· Kaufmann, Bruno: Initiative & Referendum Monitor 2004/05 (www.iri-europe.org)
· C2D – Research and Documentation Centre on direct democracy (http://c2d.unige.ch/)

SURVEY 2
DIRECT-DEMOCRATIC PROCEDURES AND PLEBISCITES IN THE CONSTITUTIONS OF 32 EUROPEAN STATES

LEGEND AND ABBREVIATIONS

TYPE OF PROCEDURE	FORM OF PROCEDURE		INSTITUTIONAL FORM
REFERENDUM	OBLR	obligatory referendum	
	POPR	popular referendum	
	AR	authorities' referendum	
	AMR	authorities' minority referendum	
	POPRP	popular referendum proposal IN = Citizens; EX = Authority	
INITIATIVE	POPI	popular initiative	
	POPIP	popular proposal (agenda initiative) IN = Citizens; EX = Authority	
ALTERNATIVE PROPOSAL	POPCP	popular counter proposal	
	ACP	authorities' counter proposal	
PLEBISCITE	APL	authorities' plebiscite	
	AMPL	authorities' minority plebiscite	

IN	the right to initiate a procedure	OBL	obligatory
EX	the right to call a referendum		

A	authorities'	P	proposal
C	counter or alternative	PL	plebiscite
I	initiative	POP	popular
M	minority	R	referendum
DDIN EUROPE	Kaufmann, Bruno & Waters, M. Dane (Ed.): Direct democracy in Europe (Durham, North Carolina 2004)		

NOTES ON THE FORM OF THE PROCEDURE:
As a rule, the launching of the process simultaneously implies that it will conclude with a popular referendum vote (In = Ex); but it is also possible for an initiative to be launched by citizens, but the decision on whether there is to be a referendum vote to be taken by parliament.
In this case In ≠ Ex. Such cases are explicitly noted; in all other cases In = Ex applies.

NOTES ON THE INSTITUTIONAL FORM:
The figures denote the relevant article in the constitution (29 = Article 29);
the Roman numerals the paragraph (II = Paragraph 2) and
Z = Number (Z3 = Number 3)
Notation: [legal effect] Procedure (Subject)

SURVEY 2
Direct-democratic procedures and plebiscites in the constitutions of 32 European states

Austria

The sole direct-democratic tools contained in the Austrian constitution are the agenda initiative (known as the "Volksbegehren") to parliament and an obligatory referendum when there is a total revision of the constitution. To date there have been two referendums: in 1978 on the start-up of the Zwentendorf nuclear power station (rejected) and in 1994 on Austria's accession to the EU (accepted). Since 1963, 32 often very widely supported "Volksbegehren" have been submitted to parliament, from which one can guess at the majority wish of the citizens for a real popular initiative. There is a clear need to complement the existing political system with more direct democracy.
More information on Austria: Survey 3, page 286

Referendum	OblR	Obligatory referendum (total revision of the federal constitution) (44 III)
Initiative	PopIP	Popular proposal (legislative proposal – federal law) to parliament ("Volksbegehren"), 100,000 voters, parliament must consider the proposal (41)
Plebiscite	APl	a) authorities' plebiscite (draft law) (43) b) authorities' plebiscite (fundamental issues of national importance) (49b)
	AMPl	Authorities' minority plebiscite (partial revisions of the federal constitution), 1/3 parliament, (44 III)

Sources:
- Austria's current federal constitutional law (status 2004) (German) www.bka.gv.at/DesktopDefault.aspx?TabID=3511&Alias=bka
- DD in Europe, pp. 33–36, Christian Schaller

Belgium

Like all the Benelux countries, Belgium has so far had a difficult relationship to national referendums. Since the end of WWII, there has been only one national plebiscite. Binding popular votes are not allowed in Belgian law. The current head of government, Guy Verhofstadt, wanted Belgium to have a consultative plebiscite on the EU constitution, like the Netherlands and Luxembourg, but failed. At the regional level, there seems to be a desire in Flanders to reach agreement on a reform which would include the right to popular initiative.
More information on Belgium: Survey 3, page 299

Referendum	PopR	The draft law of 12.2.2002 to the Chamber of Representatives includes a consultative popular referendum
Plebiscite	APl	ad hoc law of 11.2.1950

SURVEY 2
DIRECT-DEMOCRATIC PROCEDURES AND PLEBISCITES IN THE CONSTITUTIONS OF 32 EUROPEAN STATES

SOURCES:
- The Belgian constitution (in French) (as of 11.6.2004)
www.senate.be/doc/const_fr.html
- The draft law of 12.2.2002 to the Chamber of Representatives:
www.senat.fr/lc/lc110/lc1101.html
- DD in Europe, pp. 37–38, Jos Verhulst.

BULGARIA

During the years of democratic renewal the citizens of Bulgaria were never able to vote on a substantive issue. Constitutional amendments are specifically ruled out as a possible subject of popular votes, which can be initiated by a majority in parliament. Parliament is working on a fully developed initiative and referendum system, which would give 100,000 (200,000) registered voters the right to demand a referendum on a new law (basic law). The government is considering having a popular vote on accession to the EU (including the new constitution) in 2007.

PLEBISCITE	APL	Blanket norms for the authorities' plebiscite, consultative (42), parliament decides on execution (84 Z5), the president on the timetable (102 Z6), execution of the plebiscite is governed by law (42 II)

SOURCES:
- Constitution of the Republic of Bulgaria
Prom. SG. 56/13 Jul 1991, amend. SG. 85/26 Sep 2003
- National Assembly of the Republic of Bulgaria
www.parliament.bg/?page=const&lng=en
- Referendum and Civil Initiative, project of Association Balkan Assist
www.balkanassist.bg/en/ProjectDetails.jsp?prjID=2

CYPRUS

The 1960 constitution of the Republic of Cyprus was not chosen by the inhabitants of the island, but was the result of negotiations between the former occupying forces of Great Britain, Greece and Turkey. It contains no direct-democratic rights. However, consultative referendums are possible. The constitution set in place a presidential system of government and a proportional division of power between Greek and Turkish Cypriots, which never worked properly. The island has been partitioned since 1974; all attempts to end partition have so far failed. A referendum on re-unification – organised separately in the two parts of the island – was held on 24th April 2004, against the background of Cyprus' accession to the EU, which was to take place on 1st May. A majority of Turkish Cypriots voted for reunification, but a majority of Greek Cypriots rejected it.

SURVEY 2
Direct-democratic procedures and plebiscites in the constitutions of 32 European states

So partition remains for the time being; only the Republic of Cyprus (the Greek part) becoming a member of the EU. However, every Cypriot carrying a Cyprus passport do have the status of a European citizen.

Plebiscite	APL	It is possible to hold a consultative popular vote based on an ad-hoc law

Source:
- Constitution of the Republic of Cyprus
  www.kypros.org/Constitution/English/

The Czech Republic

The citizens of the Czech Republic have plenty of experience of dictatorship, little of democracy and almost none at all of direct democracy. It is not surprising, therefore, that a majority of those in political power and in the media oppose the introduction of popular initiatives and referendums, and even that many citizens do not yet trust themselves or others to play a direct role in political decision-making. Referendums are possible in principle, but in practice require an amendment to the constitution. So, for example, an addition to the 1993 constitution permitted the referendum of 13–14 June 2003 on EU accession, but no general referendum procedure has yet been adopted.

Referendum	OBLR	Obligatory referendum (accession to EU) (62 l)
Restrictions		The constitution has to be amended for each separate referendum (2 II); No change may be made to the basic form of state: a democracy based on the rule of law (9 II)

Sources:
- Constitution of the Czech Republic (as of 1st August 2002)
  www.psp.cz/cgi-bin/eng/docs/laws/constitution.html
- DD in Europe, pp. 48–51, Milan Valach with comments by Veronika Valach

Denmark

The Danish constitution requires, under certain conditions, that the transfer of national rights of sovereignty to international authorities must be decided by referendum. This rule has meant that Danish referendums on the European integration process have had a significance extending far beyond Denmark. They provoked public debate about initiative and referendum processes within the framework of European integration. In this connection, the Danish "No" to the Treaty of Maastricht in 1992 was especially important. Overall, Denmark has little experience of referendums. There is no right either of the popular initiative or the popular referendum.

SURVEY 2
Direct-democratic procedures and plebiscites in the constitutions of 32 European states

Referendum	OblR	a) Obligatory referendum (change of voting age) (29), Quorum = >50% "No" votes +≥30% of total registered electorate votes "No" (42 V) b) Obligatory referendum (change to constitution), approval quorum >50% "Yes" votes +≥40% of registered electorate votes "Yes" (88)
	AR	Authorities' referendum (transfer of sovereignty), if >1/2 and <5/6 majority in parliament (20), popular vote procedure according to 42
Plebiscite	AMPl	Authorities' minority plebiscite (law) on request of 1/3 parliament (42 I), parliament can withdraw the proposal (42 III), rejection quorum: ≥30% electorate (42 V)
Restrictions		Excluded from referendum: bills on finance, taxation, salaries and pensions, naturalisation, appropriation and expropriation, and discharge of existing treaty obligations 8-11, 19 (42 VI) + 42 VII.

Sources:
- Constitution of the Kingdom of Denmark of 5th June 1953 (unchanged since then): http://homepages.compuserve.de/constitutionen/verf/daen53.htm
- Denmark – Constitution
  www.oefre.unibe.ch/law/icl/da00000_.html
  { Adopted on: 5 June 1953 }
  { ICL Document Status: 1992 }
- DD in Europe, pp. 51–54, Steffen Kjaerulff-Schmidt

Estonia

Unlike its southern neighbour Latvia, Estonia did not resume the direct-democratic tradition of the inter-war years after independence was restored in 1991, but rather oriented itself to the model of its politically centralised northern neighbours. In Estonia there is a parliamnetary plebiscite; if the parliament loses such a plebiscite, the president has to arrange early parliamentary elections. There is, however, no right of popular initiative or popular referendum, but there is an obligatory constitutional referendum, which was called for the first time when Estonians were able to vote on accession to the EU in autumn 2003. IRI Europe assessed this referendum as being "partially free and partially fair", giving a boost to those political forces which want to expand direct democracy in this Baltic republic.

SURVEY 2
DIRECT-DEMOCRATIC PROCEDURES AND PLEBISCITES IN THE CONSTITUTIONS OF 32 EUROPEAN STATES

REFERENDUM	OBLR	Obligatory constitutional referendum (Revision of Chapters I and XV)(162, 163 I Z1, 164 + 168)
PLEBISCITE	APL	Authorities' plebiscite (draft law or important national issue); parliament decides on the submission of a bill to a popular vote: if the bill does not receive a majority of votes in favour, the president shall declare extraordinary elections to the parliament (Riigikogu) (65 Z2, 105)
RESTRICTIONS		Excluded from popular vote are issues related to the budget, taxes, the financial obligations of the state, the ratification of foreign treaties, and the enactment and ending of a state of emergency (106 I).

SOURCES:
- Estonian constitution (read 11.8.2004)
www.riik.ee/en/constitution/const_act.html
- Estonia – constitution
{ Adopted on: 28 June 1992 }
{ ICL Document Status: 28 June 1992 }
www.oefre.unibe.ch/law/icl/en00000_.html
- DD in Europe, pp. 54–58, Jüri Ruus.

FINLAND

In Finland there is only the plebiscite known as the "consultative referendum", which was adopted into the constitution in 1987. Finnish voters have no direct-democratic rights. To date, only two national referendums have been held in Finland, in 1931 on the prohibition of alcohol, and in 1994 on EU membership. The ruling elites and the public which supports them have always resisted the introduction of direct democracy. However, since the 1990s, a new understanding of direct democracy has been developing, which no longer sees it only as the antithesis of representative democracy, but as a complement to it. The will to hold a referendum on the EU constitution was underlined by a petition of 50,000 citizens in spring 2006 but the Finnish parliament opted for ratifying the new treaty without referendum.

PLEBISCITE	APL	"Consultative popular vote" (important issues) (53). Each national plebiscite is governed by a separate law, which has to be approved by parliament. The law specifies the timing of the plebiscite and the ballot text

SURVEY 2
Direct-democratic procedures and plebiscites in the constitutions of 32 European states

Source:
- Suomen perustuslaki, Annettu Helsingissä 11 päivänä kesäkuuta 1999 (vgl. www.om.fi/21910.htm)

France

Modern democracy has its roots in the American and French revolutions. However, it was not direct democracy which established itself in France, but a plebiscite governed by the authorities. This is a tool of the ruling elites, not of the citizens. But there is also a tradition of legitimising constitutional changes by popular vote, and under the weight of this tradition president Chirac has decided, not without strong hesitation, to order a plebiscite on the EU constitution, which he lost on May 29, 2005. The political elite has repeatedly promised to introduce genuine initiative and referendum rights.
More information on France: Survey 3, page 302

Plebiscite APL	a) Plebiscite (draft law), the holding of a referendum is decided by the president, at the suggestion of the government or of both chambers of parliament (référendum législatif, 11, 53 III, 60); in the event of "cohabitation", the presidential power is reduced b) Plebiscite (amendment to the constitution), avoidance of the plebiscite is at the discretion of the president (référendum constituant, 89)
Restrictions	No change can be made to the republican form of government (89).

Sources:
- La Constitution du 4 octobre 1958 (copied July 2004) á jour des révisions constitutionnelles:
  - mandat d'arrêt européen
  - organistion décentralisée de la République
  www.conseil-constitutionnel.fr/textes/c1958web.htm
- La Constitution de 1958 a quarante ans
  Question n° 17: Le référendum sous la Ve République
  Auteur: Michel de Villiers
  www.conseil-constitutionnel.fr/dossier/quarante/q17.htm

Germany

In 2006, a third attempt (after the first two in 2002) to introduce direct democracy at the federal level failed because it was resisted by the co-governing Christian Democrats, leaving Germany for the time being without direct-democratic rights at the national level. However, over the last 15 years, citizens' rights at the regional (Länder) and local levels have been greatly expanded, although direct-democratic procedures are often not

SURVEY 2
DIRECT-DEMOCRATIC PROCEDURES AND PLEBISCITES IN THE CONSTITUTIONS OF 32 EUROPEAN STATES

very citizen-friendly and the political elites have so far firmly resisted further reforms. More information on Germany: Survey 3, page 277

REFERENDUM	OBLR	Obligatory referendum in states (Länder) affected (new delimitation of federal territory) (29 II, III, IV, V+VI); majority agreement required from all regions affectedor a 2/3 majority in the directly affected smaller entities (29 III); additional quorum = 25 % of all the voters in each area affected (29 VI)
	PopIP	Popular initiative (new delimitation of federal territory) (29 IV)

SOURCES:
- Grundgesetz der Bundesrepublik Deutschland (Stand Juli 2002): www.bundestag.de/Parlament/Gesetze/index.html
- The Basic Law (Constitution) (2002: www.oefre.unibe.ch/law/icl/gm__indx.html
- DD in Europe, pp. 63–67, Ralph Kampwirth, with additional remarks by Otmar Jung

GREAT BRITAIN

Uniquely within Europe, Great Britain has no written constitution. Sovereignty belongs to parliament rather than the people, and the democratic system is almost purely indirect. Nonetheless, some significant changes have occurred in recent years, in particular the devolution of certain powers to Scotland, Wales and Northern Ireland which was decided by plebiscites. A plebiscite in the North East on the establishment of an elected regional assembly took place in November 2004. A number of local popular votes have also been held. The only UK-wide plebiscite was held in 1975, on whether to stay in the European Community. In 2006 a Power Inquiry led by Helena Kennedy clearly recommended the establishment of a citizen initiative right.

PLEBISCITE	APL	Authorities' plebiscite

SOURCES:
- ICL-Document on the U.K. legal system (1992) www.oefre.unibe.ch/law/icl/uk__indx.html
- Referendum law: Political Parties, Elections and Referendums Act 2000 www.hmso.gov.uk/acts/acts2000/20000041.htm
- North East assembly referendum: The Electoral Commission www.electoralcommission.org.uk/referendums/keyissues.cfm

SURVEY 2
DIRECT-DEMOCRATIC PROCEDURES AND PLEBISCITES IN THE CONSTITUTIONS OF 32 EUROPEAN STATES

GREECE

The constitution of the Third Greek Republic founded in 1975 contains no direct-democratic rights, but only two forms of plebiscite, which to date have never been used. So far, the parties of government have expected the citizens to agree with their decisions, but not to play an active part in making them. Direct democracy is not one of the priorities of the Nea Dimokratia party under Kostas Karamanlis, which came to power in March 2004. It was only at the eve of election defeat that George A. Papandreou, president of the PASOK socialist party which had been in power previously, announced that he was making citizen participation and the introduction of direct democracy a key element of his party's policy for 2004–2008. In recent years, the call for more, and direct, democracy has become louder within Greek society in general.

PLEBISCITE	APL	a) Plebiscite (national questions of crucial importance): the president may issue a decree on holding a plebiscite vote if 3/5 of the parliament have voted for it and the government has proposed it to the president (44 II) b) Plebiscite (draft law on serious social issues): the president may issue a decree on holding a plebiscite if 2/5 of the parliament have proposed it and 3/5 of the parliament have voted for it (44 II) a) + b) the proclamation of a plebiscite on a bill is countersigned by the Speaker (35 III)
RESTRICTIONS		Fiscal bills may not be the subject of a plebiscite; the proposition of more than one referendum on bills in the same parliamentary term is prohibited (44 II).

SOURCES:
- Greek constitution (2001) www.oefre.unibe.ch/law/icl/gr__indx.html
- Die Verfassung der Griechischen Republik in Kraft getreten am 11. Juni 1975 (Stand 2001), www.constitutionen.de/griech/verf75.htm

HUNGARY

Hungary has successfully restructured its economic and political system. A set of democratic institutions has been put in place, but there is a lack of practical experience and there are mental blocks to be overcome. The constitution allows for the legislative popular referendum and initiative and sets rather strict limitations on their use; for example, popular initiatives cannot be used to revise the instruments of direct democracy. This shows that initiatives and referendums have been given only a limited and auxiliary role within Hungarian representative democracy. In 1997, the participation quorum was cut from 50% to 25%; without this change both referendums – 1997 on NATO membership and 2003 on EU accession – would have been invalid due to too low turnout. Prime Minister Ferenc Gyurcsány has proposed to hold a popular vote on EMU accession in 2008 or 2009.

SURVEY 2
DIRECT-DEMOCRATIC PROCEDURES AND PLEBISCITES IN THE CONSTITUTIONS OF 32 EUROPEAN STATES

REFERENDUM	PopR	Popular referendum (any question within competence of parliament), at request of 200,000 registered voters (28/C II), signature collection period 4 months, referendum must be held and is binding (28/E)
	AR	Authorities' referendum at suggestion of president or government or 1/3 parliament, referendum at discretion of parliament (28/B II + 28/C IV + 28/E)
	PopRP	Popular referendum proposal, 100,000 voters, signature collection period 2 months, referendum at discretion of parliament (28/B II + 28/C IV + 28/E)
INITIATIVE	PopI	Popular initiative (any question within competence of parliament), 200,000 voters (28/C II), signature collection period 4 months, referendum must be held and is binding (28/E)
	PopIP	a) Popular proposal, 100,000 voters, signature collection period 2 months, referendum at discretion of parliament (28/B II + 28/C IV + 28/E) b) Popular proposal, 50,000 voters, issue dealt with by parliament, no referendum (28/D)
RESTRICTIONS		Extensive list of exclusions (28/C V a) – j)), excluded from referendum are among others the state budget, central taxes, and the provisions of the constitution on national referendums and popular initiatives; approval quorum for popular initiative and popular referendum: >25% registered voters + majority of votes cast.

SOURCES:
- Verfassung der Republik Ungarn 1949, Law Nr. XX von 1949:
  www.mkab.hu/content/de/decont5.htm
- Hungary Constitution: The ICL-edition of the Constitution is based on an improved (though inofficial) translation. It also consolidates all amendments until 2003.
  www.oefre.unibe.ch/law/icl/hu__indx.html
- The Constitution of the Republic of Hungary: Act XX of 1949 as revised and restated by Act XXXI of 1989 as of 1 December 1998
  www.kum.hu/Archivum/Torvenytar/law/const.htm
- Referendum und initiative law:
  Act XVII of 1989 on Referendum and Popular Initiative
  www.election.hu/nep97/jo/to/nep89_en.htm
- DD in Europe, pp. 67–70, Pal Reti, with comments by Kristina Fabian

SURVEY 2
Direct-democratic procedures and plebiscites in the constitutions of 32 European states

Iceland

During the first 60 years of its independence, 1944–2004, Iceland has not had a referendum – after having voted for independence by referendum. There is the possibility of a plebiscite if the president is rejecting a bill passed by parliament. This happened in summer 2004, when President Olafur Grimsson rejected a highly controversial Media Bill. However, the centre-right government chose to redraw the bill and to avoid a citizens decision at this time.

Referendum	OblR	Obligatory referendum (article 62 of the constitution = status of the Evangelical Lutheran Church), (79)
	AR	Authorities' referendum (Impeachment of the President vs. Dissolution of the parliament) on request of 3/4 Althingi, (11)
Plebiscite	APl	a) Plebiscite (removal of the president from office before his term expires) on request of 3/4 Althingi (parliament); if the plebiscite is not accepted, new elections for parliament are called (11) b) plebiscite (bill rejected by the president) (26)

Source:
- Constitution of the Republic of Iceland
(No. 33, 17 June 1944, as amended 30 May 1984, 31 May 1991, 28 June 1995 and 24 June 1999), http://government.is/media/Skjol/constitution_of_iceland.doc

Ireland

In Ireland the citizens vote on all amendments to the constitution. They have the last word on important questions, including European Integration. Referendum topics were among others abortion, the introduction of divorce laws, the relationship of the state to the Roman-Catholic Church and European Integration. The Irish have provoked attention throughout Europe when they first rejected the Treaty of Nice in a referendum in 2001 and only after reaffirmation of Irish military neutrality by the EU accepted it in a second referendum in 2002. In Ireland the obligatory constitutional referendum is firmly rooted; however, the citizens themselves have no right to initiate referendums.

Referendum	OblR	obligatory referendum (amendments to the constitution) (46); the referendum is accepted by a simple majority of the votes cast (47 I)

SURVEY 2
DIRECT-DEMOCRATIC PROCEDURES AND PLEBISCITES IN THE CONSTITUTIONS OF 32 EUROPEAN STATES

PLEBISCITE	AMPL	Authorities' (minority) plebiscite (bill – question of national importance); initiated by: Senate + ≥1/3 House of Representatives; execution decided on by: president after consultation with the government (In ≠ Ex) (27); the referendum is rejected if a majority of the votes cast reject it + ≥1/3 electorate reject it (47 II)

SOURCES:
- Constitution – Ireland
  { Adopted on: 1 July 1937 }
  { ICL Document Status: 1995 }
  www.oefre.unibe.ch/law/icl/ei00000_.html
- Referendum Acts 1994, 1998, 2001 (www.oireachtas.ie)
- DD in Europe, pp. 70–73, Dolores Taaffe, with additional remarks by Anthony Coughlan

ITALY

Italy, with a population of 58 million, is one of the few countries with a lot of practical experience in popular referendums. Since 1974 more than 50 abrogative referendums were held; like popular initiatives abrogative referendums aim at improving existing laws. However, as a direct democratic procedure the abrogative referendum has its shortcomings like for example the high turnout quorum of 50% which led to the invalidation of too many referendums. The referendum flaws produce bad experiences with direct democracy and a growing disaffection with referendums. There are forces who strive to reform the abrogative referendum towards the more constructive popular initiative. After the new center-left government of Romano Prodi took office in 2006, they initiated a new move for more direct democracy on the federal level, but they are not strong enough yet.
More information on the Province of South Tyrolea: Survey 3, page 294

REFERENDUM	PopR	a) abrogative referendum (total or partial repeal of a law or other acts with legal force) requested by 500,000 voters (75 I); referendum accepted if it is supported by a majority of the votes and if a majority of the electorate has participated (75 IV) b) popular referendum (constitutional amendment) requested by 500,000 voters (138 II); if the law has been approved by each chamber with a 2/3 majority of its members, no referendum may be held (138 III)
	AMR	Authorities' minority referendum (constitutional amendment) requested by 1/5 of the members of either chamber or by five regional councils (138 II); if the law has been approved by each chamber with a 2/3 majority of its members, no referendum may be held (138 III)

SURVEY 2
Direct-democratic procedures and plebiscites in the constitutions of 32 European states

INITIATIVE	PopIP	popular proposal supported by 50,000 voters (71 II); parliament consideres the initiative proposal
RESTRICTIONS		abrogative referendums not allowed for tax or budget laws, amnesties, pardons, or ratification of international treaties (75 II).

SOURCES:
- Italy constitution 2001 www.oefre.unibe.ch/law/icl/it__indx.html
- Costituzione della Repubblica Italiana 2003 www.senato.it/funz/cost/home.htm
- DD in Europe, pp. 73–77, Roland Erne with comments by Bruno Kaufmann

Latvia

Although the current state of Latvia only regained its independence in 1991, its citizens enjoy fairly extensive rights of initiative and referendum, dating originally from the first period of independence between the two world wars. 10 per cent of the electorate can propose a new law and parliamentary decrees can be submitted to referendum. However, important subject areas remain out with the scope of the referendum, and the situation is aggravated by the condition that turnout must be at least 50% of the number who voted in the last parliamentary elections. On the 20th of September 2003 there was a referendum on accession to the EU.

REFERENDUM	OBLR	Obligatory constitutional referendum for changes to 1 (democratic republic), 2 (popular sovereignty), 3 (territory), 4 (language, flag), 6 (election) or 77 (referendum about amendment) (77)
	AR	Authorities' referendum (draft laws) initiated by the president or 1/3 parliament and carried out at the request of 1/10 of the electorate; within 2 months; BUT: no referendum, if parliament votes again and passes the law with a 3/4 majority. (72); repeal of a law according to 72 requires a turnout of at least 50% of the last parliamentary elections (74) and that the majority has voted for repeal of the law (79)
INITIATIVE	PopI	Popular initiative (fully elaborated draft of constitutional amendment or law), supported by 1/10 electorate (78); an amendment to the constitution is adopted if at least half of the elecotrate has voted in favour (79); a draft law is adopted if the number of voters is at least half of the number of electors as participated in the previous parliament election and if the majority has voted in favour (79)

250

SURVEY 2
DIRECT-DEMOCRATIC PROCEDURES AND PLEBISCITES IN THE CONSTITUTIONS OF 32 EUROPEAN STATES

RESTRICTIONS	Authorities' referendum: the budget, laws concerning loans, taxes, customs duties, railroad tariffs, military conscription, declaration and commencement of war, peace treaties, declaration of a state of emergency and its termination, mobilisation and demobilisation, as well as agreements with other nations (73) and laws declared to be urgent by not less than a 2/3 majority of parliament (75) cannot be put to referendum.

SOURCES:
- Latvia Constitution
  { Adopted on: 15 Feb 1922 }
  { Amended in: 1933, 1994, 1996, 1997, 1998, 2002, 2003 }
  { Official name: Constitution of the Republic of Latvia }
  { ICL Document Status: 2003 } www.oefre.unibe.ch/law/icl/lg__indx.html
- Die Verfassung der Republik Lettland 2002
  www.muench-dalstein.de/lvconstgr.html
- DD in Europe, pp. 77–82, Gita Feldhune

LIECHTENSTEIN

The tiny principality between Austria and Switzerland has a well-developed direct democracy and regularly uses the three basic procedures – popular initiative, facultative and obligatory referendums. However, the Prince of this unique direct-democratic hereditary monarchy dominates the politics of his country in a way which is irreconcilable with a modern democracy – and not merely on account of his extensive veto rights. For this reason Liechtenstein has come under "observation" by the international democracy watchdog, the Council of Europe.
More information on Liechtenstein: Survey 3, page 295

REFERENDUM	PopR	a) Facultative popular referendum (financial decrees, laws), requested by 1,000 registered voters in 30 days, (65 II +66 I)
		b) Facultative popular referendum (state treaties), (66bis)
	AR	Authorities' referendum (state treaties), (66bis)
INITIATIVE	PopI	a) Popular initiative (enactment, amendment or repeal of a law) 1,000 registered voters, (64 Ic, II + 66 VI);
		b) Popular initiative (constitutional amendment) 1,500 voters, (64 Ic, IV + V, 66 VI)
PLEBISCITE	APL	Authorities' plebiscite (principles of a law to be enacted) at the request of parliament, (66 III)

SURVEY 2
Direct-democratic procedures and plebiscites in the constitutions of 32 European states

Sources:
- Principality of Liechtenstein Constitution 2003
  www.fuerstenhaus.li/constitution.0.html
- Rechtsgutachten im Rahmen der Verfassungsdiskussion im Fürstentum Liechtenstein zuhanden der Regierung des Fürstentums Liechtenstein, erstattet von Rhinow, René, Schinzel, Marc & Besson, Michel. Basel, 18. April 2000
  www.dese.li/GesetzeMaterialien/Resources/Gutachten_Rhinow.pdf
- DD in Europe, pp. 83–86, Sigward Wohlwend

LITHUANIA

This Baltic republic has the obligatory constitutional referendum, the popular initiative and the facultative referendum. Ten national referendums were held between 1991 und 1996. These revealed the weaknesses in the design of the procedures: the high turnout quorum (50% of the electorate) led to many referendums being declared invalid. A new referendum law (4th June 2002 – amended 25th February 2003) partially removed the approval quorums e.g. for referendums on accession to international organisations where there is transfer of sovereignty. This meant that the referendum of 11th May 2003 on EU accession was not threatened by too low a turnout.

Referendum	OblR	a) Obligatory constitutional referendum (amendments to Art. 1 and Chapters I and XIV), (148); b) Obligatory referendum (introduction of the new constitution of 1992) (151, 152, 154); the constitution is accepted if more than half of the electorate voted in favour (151)
	PopR	Popular referendum (the most significant issues concerning the life of the state and the people), 300,000 registered voters, 3 months, (9 + referendum law)
	AR	Authorities' referendum (the most significant issues concerning the life of the state and the people) (9)
Initiative	PopI	Popular initiative (amendment to constitution), 300,000 registered voters (147 I); except during state of emergency or war (147 II)
	PopIP	Legislative initiative as a popular proposal presented as a detailed draft, 50,000 registered voters (68 II); parliament decides on the organization of referendums (67 + 69 IV)

SURVEY 2
DIRECT-DEMOCRATIC PROCEDURES AND PLEBISCITES IN THE CONSTITUTIONS OF 32 EUROPEAN STATES

| RESTRICTIONS | Referendum law 2002–3:Form of the Lithuanian state (Article 1 of the constitution): may only be changed by a 3/4 majority of all voters in an obligatory referendum (148 I); amendment to Chapters I and XIV: turnout >50% electorate; binding referendum on accession to international organisations: simple majority of the voters (i.e. no turnout quorum e.g. referendum on EU accession on 11.5.2003); consultative referendums: turnout >50% electorate. |

SOURCES:
- Constitution of the Republic of Lithuania 2003.03.20,Translated by: Office of the Seimas of the Republic of Lithuania Document Department (Approved by the citizens of the Republic of Lithuania in the Referendum on 25 October 1992) (as amended by 20 March 2003, No. IX–1379)
http://www3.lrs.lt/c-bin/eng/preps2?Condition1=21892&Condition2=
- Law on Referendum, June 4, 2002 – amended February 25, 2003:
http://www3.lrs.lt/cgi-bin/preps2?Condition1=206332
- DD in Europe, pp. 86–89, Algis Krupavicius

LUXEMBOURG

The Grand Duchy of Luxembourg with its princely traditions hardly presents the most propitious conditions for the development of direct democracy. Perhaps predictably, therefore, its constitution so far includes only the possibility for a plebiscite. To be sure, in 1999 the government did declare its intention of introducing some direct democracy, but the draft law presented in 2003 (projet de loi 5132) clearly reveals the continuing lack of willingness to include the citizens directly in decision-making. However, a popular vote on the proposed EU Constitution was held in mid-2005, delivering a clear yes-vote.

PLEBISCITE	APL	Authorities' plebiscite according to 51 VII
RESTRICTIONS		During a regency, no amendment can be made to the constitution concerning the constitutional prerogatives of the Grand Duke, his status as well as the order of succession (115).

SOURCES:
- Constitution of the Grand-Duchy of Luxembourg 1999 (French); Text as of 2 June 1999; www.etat.lu/SCL/CNST0999.PDF
- Luxembourg constitution 1998; www.oefre.unibe.ch/law/icl/lu__indx.html
- Draft law:
5132/Draft law relating to the popular legislative initiative and to the referendum Dépôt: Premier Ministre, Ministre d'Etat, le 20/05/03 www.chd.lu/fr/portail/role/lois/detail.jsp?order=descend&project=0&mode=number&page=5
- DD in Europe, pp. 90–92, Alfred Groff

SURVEY 2
DIRECT-DEMOCRATIC PROCEDURES AND PLEBISCITES IN THE CONSTITUTIONS OF 32 EUROPEAN STATES

MALTA

Malta's political system is that of a majority democracy after the model of Great Britain. The country received its independence from Great Britain in 1964 and became a republic in 1974. The sole plebiscite to date was the one on accession to the EU of 8th March 2003.

REFERENDUM	OBLR	Obligatory constitutional referendum (general extension of the legislature) (66 III+IV, 76 II)

SOURCE:
- Constitution of Malta (Stand 2001)
  http://docs.justice.gov.mt/lom/legislation/english/leg/vol_1/chapt0.pdf

THE NETHERLANDS

In the Netherlands the referendum issue has dominated the political debate for many decades. However, the very first popular vote on an issue took place as late as mid-2005 on the proposed EU Constitution. After having experienced and developed initiative and referendum procedures on the local level an agenda initiative was introduced in 2006 offering 40,000 citizens the right to put an issue into parliament. The first issue of this new instrument was the proposal to ban smoking in restaurants.

INITIATIVE	PopIP	Agenda initiative right for 40,000 voters. Free signature gathering. Excluded are the topics: taxes and budget. The Parliament can decide whether the initiative committee can explain their case in Parliament. After the launch of an initiative the same issue cannot be the topic of another initiative during 2 years.
RESTRICTIONS		No referendums on constitutional changes, laws on the monarchy, the royal house, the budget (but not taxes), laws which are valid in the entire Kingdom (including the Dutch Antilles and Aruba), and laws which only serve to implement international decisions.

SOURCES:
- The Constitution of the Kingdom of the Netherlands
  { Adopted on: 17 Feb 1983 }
  { ICL Document Status: 1989 }
  www.oefre.unibe.ch/law/icl/nl__indx.html
- The Constitution of the Kingdom of the Netherlands 2002
  www.minbzk.nl/uk/constitution_and/publications/the_constitution_of
- DD in Europe, pp.94–98, Arjen Nijeboer

SURVEY 2
DIRECT-DEMOCRATIC PROCEDURES AND PLEBISCITES IN THE CONSTITUTIONS OF 32 EUROPEAN STATES

NORWAY

Norway's constitution dates from 1814 and contains no direct-democratic rights. But six countrywide plebiscites have been held; in 1972 and 1994 the Norwegians were asked to give their opinion on EU membership. There is also a tradition of popular consultation at the local level, where more than 500 popular votes have been held since 1972. In 2003, the national parliament introduced the right to an agenda initiative at the communal (local) level – giving 300 citizens the right to put an issue on the political agenda.

PLEBISCITE	APL	Ad-hoc law possible for plebiscites without constitutional basis (50 I)

SOURCES:
- Norway constitution
  { Adopted on: 17 May 1814 }
  { Adopted by the Constituent Assembly at Eidsvoll }
  { Official Title: The Constitution of the Kingdom of Norway }
  { ICL Document Status: 29 Feb 1996 }
  www.oefre.unibe.ch/law/icl/no__indx.html
- DD in Europe, pp. 98–101, Tor Björklund with additional remarks by Aimée Lind Adamiak

SURVEY 2
DIRECT-DEMOCRATIC PROCEDURES AND PLEBISCITES IN THE CONSTITUTIONS OF 32 EUROPEAN STATES

POLAND

In 1997, a democratic constitution was approved by the National Assembly (parliament) and ratified by popular vote. The law requiring a turnout of at least 50% of the registered electorate for a plebiscite to be valid was set aside for this popular vote. The new constitution is the first constitution in the history of Poland to have been subjected to popular vote. In a plebiscite held on 7th and 8th June 2003, Poland's accession to the EU was approved. This plebiscite demonstrated that the citizens were perfectly capable of distinguishing between the issue – in this case, EU accession – and their antipathy to the government. Although Poland's constitution contains no rights of popular initiative or popular referendum, efforts are nonetheless being made at both national and local levels to involve citizens more, and directly, in politics.

INITIATIVE	PopIP	Popular proposal (law), 100,000 voters (118 II); procedure governed by law (The Act of 14th March 2003 on nationwide referendums)
PLEBISCITE	APL	a) Authorities' plebiscite (issues of special state interest (125) or state treaties involving transfer of sovereignty (90)) at request of parliament or president + senate (125 II); binding if turnout is > 50 % (125 III) b) Authorities' plebiscite (changes to the constitution: Chapter I [the republic], II [Basic rights] or XII [revision of the constitution]) at the request of 1/5 parliament or the senate or the president of the republic; within 60 days; majority of the votes cast (235 I, VI–VII)

SOURCES:
- Poland – Constitution
  { Adopted by National Assembly on: 2 April 1997 }
  { Confirmed by Referendum in: Oct 1997 }
  { ICL Document Status: Oct 1997 }
  www.oefre.unibe.ch/law/icl/pl00000_.html
- The Constitution of the Republic of Poland (Status 2004)
  www.sejm.gov.pl/english/konstytucja/kon1.htm
  The Act of 14th March 2003 on nationwide referendums (unofficial translation)

SURVEY 2
DIRECT-DEMOCRATIC PROCEDURES AND PLEBISCITES IN THE CONSTITUTIONS OF 32 EUROPEAN STATES

PORTUGAL

In 1998 there were two badly prepared attempts to hold popular votes, one on the abortion issue, the other on European integration. The first was steamrollered through in a matter of weeks, the second was declared invalid by the Constitutional Court. Leading politicians now try to use these bad experiences to discredit citizens' rights. On the other hand, the then head of government José Manuel Barroso announced that there would be a popular vote on the EU Constitution – a commitment, which was drawn back after the No-votes in France and the Netherlands. Portugal is an example of how direct democracy can be falsely branded through badly designed popular vote procedures and its progress held up.

REFERENDUM	PopRP	Popular proposal to parliament (popular vote on existing law or parliamentary bill or citizen's draft law), 75,000 registered voters; parliament considers the proposal and then the president – after consulting the Constitutional Court – makes the decision on execution of the popular vote (115 + referendum law No. 15-A/98)
INITIATIVE	PopIP	cf. popular referendum proposal
PLEBISCITE	APL	Plebiscite (law or issues of national importance); the president decides whether to order a popular vote following a proposal by the parliament or by the government (115 I); the result of the vote is binding if turnout >50% (115 XI)
RESTRICTIONS		referendum not permitted for a. amendments to the constitution; b. budgetary, fiscal and financial matters and actions; c. Art. 161 and d. Art. 164 of the constitution (115 IV); waiting time: the renewal of a referendum proposal during the same term of the legislature is not allowed (115 X).

SOURCES:
- Constituição Da República Portuguesa (status of 1.1.1999)
  www.cea.ucp.pt/lei/const/constind.htm
- Constitution of the Portuguese Republic
  Since its adoption in 1976, the constitution has been revised five times. This translation does not reflect the most recent revision, which occurred through Constitutional Law 1/2001 of 12 December 2001, and changed Articles 7, 11, 15, 33, 34, and 270.
  www.parliamento.pt/ingles/cons_leg/crp_ing/index.html
- Referendum law:
  Lei Orgânica Do Regime Do Referendo; Law nº 15-A/98 of 3rd April
  www.parliamento.pt/const_leg/referendo/index.html
- DD in Europe, pp. 102–105, Elisabete Cidre and Manuel Malheiros

SURVEY 2
DIRECT-DEMOCRATIC PROCEDURES AND PLEBISCITES IN THE CONSTITUTIONS OF 32 EUROPEAN STATES

Romania

Of all the former Eastern-block countries, Romania was the one with the bloodiest regime change. The country still suffers from the legacy of totalitarianism. This includes a plebiscitarian tradition which, on the one hand, has served dictatorships such as that of Nikolai Ceaucescu and, on the other, may contain the seed of an obligatory constitutional referendum: in 1864, 1938, 1991 and 2003 constitutional plebiscites were held. The one in autumn 2003 resulted in a clear "Yes" to commencing the process of EU accession – but the campaign also revealed the inability of the authorities to mobilize the voters and to do this within the limits of fairness. The gap between citizens and their government is still large and empowering the citizens is a necessary but probably distant aim.

Referendum	AR	Suspension from office of the president by parliamentary majority + referendum (95)
Initiative	PopIP	a) popular proposal (bill), 100,000 voters from at least 1/4 of the country's 41 counties + in each county or the municipality of Bukarest at least 5,000 supporters; signature collection within 3 months; parliament makes the final decision on whether a referendum will be held (74 I –II + law No. 189/1999) b) Popular proposal (revision of the constitution), 500,000 voters from at least half of the country's 41 counties + in each county or the municipality of Bukarest at least 20,000 supporters (150); parliament considers proposal and decides on it (by a 2/3 majority in each chamber, or a 3/4 majority of both chambers in joint session); finally there is a popular vote (151); limits to revision of the constitution (152)
Plebiscite	APl	Plebiscite (issue of national importance) by decision of the president, after consultation of the parliament; result of referendum valid if turnout >50% (90 +law no. 3/2000)
Restrictions		Popular proposal may not touch on matters concerning taxation, international affairs, amnesty or pardon (74 II).

Sources:
- Romanian constitution (status 2003 www.oefre.unibe.ch/law/icl/ro__indx.html
- DD in Europe, pp. 105–108, Horia Paul Terpe

SURVEY 2
Direct-democratic procedures and plebiscites in the constitutions of 32 European states

Slovakia

In Slovakia, voters enjoy direct-democratic rights. In this respect, the country has made enormous progress. On the other hand, the conditions for these direct democratic rights are not yet well developed; the approval quorum of 50% of the electorate threatens the validity of referendums. In 2003, there was a referendum on EU accession, but the referendum process was strongly criticised as lacking fairness.

Referendum	OblR	Obligatory referendum (constitutional law on accession or withdrawal from a league of nations) (7, 86d, 93 I)
	PopR	Popular referendum (important issues of public interest), 350,000 registered voters, (93 II, 95 I)
	AR	Authorities' referendum (important issues of public interest) at the decision of the National Council (93 II, 95 I), request for referendum: government or parliament (96)
Initiative	PopI	Popular initiative (important issues of public interest), 350,000 voters (93 II, 95 I)
Restrictions		a) No referendum on fundamental rights and freedoms, taxes, duties and budget (93 III); b) Referendum result valid: turnout >50%, simple majority (98 I–II).

Sources:
- The Constitution of the Slovak Republic (status 2004) www.government.gov.sk/VLADA/USTAVA/en_vlada_ustava.shtml
- The Act on Referendum /No. 564/1992 Zb Referendum Law of the National Council of the Slovak Republic – 1992, 1994, 1995 http://www2.essex.ac.uk/elect/database/legislationAll.asp?country=SLOVAKIA &legislation=skref&print=true

Slovenia

As a young, independent republic, Slovenia instituted in 1991 a representative democracy, which includes direct democratic rights, most importantly the popular referendum and the popular proposal. Slovenia is the most prosperous of all the Eastern European countries with transition economies. It established a market economy cautiously, instead of applying shock therapy. After successful binding referendums in March 2003, it became a member of the EU and of NATO in 2004. Direct democracy appears to have considerable potential, but there are also limiting factors. Lack of democratic experience creates a lack of democratic habits and behaviour on both sides, among both citizens and politicians. The referendum of April 2004 ,which rejected (95% in favour, 31% turnout) the adoption of a law restoring basic rights to thousands of people erased from the register of citizens after independence, was an illustration of this.

SURVEY 2
DIRECT-DEMOCRATIC PROCEDURES AND PLEBISCITES IN THE CONSTITUTIONS OF 32 EUROPEAN STATES

REFERENDUM	PopR	Popular referendum (law), 40,000 voters, majority of valid votes cast (90)
	AR	Authorities' referendum (law) launched by the government (90)
	AMR	Authorities' minority referendum (law) launched by 1/3 parliament (90)
INITIATIVE	PopIP	a) Popular proposal (law), 5,000 registered voters (88); b) Popular proposal (constitution), 30,000 registered voters (168) a)+b): 2/3 majority of parliament decides on the proposal
PLEBISCITE	APL	a) Authorities' plebiscite (international agreement) launched by parliament, result binding, simple majority of votes cast (3a) b) Consultative referendum (issue within the sphere of competence of parliament)[1]
	AMPL	Authorities' minority plebiscite (constitution) launched by 30 members of parliament, simple majority + turnout >50% (170)

SOURCES:
- Constitution of the Republic of Slovenia (status 2001) www.dz-rs.si/en/aktualno/spremljanje_zakonodaje/ustava/ustava_ang.pdf
- DD in Europe, pp. 108–110, Igor Luksic
- [1]Doors to Democracy. 1998. The Regional Environmental Center for Central and Eastern Europe, p. 383, www.rec.org/REC/Publications/PPDoors/CEE/cover.html

SPAIN

The last time when the Spanish people were able to vote on an important substantive issue was in 2005 – in a popular vote on the country's adoption of the proposed EU Constitution. The constitution includes a so-called "legislative popular initiative", which is an agenda initiativel and does not lead to a referendum. One positive aspect is that initiative committees can receive a refund of their expenses. On June 18 the Catalan people could vote on the new rules for their autonomy. At the same time the conservative national opposition launched a nationwide signature-gathering for a popular vote on autonomy in the whole of Spain.

SURVEY 2
DIRECT-DEMOCRATIC PROCEDURES AND PLEBISCITES IN THE CONSTITUTIONS OF 32 EUROPEAN STATES

REFERENDUM	OBLR	Obligatory referendum (total revision of the constitution, or a partial revision affecting Articles 1–9, 15–29, 56–65) (168 III)
INITIATIVE	PopIP	"Legislative popular initiative" (87 III), really a popular proposal, which does NOT lead to a referendum (cf. ley organica Art. 3 + 13)*
PLEBISCITE	APL	a) Consultative popular vote (issues of considerable political scope) declared by the King at the suggestion of the head of government after authorisation by the House of Representatives (92) b) popular vote on autonomy (149 I Z 32, 151 I+ II Z 3+5, 152 II)
	AMPL	Authorities' minority plebiscite (amendment to the constitution) on request by 1/10 of the members of either chamber (167 III)
RESTRICTIONS		*ley organica 26.3.1984: the following subjects are excluded from the "popular legislative initiative": 1. issues which are determined in "organic laws", 2. taxes, 3. international affairs, 4. pardon, 5. issues which are covered by articles 131 and 134 of the constitution.

SOURCES:
- Spanish constitution (in English, status 1992)
www.oefre.unibe.ch/law/icl/sp00000_.html
- Constitución española (status 2004)
www.congreso.es/constitucion/constitucion/indice/index.htm
- Synopsis Article 87
www.congreso.es/constitucion/constitucion/indice/sinopsis/sinopsis.jsp?art=87&tipo=2
- Referendum law:
Ley Organica 3/1984, De 26 De Marzo, Reguladora De La Iniciativa Legislativa Popular («BOE», num. 74, de 27 de marzo de 1984).
http://noticias.juridicas.com/base_datos/Admin/lo3-1984.html
- DD in Europe, pp. 111–114, Guillem Rico and Joan Font, with additional remarks by Juan Pablo de Soto

SURVEY 2
DIRECT-DEMOCRATIC PROCEDURES AND PLEBISCITES IN THE CONSTITUTIONS OF 32 EUROPEAN STATES

SWEDEN

Like France, Sweden has used the plebiscite. While in France it is the president who controls the use of the plebiscite, in Sweden it has been the Social Democratic party. It uses popular votes – the results of which are only binding under certain circumstances – as instruments of power. The citizens have no right to take part directly in decision-making on issues. The so-called "initiative right" at the local (communal) level is in reality only an agendasetting right and it has resulted in a great deal of frustration with many people. In the context of rewriting the nations constitutional texts until 2010 the introduction of direct democratic rights has been launched.

PLEBISCITE	APL	consultative popular vote, procedure determined by law, for each popular vote parliament makes a separate law, government formulates the ballot text, (chapter 8 § 4 + special law on referendums SFS 1979:369)
	AMPL	binding popular vote (change to the constitution) if 1/3 parliament supports the holding of a popular vote (chapter 4 §15 III+V)

SOURCES:
- Swedish constitution (status 2004)
www.riksdagen.se/english/work/constitution.asp
- Constitution in Swedish:
www.riksdagen.se/arbetar/demgrund/grund_k.asp
- DD in Europe, pp. 115–118, Mattias Goldmann, with additional remarks by Bruno Kaufmann

SWITZERLAND

Switzerland has the most extensive system and the longest tradition of direct democracy. The procedures of citizen lawmaking are designed in a genuinely user-friendly way. They give citizens real power to make political decisions, something with which elected politicians and others wielding power in the country have to reckon. But even in Switzerland, the procedures for citizen participation in decision-making are, of course, not perfect. Too little is done to ensure the fairness and transparency of referendum campaigns; there is a lack of political education; and more ought to be done to research and further develop direct democracy.

SURVEY 2
DIRECT-DEMOCRATIC PROCEDURES AND PLEBISCITES IN THE CONSTITUTIONS OF 32 EUROPEAN STATES

REFERENDUM	OBLR	a) Obligatory referendum to the people + states (cantons) (the changes to the federal constitution, accession to organisations for collective security or supranational communities, federal laws declared urgent which are not grounded in the constitution and are valid for more than 1 year) (140 I a–c) b) Obligatory referendum to the people (the popular initiatives for total revision of the federal constitution, the draft law + counter-proposal of federal assembly to a general popular initiative, the general popular initiatives rejected by federal assembly, issue of possible total revision of the federal constitution when the two chambers of parliament disagree) (140 II a, a^{bis}, b, c)
	PopR	Facultative referendum to the people (federal laws, federal laws declared urgent + valid for more than one year, federal decrees based on constitution or law, international treaties), 50,000 registered voters, 100 days, simple majority of valid votes cast (141)
	AR	facultative referendum on request of 8 cantons, otherwise like popular referendum, (141)
INITIATIVE	PopI	a) General popular initiative (adoption, amendment, repeal of constitutional and legislative determinations), 100,000 voters within 18 months (139a I); unity of form and matter + international law must be respected (139a II); parliament accepts initiative and implements it; parliament may present a counter-proposal to the initiative and submit both to the people + cantons for a referendum (139a III+IV); parliament rejects initiative and submits it to the people for a referendum, if the initiative is accepted, parliament implements it (139a V) b) Popular initiative (partial revision of federal constitution, detailed draft), 100,000 voters within 18 months (139 I); unity of form and matter + international law must be respected (139 II); parliament may present a counter-proposal, parliament recommends adoption or rejection of initiative, the proposal is submitted to the people + cantons for a referendum (139 III) c) Popular initiative (proposal for total revision of federal constitution), 100,000 voters within 18 months, the proposal is submitted to the people for a referendum (138 II)

SURVEY 2
Direct-democratic procedures and plebiscites in the constitutions of 32 European states

Alternative proposal	PopCP	Counter-proposal to popular initiatives (139, 139a); referendum procedure: double "Yes"+ deciding question (139b)
Restrictions		Required majorities: proposals submitted to the vote of the People shall be accepted if the majority of those voting approves them (142 I); proposals submitted to the vote of the People and the cantons shall be accepted if the majority of those voting and the majority of the cantons approve them ("double majority") (142 II).

SOURCES:
- Federal Constitution 1999 (as of 11th May 2004) (in German) www.admin.ch/ch/d/sr/101/
- Swiss Constitution (in English) www.oefre.unibe.ch/law/icl/sz__indx.html
- Federal law on political rights (as of 14th October 2003) (in German) www.admin.ch/ch/d/sr/161_1/
- DD in Europe, pp. 118–121, Paul Ruppen, with additional remarks by Hans-Urs Wili, Rolf Büchi, Bruno Vanoni, and Bruno Kaufmann

Turkey

In 1999, Turkey was officially recognised by the EU as an accession candidate and the prospect of joining the EU acted as a catalyst for a process of reform and democratisation. In the parliamentary elections of November 2002, the political landscape was completely changed. The Justice and Development Party (AKP) of moderate Islamists under Reçep Tayyip Erdogan, which won the elections, has accelerated and deepened the process of reform and democratisation and begun a shift away from the traditional idea of the state which was the legacy of Kemal Ataturk. Crucial to the reform process is the EU's policy towards Turkey; a positive development of the negotiations on accession will strengthen the continuation of Turkish democratisation and "Europeanisation".

Plebiscite	APl	a) plebiscite possible, governed by law (67) b) plebiscite (changes to constitution), (104, 175)
Restrictions		Articles 1–3 of the constitution may not be changed (4).

SOURCES:
- The Constitution of the Republic of Turkey (2002) www.oefre.unibe.ch/law/icl/tu__indx.html
- The Constitution of the Republic of Turkey as amended on October 17, 2001) (published by the Grand National Assembly) www.tbmm.gov.tr/anayasa/constitution.htm

SURVEY 3
GLOBAL OVERVIEW OF DIRECT DEMOCRACY IN SELECTED REGIONS OF THE WORLD

LATIN AMERICA

Most Latin American countries have incorporated provisions for the use of direct democracy in their constitutions. The date and scope of the constitutional introduction of direct democracy in Latin America vary considerably among the different countries in the region. By the 1990s, however, instruments of direct democracy had been incorporated into the majority of the Latin American constitutions. In the crisis of representation that has characterised the region since the late 1980s, neo-populist politicians and newly created parties came to challenge the traditional political parties. Capitalizing on the widespread loss of trust in the political establishment, the winning formula of these political newcomers was a discourse that professed to let the people decide directly on issues that affected them. There are indeed many examples from the 1980s and 1990s where instruments of direct democracy were incorporated when the process of constitutional reform or rewriting was notably influenced or wholly controlled by such newcomers. The success of this strategy soon led to a rhetorical appropriation by traditional political parties of the new discourse of direct forms of democratic government. Instruments for direct democracy continued to be included in the constitution, even when neo-populist politicians or newly created parties failed to assume control. The introduction of direct democracy instruments into the legal framework of a country raises issues regarding their design and administration, frequency of use and participation.

THE INSTRUMENTS
An overview of various aspects of direct democracy in the eighteen Latin American countries allows us to make the following remarks:

1. Sixteen countries have provisions in their constitutions for referendums and plebiscites at the national level. The Dominican Republic and Mexico have no such provisions.

2. Twelve countries have provisions for initiatives at the national level.
Chile, the Dominican Republic, El Salvador, Honduras, Mexico and Panama do not.

3. Panama and Venezuela are the only countries that have provisions for recalling elected officials at the national level.

4. Argentina, Colombia, Ecuador, Peru and Venezuela have provisions for recalling elected officials at the first tier authority level (regions/states/provinces, etc).

5. Colombia, Costa Rica, Ecuador, Panama, Peru and Venezuela have provisions for recalling elected officials at the local level.

6. Five countries that do have provisions for direct democracy have yet to put them into practice: Costa Rica, El Salvador, Honduras, Nicaragua and Paraguay.

7. In Argentina, Colombia and Guatemala, both the president and the congress can initiate referendums and plebiscites (in Colombia, however, the president needs congressional approval of a law that calls

SURVEY 3
GLOBAL OVERVIEW OF DIRECT DEMOCRACY IN SELECTED REGIONS OF THE WORLD

the referendum). In Chile only the president can initiate such. In Brazil only the congress can initiate such. In Bolivia, Costa Rica, Uruguay and Venezuela referendums can be initiated by the president, the congress or a percentage of the registered citizens. In Ecuador either the president or 8% of the registered voters can initiate such.

8. In Ecuador, Paraguay, Peru, and Venezuela a mandatory referendum or plebiscite is required for constitutional reform (although in Peru this is the case only if the Congress does not obtain the support of two thirds of its members); El Salvador requires such for decision-making with regard to political integration among Central American countries; in Guatemala, such is required for any law concerning the border with Belize; in Panama, for issues relating to the Panama Canal. In Ecuador, mandatory referendums or plebiscites are required for a variety of issues of public policy such as taxes and public expenditure. In Chile, referendums or plebiscites are mandatory for constitutional reforms only if there is no agreement between the congress and the president.

9. In Colombia, Costa Rica, Paraguay, Peru, Uruguay and Venezuela certain issues, such as public expenditure, taxes and the adoption of international treaties (Uruguay, Costa Rica and Venezuela are excepted from the latter), have been specified as ineligible for referendums or plebiscites. Colombia further excludes issues such as giving amnesties, and preserving and re-establishing public order. Uruguay further excludes legislative measures, which are exclusive initiatives of the executive. In Paraguay, electoral matters and national defence are excluded, and in Peru human rights issues are excluded. Costa Rica further excludes pensions, security and administrative acts. Venezuela further excludes amnesties, human rights issues and restrictions or suspensions of constitutional guarantees.

10. In some countries, a certain number of valid signatures are required for the formal initiation of the decision-making process for referendums. For example, Peru requires 10%, Bolivia 6% and Uruguay 25%.

11. Some countries ask for a minimum participation or turnout quorum for a referendum to be valid. For example, Costa Rica requires the turnout of 30% of the registered voters for ordinary legislation and 40% for partial reforms of the constitution; Colombia requires the turnout of 25% of the registered citizens and Uruguay 35% of the registered voters.

12. In order for a referendum to be valid some countries also require an approval quorum. Colombia, Ecuador, Peru and Uruguay require a qualified majority of the votes (50% + 1).

13. Common requirements for registration of initiatives are: a) the support of a certain percentage of the total of the electorate (Argentina 1.5% in at least six electoral districts); b) a percentage of the census (Brazil 1% in at least 5 provinces, Colombia 5%); c) a percentage of the registered citizens or voters (Ecuador 8%, Guatemala 5,000 registered citizens, Peru 0.3% of the registered voters).

14. In Argentina, Ecuador and Peru, the following issues are ineligible for initiatives: constitutional reforms, budgetary issues and taxes. Peru also excludes human rights issues and the adoption of international treaties. In addition to budgetary issues and taxes, Costa Rica also excludes administrative acts.

SURVEY 3
Global overview of Direct Democracy in selected regions of the world

The experience
When talking about "instruments of direct democracy", it is important to clarify that in the Latin American context the terms plebiscite and *consulta popular* are often used as synonyms for referendums and *peticiones legislativas* as a synonym for initiatives.

1. Argentina
The Argentine constitution did not include any provisions for direct democracy when, in 1984, president Raúl Alfonsín convoked a referendum on a proposed treaty with Chile over the Beagle Channel Islands. The government faced strong opposition from various sectors, which considered the issue as one for specialists rather than the general public. More to the point, the referendum was not compulsory, nor was the result binding. Even so, voter turnout was high (73%), and a large majority (81%) voted in favour of the treaty. Constitutional provisions for direct democracy were established ten years later, in 1994, towards the end of Carlos Menem's first presidential term. Paradoxically, the 1984 referendum remains the only Argentine experience of direct democracy at the national level, supporting the view that the constitutional introduction of direct democracy instruments formed part of Menem's neo-populist strategy to pull in the Argentine people.

2. Bolivia
Following a year of political unrest and national demonstrations, the Bolivian constitution was reformed in February 2004. Providing measures for democratic improvement, the new constitution included provisions for holding referendums *(consultas populares)* on matters of national interest. A subsequent referendum on the management of gas reserves, the first ever to be held at the national level, saw a voter turnout of 60%, that is, only slightly lower than the last national election. After this first experience, Bolivia will have to continue to improve its legal framework for holding future referendums. In July 2006 a devolution-referendum was hold, defining the autonomy status of the countries regions.

3. Brazil
In 1988, three years after the transition to democracy, the Congress resolved that the future nature of the form of government was to be decided by means of a referendum. In 1993, the electorate was presented with the choices between a monarchy and a republic, and a presidential or a parliamentary system. The result favoured the republic over the monarchy (87%–13%), and the presidential over the parliamentary system (69%–31%). This remains the only referendum to be held in Brazil at the national level. However, at the regional and local levels Brazil's experience with direct democracy is much richer. Indeed, since 1989, the municipality of Porto Alegre has settled its budget in so-called participatory assemblies. Though very limited in the beginning, turnout has steadily increased. In 1998, 20,000 individuals out of a population of 1.2 million people took part in these assemblies. However small a percentage this may seem, it is important to acknowledge that participants are likely to come and go according to individual interests.

SURVEY 3
GLOBAL OVERVIEW OF DIRECT DEMOCRACY IN SELECTED REGIONS OF THE WORLD

4. CHILE

Four national plebiscites have been held in Chile to date. The first took place in 1978, five years after Augusto Pinochet had seized power in a military coup. The turnout reached 91.4%, with an approval rate of 75%. However, this compulsory and highly questionable plebiscite presented the electorate with one of the most "loaded" questions in the history of direct democracy (Butler and Ranney 1994:6): "In the face of international aggression unleashed against the government of the fatherland, I support President Pinochet in his defence of the dignity of Chile, and I reaffirm the legitimate right of the republic to conduct the process of institutionalisation in a manner befitting its sovereignty."

The next plebiscite, also convoked by Pinochet, was held in 1980. This time voters were called upon to decide on a new constitution, which was to become the foundation for the new government. Pinochet achieved a 92.9% turnout in a compulsory referendum that produced a result favourable to his military regime. Again, the organization and the conduct of the plebiscite have been questioned. The new constitution obliged Pinochet to seek continued endorsement in yet another plebiscite or to call new elections within a period of eight years. So, in 1988, Pinochet convoked one of the most important referendums to have been held in Latin America to this day. The opposition gained 56% of the votes, and was thus able to put an end to a dictatorship that had lasted for 15 years. Counting on a strong economy and a controlled media, Pinochet had hoped to legitimise his position through a "democratic" vote. Ironically, Pinochet had to accept defeat in and by a plebiscite that he himself had instituted. Chile's fourth national plebiscite was held the following year. Centering on constitutional reform, the referendum confirmed and furthered the transition to democracy.

5. COLOMBIA

In Colombia, constitutional provisions for direct democracy were introduced in 1991. The reform of the earlier constitution was largely motivated by a general crisis of democratic institutions, a crisis deepened by the ever increasing numbers of political murders carried out by drug cartels and guerrilla movements.

In 1990, students promoted an informal *consulta* with the aim of convoking a constituent assembly. With the *consulta* "approved", the composition of the assembly changed so as to include representatives from a wider social range. In the light of Colombia's historical lack of social cohesion, the introduction of instruments of direct democracy was surely meant to promote citizen participation and "societal reconciliation". However, it has also been argued that "the effective operation of government" has served as an additional aim (Van Cott in Barczak 2001:52).

Colombia has seen a number of different kinds of referendums since 1991. The most (in)famous took place in 2003, when president Alvaro Uribe presented the electorate with 15 different proposals in one and the same referendum. The proposals covered a wide range of political and administrative issues: actions against corruption, reductions of government expenditure, and increases in state funding for sanitation and education – only the proposal on anti-corruption reached the required turnout quorum of 25%.

SURVEY 3
GLOBAL OVERVIEW OF DIRECT DEMOCRACY IN SELECTED REGIONS OF THE WORLD

The discouragingly low turnout has been explained in different ways. The sheer number and the complexity of the proposals, and the Colombian tendency for absenteeism, which gives an average turnout of 45–50%, are certainly among the contributing factors. In addition, the referendum was partly perceived as concerning the president himself, as boiling down to the simple terms of "for or against". In this connection, the opposition's promotion of active absenteeism may also be said to have affected the turnout negatively.

The low turnout of the 2003 referendum sparked extensive discussions on the principles and the procedures of the practices and instruments of direct democracy. In this way, the outcome of the referendum might just have been positive after all (De la Calle 2004).

6. Dominican Republic
No constitutional provisions.

7. Ecuador
The first referendum to take place in Ecuador was organized by the military regime in 1979, during the country's gradual development from authoritarian rule to democratic government. The aim was to replace the constitution of 1949 with a constitution that was to include a few provisions for direct democracy. The new constitution was approved, but constitutional reforms stagnated until León Febres took office as president in 1984. Confronted by a hostile legislature, Febres proposed to strengthen presidential powers so as to enable him to call referendums on constitutional reform, should the legislature fail to rule within 75 days. The proposal was turned down, but in 1986 Febres nonetheless called a referendum in which he proposed to the electorate that independent candidates should be allowed to run in elections. Although opinion polls predicted presidential victory, the proposal was rejected by 68.8% of the votes.

In 1994, during a period of unprecedented public disapproval rates as well as difficulties with the legislature, president Sixto Durán similarly resorted to a referendum in an attempt to boost his bargaining power, and to regain public support. In sharp contrast with the case of Febres, a poll taken by the private polling firm Cedatos five days prior to the referendum had suggested that 72% of the voters were either confused or undecided on how to vote. The ballot was presented as too complicated or indeed impossible to understand for a large percentage of Ecuadorians: in 1994, 12% of Ecuadorians were illiterate and another 51% had only basic education. Yet, of the seven proposals put forward in the referendum, all but one were approved, the exception being a proposal to turn budget management over to the parliament.
Relations between the president and the legislature remained strained. In 1995 Durán called for a *consulta*, hoping to gain powers to dissolve the parliament and to extend the mandate of the provincially elected parliamentarians from 2 to 4 years. The proposal was firmly rejected by the voters.

A constitutional crisis triggered the next use of direct democracy in Ecuador. Removing neo-populist president Abdalá Bucarám from office in February 1997, the legislature paved the way for Fabián Alarcón to serve as interim president. In May 1997, Alarcón called a referendum, effectively

SURVEY 3
GLOBAL OVERVIEW OF DIRECT DEMOCRACY IN SELECTED REGIONS OF THE WORLD

asking the electorate whether or not it had agreed with the removal of Bucarám, and with his own placement as president. Both measures met with the voters' approval.

8. GUATEMALA

In 1996, a peace accord between the government and guerrilla forces was signed. Many of the provisions of the peace accord were presented as proposals for constitutional amendments in a referendum held in May 1999. The amendments intended to make Mayan languages, religions and traditional laws equal in status to their ladino counterparts. It was moreover suggested that the army be placed under civilian control, and that internal security be removed from the army's jurisdiction. However, less than 20% of the population turned out to the polls, and the majority of the votes rejected the reforms. Indigenous leaders attributed the low turnout to poor political organization, to a general mistrust of the government, and to the fact that information about the referendum was available in the Spanish language only.

9. MEXICO

Constitutional and legal provisions for direct democracy exist at the local level for 8 of the 32 federal entities.

10. PANAMA

Three national referendums have been held in Panama to date. The first referendum, held in 1983, proposed a number of amendments to the 1972 Constitution, such as the replacement of the 505-member National Assembly of Municipal Representatives by a national legislature of 70 members. The proposals were approved by 88% of the votes, a result that strengthened the authoritarian regime of Manuel Noriega. In 1992, a referendum was held on further constitutional reforms. With a turnout of 40%, and with 64% of the cast votes rejecting the proposals of the government of Guillermo Endara and its allies, the suggested reforms were rejected. The vote was seen as an expression of a widespread discontent with the administration. At the same time, it did not shed much light on where the people wanted to go, a need felt in particular with regard to the proposal to demilitarise politics by abolishing the military. The third referendum was held in 1998 by the government of Pérez Balladares. Sixty-four percent of the voters rejected a proposal to change the constitution so as to allow the immediate re-election of the president. Coming after the end of a military rule, voters appear to have been concerned about the possibility of entrenching a "civil dictatorship".

SURVEY 3
Global overview of Direct Democracy in selected regions of the world

11. Peru

In 1993, a referendum was held on a new constitution, drawn up by a constituent assembly formed only the year before in an election called by president Alberto Fujimori. The election had been called during a peak in the president's popularity, and had resulted in an assembly of presidential loyalty. The new constitution was indeed criticized for being "authoritarian" by the opposition political parties, which even tried to block the referendum. The opposition was met with disparagement from the president, who pushed hard not only for the referendum, but also for the new constitution itself. The new constitution was in fact approved. Although it includes direct democracy instruments such as referendums, legislative initiatives and the removal or renewal of authorities, the referendum in which it was ratified was seen as giving legitimacy to Fujimori's rule, rather than empowering the Peruvian people through powers of direct democracy.

12. Uruguay

Nowhere in Latin America have instruments of direct democracy been used more often than in Uruguay, which established a semi-representative or semi-direct system of government in its constitution of 1934. Since the 1973-1985 dictatorship, examples of referendum issues include questions of revocation of amnesty laws (1989), measures to safeguard pensions (1989), privatisation of state-owned companies (1992), constitutionally fixed budgets for the education system (1994), legal restrictions for workers' claims against their employers (1998), and privatisation of water assets (2004).

The 1994 elections triggered a constitutional reform process, as two traditional political parties, Blancos and Colorados, united forces against a new party, Frente Amplio. They proposed the introduction of a majority runoff system for the presidential elections, according to which a candidate would need 40% of the votes and a 10% lead over the nearest opponent to avoid a second round. The results of this reform, which was approved in a referendum held in 1996, were to become obvious in the following elections. In 1999, the Frente Amplio candidate, Tabaré Vázquez, who had won the first round with 38.1% of the votes, was forced under the new system to compete in a second round against the Colorados candidate, Jorge Batlle, who had obtained 31.5% in the first round. The Blancos aligned themselves with the Colorados, thereby securing presidential victory for Batlle. The Uruguayan experience of direct democracy has often suggested that voters remain politically loyal to the parties that they support (Altman 2002).

13. Venezuela

The 1998 elections, in which Hugo Chávez was elected president, formed a turning-point for direct democracy in Venezuela. The promise to include instruments of direct democracy in the constitution, so as to overcome the claimed limitations of representative democracy, had been central to Chávez's electoral platform. In April 1999, he held a referendum asking voters to authorize elections for a new assembly. The voters complied, and Chávez-supporters were able to take 90% of the assembly seats in the elections that followed in July of the same year. The Venezuelan constitution was then reformed through a plebiscite held in December 1999. The new constitution stated that Venezuelan citizens have the right to a wide range of direct democracy instruments such as plebi-

SURVEY 3
**GLOBAL OVERVIEW OF DIRECT DEMOCRACY
IN SELECTED REGIONS OF THE WORLD**

scites, *consultas*, referendums, constitutional initiatives, indirect legislative initiatives, recalls and powers to revoke existing laws. However, legal frameworks setting the conditions for the different types of referendums have yet to be developed.

In 2004, the opposition convened a presidential recall, the only presidential recall ever to take place in the world. The electoral process has been described as the worst ever in the history of the country. A detailed examination has highlighted several shortcomings, such as arbitrary delays in the verification and validation of the signatures collected (Kornblith 2004). Indeed, the process provoked violent protests against the electoral commission, which, after much manoeuvring, had to validate a sufficient number of signatures so that the referendum could finally be activated six months later. This contrasted sharply with the law, which states that signature verification should take no longer than 30 days. Failing the expectations from both within and outside the country, the referendum worsened existing tensions and polarisation. It did little to restore trust in the democratic institutions and in the electoral processes, but was rather marred by the very weaknesses that it feigned to overcome.

Conclusion

Most Latin American countries have incorporated provisions for the use of direct democracy in their constitutions. Initially, direct democracy instruments were employed mainly for constitutional ratification, but they have come to be used for a wide range of issues. While direct democracy is here to stay, the design and implementation of its instruments need to be developed further. Direct democracy instruments are still being employed "from above", that is by the state powers, not least due to the complexity of the requirements for their utilization. As outlined above, the experiences of individual countries highlight a number of issues that have proven problematic, and that will need to be taken into renewed account for the future:

- The questions put to the electorate should not be loaded or too complex or too long.
- The requirements for initiating an instrument of direct democracy, such as the number of signatures, should be clear from the outset.
- The time allocated for collection and verification of signatures should be specified in the law, and allowed to vary according to the number of signatures required.
- Voter education must be conducted with an understanding of the linguistic and educational particularities of each country. In referendums held to this date, the indigenous, the illiterate and the young voters have often been neglected.

In Latin America, direct democracy instruments have been most successfully employed in countries where the institutions of representative democracy are most solid. In these cases, representative democracy has been complemented and strengthened, rather than replaced, by direct democracy (Zovatto 2004). Many of the potential limitations of direct democracy instruments can be reduced through the transparency, impartiality, efficiency and accountability of public institutions. As illustrated by some of the above country-specific examples, the employment of these instruments may provoke deeper division in a society already divided, or even be abused as tools of political manoeuvring to cling on to power. Although it has not always been the case, direct democracy instruments

SURVEY 3
GLOBAL OVERVIEW OF DIRECT DEMOCRACY IN SELECTED REGIONS OF THE WORLD

should pertain to and focus on specific issues rather than the performance of a particular government. As consensus builders, direct democracy instruments rely on the fairness and transparency of their legal frameworks and operational processes. By allowing for equal possibilities for opposing campaigners, and enabling all voters to participate without discrimination, the democratic outcome stands a better chance of being accepted.

Future developments in the region may not only see more frequent use of direct democracy instruments at the national, regional and local levels, but also their introduction on the transnational stage, possibly through the Mercosur (Common Market of the South), as a parallel to the European Union.

MORE INFORMATION:
- Altman, David (2002) "Popular initiatives in Uruguay: confidence votes on government or political loyalties?', *Electoral Studies* 21.
- Barczak, Monica (2001) "Representation by Consultation? The Rise of Direct Democracy in Latin America', *Latin American Politics and Society* 43:3 (Autumn).
- Butler, David and Ranney, Austin (eds.) (1994) *Referendums around the world: the growing use of direct democracy.* The Macmillan Press Ltd: London.
- Carranza, Mario (2003) "Can Mercosur Survive? Domestic and International Constraints on Mercosur', *Latin American Politics and Society* 45:2 (Summer).
- Cepeda Ulloa, Fernando (2005) *Removal of Congresspersons from public office: an effective tool against corruption*, paper presented at the *6th Global Forum on Reinventing Government: toward participatory methods and transparent governance* (May 2005, Seoul).
- De la Calle, Humberto (2004) *Democracia Directa: El caso de Colombia*, Case Study commissioned by International IDEA for the Direct Democracy Project.
- Kornblith, Miriam (2004) *La democracia directa y el referendo revocatorio presidencial en Venezuela*, Case Study commissioned by International IDEA for the Direct Democracy Project.
- González Rissotto, Rodolfo (2004) *Democracia Directa: El caso de Uruguay*, Case Study commissioned by International IDEA for the Direct Democracy Project.
- Payne, Mark J., Zovatto, Daniel et al. (2002) *Democracies in Development: Politics and Reform in Latin America*. Inter-American Development Bank: Washington DC.
- Thibaut, Bernhard (1998) "Instituciones de Democracia Directa', in Dieter Nohlen, Sonia Picado and Daniel Zovatto (eds) *Tratado de Derecho Electoral Comparado de América Latina.* Fondo de Cultura Económica: México.
- Zovatto, Daniel (2004) *Las Instituciones de Democracia Directa a Nivel Nacional en América Latina. Un Balance Comparado 1978-2004*, paper presented at International IDEA's Seminar on Direct Democracy (March 2004, London).

SURVEY 3
GLOBAL OVERVIEW OF DIRECT DEMOCRACY IN SELECTED REGIONS OF THE WORLD

Country	Country-wide	Regional	Local	Excluded Issues for referendum/plebiscite votes	Popular votes (p, r) initiated by
Argentina	R/I	AI/Recall		Not specified	Cg, Pr
Bolivia	R/I	R	R		Cg, Pr, El
Brasil	R/P/I	PA/P	PA/P		Cg
Chile	P	P	P		Pr
Colombia	R/P/I (Recall)	Recall	Recall	National budget, taxes, international agreements, amnesties, preservation and reestablishment of public order	Cg, Pr
Costa Rica	R/P/I		P/Recall	Taxes, Budget, Pensions, Security, Administrative acts	Cg, Pr, 5% registered citizens
Dominican Republic	NA				
Ecuador	R/I	R/I/Recall	R/I/Recall		Pr, 8% electoral register
El Salvador	R				
Guatemala	R/I				Cg, Pr
Honduras	R/P				
México	NA		R/P/I		
Nicaragua	R/P/I				
Panamá	R/Recall		R/I/Recall		
Paraguay	R/I			International relations and treaties, expropriations, national defence and budget, fiscal policies, electoral matters	
Perú	R/I	R/I/Recall	I/Recall	Adoption of international treaties, taxes and public expenditure, other public policy issues, human rights	
Uruguay	R/P/I	R/I		Taxes, legislative measures which are exclusive initiatives of the executive	Cg, Pr, El
Venezuela	R/I/Recall	R/Recall	R/Recall	Budget, taxes, amnesties, human rights	Cg (agreement by 2/3 of its members), Pr, 10% registered voters

R = Referendum, P = Plebiscite, I = Initiative, AI = Agenda initiative, PA = Participatory assemblies
Cg = Congress, Pr = President, El = Electorate, SM = Simple majority, QM = Qualified majority

SURVEY 3
GLOBAL OVERVIEW OF DIRECT DEMOCRACY IN SELECTED REGIONS OF THE WORLD

REQUIRED SIGNATURES FOR INITIATING A REFERENDUM PROCESS AT NATIONAL LEVEL	TURNOUT QUORUM	APPROVAL REQUIREMENTS	EXPLICITLY ALLOWED ISSUES FOR INITIATIVE PROCESS
6% electorate			
	50% electorate	SM	
	(voting is compulsory)		
	No quorum required		
	25% registered citizens	QM	
	30% registered voters for ordinary legislation, 40% for partial constitutional reforms and matters which require legislative approval by a qualified majority		
	(voting is compulsory)	QM	Issues of transcendental importance for the country
			Political decisions of transcendental importance for the country and constitutional reforms
10% registered voters		QM	Constitutional reforms, legislative proposals
25% registered voters	35% registered voters	QM	
	25% registered voters		

R = Referendum, P = Plebiscite, I = Initiative, AI = Agenda initiative, PA = Participatory assemblies
Cg = Congress, Pr = President, El = Electorate, SM = Simple majority, QM = Qualified majority

SURVEY 3
GLOBAL OVERVIEW OF DIRECT DEMOCRACY IN SELECTED REGIONS OF THE WORLD

COUNTRY	EXPLICITLY EXCLUDED ISSUES FOR INITIATIVE PROCESS	REQUIRED SIGNATURES FOR FILING AN INITIATIVE	I&R PRACTICE
Argentina	Taxes, national budget, international treaties, penal laws, constitutional reforms	1.5% in at least 6 electoral districts	R 1984
Bolivia		1% of census in at least 5 provinces	R 2004, 2006
Brasil			R 1993, 2005
Chile			P 1978, 1980, 1988, 1989
Colombia		5% census	
Costa Rica	Taxes, Budget, Pensions, Administrative acts	5% registered citizens	
Dominican Republic			
Ecuador	Constitutional reforms, Taxes, Public expenditure	8% electoral register	R (consultas) 1979, 1986, 1994, 1995, 1997
El Salvador			
Guatemala		5.000 registered citizens	R 1994, 1999
Honduras			
México			
Nicaragua			
Panamá			R 1983, 1992, 1998
Paraguay			
Perú	Adoption of international treaties, taxes and public expenditure, other public policy issues, human rights	0.3% registered voters	R 1993
Uruguay			R, P 1980, 1989 (×2), 1992, 1994 (×3), 1996, 1998, 1999, 2003, 2004
Venezuela			R 1999 (×2), 2000, 2004

R = Referendum, P = Plebiscite, I = Initiative, AI = Agenda initiative, PA = Participatory assemblies
Cg = Congress, Pr = President, El = Electorate, SM = Simple majority, QM = Qualified majority

SURVEY 3
Global overview of Direct Democracy in selected regions of the world

EUROPE & NORTH AMERICA

Germany

There has been a strong trend towards more direct democracy in Germany since 1990. There have been several attempts at the national (federal) level to incorporate initiatives and referendums into the Constitution – all of which have so far been frustrated by opposition from the Christian Democrats. At the state ("Länder") and communal level, however, reform has been widespread: direct-democratic procedures have now been introduced in all the federal states and in all local authority areas (except for the districts of Berlin). In part, they have also been well used: there have been 204 initiative/referendum processes at the state level and around 3,200 citizens' initiatives (so-called "Bürgerbegehren") and 1,600 referendums at the local authority level.

In respect of their "citizen-friendliness", there are wide differences between the different federal states, as the procedural rules in the states and local authority areas were determined by the different state legislatures.

National (federal) level
Germany has no initiatives or referendums at the national level, except only for the obligatory referendum on any proposed new delimitation of the "Länder" (federal states) boundaries according to Article 29 of the constitution.
Germany did have national direct-democratic procedures during the Weimar Republic (1919-1933), when a referendum would be called if 10% of the registered voters requested it. However, a referendum was only valid if at least 50% of all registered voters took part in it (for simple laws). For changes to the constitution there was an even higher hurdle – at least 50% of the registered voters had to approve the proposal. Both of the referendums held during this period failed to reach the approval quorum.

Subnational (state and district/commune) Level
Below the 16 federal states or "Länder", forming the third tier of government, are the local authorities: districts, cities and communities.

Rules of procedure

Federal State level
The states of Hesse and Bavaria are unique in having the obligatory constitutional referendum (on the Swiss and US model): any proposed alteration to the state constitution must be ratified by the people. In Bremen, there was until 1994 a ruling that constitutional changes had to be decided by the people in a referendum if the parliament was not unanimously in favour.

Six federal states have non-binding popular petitions, which represent a right to make a submission to the parliament, but which do not lead to a referendum (cf. Austria, federal level).

SURVEY 3
GLOBAL OVERVIEW OF DIRECT DEMOCRACY IN SELECTED REGIONS OF THE WORLD

All German states have initiatives and referendums ("Volksbegehren" and "Volksentscheide"), which allow the public to initiate a process. Constitutional issues may be the subject of initiatives in all the states except Berlin, Hesse and the Saarland. Other than this a limited number of issues are "off-limits": popular initiatives which relate to a significant extent to the state budget, or to taxes, excise and other duties and officials' salaries, are inadmissible (the so-called "finance taboo"). This exclusion of issues is often the subject of court cases.

The rules of procedure in all of the federal states have a three-stage structure, but there are big differences in the quorums and time periods allowed:
The first stage has two forms: the popular initiative and the application for a popular submission (the "Antrag auf Volksbegehren"). In the former case only, the proposal goes first to the state parliament for consideration. In both cases, the signatures of between 0.4% and 1% of the registered voters are normally needed (North-Rhine Westphalia has a very low signature threshold of 0.02%, while Hesse is relatively high at 3%). After the Interior Ministry has checked that the submission is admissible, the process moves to the next stage of the Volksbegehren (popular demand). If this is successful, the proposal is debated in parliament. If parliament does not accept the proposal, there is a binding referendum. Unlike in Switzerland and most of the states of the USA, in many German states ("Länder") the referendum is not decided by simple majority: there is also an approval quorum. In addition, the state parliament can always present a counter-proposal, which is voted on at the same time. The table below lists the various quorums and time allowances:

Table 1: Initiatives and referendums in the federal states of Germany

STATE	INITIATIVE (VOLKSBEGEHREN)		REFERENDUM (VOLKSENTSCHEID)	
	ENTRY QUORUM	TIME ALLOWED FOR SIGNATURE COLLECTION OFFICIAL [O] OR FREE COLLECTION [F][1]	APPROVAL QUORUM SIMPLE LAW	APPROVAL QUORUM AMENDMENT TO CONSTITUTION
Baden-Württemberg	16.6 %	14 days [O]	33%	50%
Bavaria	10 %	14 days [O]	no quorum	25%
Berlin	10 %	2 months [O]	33%[2]	not possible
Brandenburg	c. 4 %	4 months [O]	25%	50% + 2/3 majority
Bremen	10 %/ 20 %[3]	3 months [O]	25%	50%
Hamburg	5 %	14 days [O+F]	20%	50% + 2/3 majority
Hesse	20 %	14 days [O]	no quorum	not possible

278

SURVEY 3
GLOBAL OVERVIEW OF DIRECT DEMOCRACY IN SELECTED REGIONS OF THE WORLD

STATE	INITIATIVE (VOLKSBEGEHREN)		REFERENDUM (VOLKSENTSCHEID)	
	ENTRY QUORUM	TIME ALLOWED FOR SIGNATURE COLLECTION OFFICIAL [O] OR FREE COLLECTION [F][1]	APPROVAL QUORUM SIMPLE LAW	APPROVAL QUORUM AMENDMENT TO CONSTITUTION
Mecklenburg-Western Pommerania	c. 10 %	unlimited [F][4]	33%	50% + 2/3 majority
Lower Saxony	10 %	12 months [F]	25%	50%
North Rhine-Westphalia	8 %	8 weeks [O]	15%	50% turnout quorum + 2/3 majority
Rhineland-Palatinate	c. 10 %	2 months [O]	25% turnout quorum	50%
Saarland	20 %	14 days [O]	50%	not possible
Saxony	c. 12.5 %	8 months [F]	no quorum	50%
Saxony-Anhalt	11 %	6 months [F]	25%[5]	50% + 2/3 majority
Schleswig-Holstein	5%	6 months [O][6]	25%	50% + 2/3 majority
Thuringia	14 %	4 months [F]	33%	40%

Notes: in some states entry quorums are expressed as real numbers. They are expressed here as percentages.

[1] Signatures may be either freely collected (F), or have to be registered in official offices (O)
[2] If turnout is more than 50%, the approval quorum of 33% is dispensed with
[3] The 20% figure refers to the number of signatures required for constitutional amendment initiatives
[4] In addition to free signature collection, a two-month long official signature collection can be requested
[5] The approval quorum is dropped if the parliament submits a counter-proposal to the referendum
[6] Other signature registration centres can be requested, in addition to government and local authority offices

The table reveals the wide variation in procedural rules. In respect of the citizens' initiative (Bürgerbegehren), only four states have a citizen-friendly signature quorum of less than 10%. Free signature collection is often forbidden, and the time allowed for collection varies from a very short two weeks to as much as several months.

There are also wide differences in relation to the popular referendum (Volksentscheid): Bavaria, Hesse and Saxony have no quorum for simple laws; most of the other states have a 25% approval quorum. Rhineland-Palatinate and North-Rhine Westphalia have recently introduced innovative reforms, opening up new possibilities with a 15% approval quorum (NRW) and a 25% turnout quorum (RP).

SURVEY 3
**GLOBAL OVERVIEW OF DIRECT DEMOCRACY
IN SELECTED REGIONS OF THE WORLD**

Securing constitutional amendments via initiative and referendum is virtually impossible in all the states, with the sole exception of Bavaria. Nearly all states impose a 50% approval quorum (Bavaria: 25%; Thuringia: 40%). In several states there is an additional requirement of a 2/3 majority.

LOCAL AUTHORITY/COMMUNAL LEVEL
Up to 1989, only Baden-Würrtemberg had any direct-democratic instruments at the local level. Since then, citizens' initiatives and referendums have been introduced everywhere (Berlin will do so in 2005). It is no coincidence that the most citizen-friendly regulations are to be found in Bavaria and Hamburg: the decisions on the procedures were made by the citizens themselves in state-wide referendums in 1995 and 1998 respectively – in each case against the views of the state government of the time. That is why Bavaria and Hamburg became role models and set a new standard for citizen-friendliness.

The way the process unfolds at the communal level is similar to that at the state level, except that there are only two stages: initiative (Bürgerbegehren) and referendum (Bürgerentscheid). There is a time limit on signature collection only for initiatives which aim at overturning a decision of the local council (the elected representatives). This so-called "corrective initiative" is known in Switzerland as the "facultative referendum". Unlike the practice at the state level, the local council may not present its own counter-proposal to be voted on simultaneously in the referendum. It is, however, possible for this to happen "indirectly": in seven federal states (Baden-Württemberg, Bavaria, Bremen, Mecklenburg-Western Pomerania, Saxony, Saxony-Anhalt and Schleswig-Holstein) the local council (normally by a 2/3 majority) is allowed to call a referendum on its own proposal. In Germany, this plebiscitary form of direct democracy is known as a "council initiative" (Ratsbegehren).

STATE YEAR OF INTRODUCTION	EVALUATION OF PERMISSIBLE ISSUES RATINGS[1]	CITIZENS' INITIATIVE (BÜRGERBEGEHREN)		REFERENDUM (BÜRGERENTSCHEID)
		ENTRY QUORUM %	TIME ALLOWANCE FOR CORRECTIVE INITIATIVES	APPROVAL QUORUM %
Baden-Württemberg (1956)	inadequate	5–10	4 weeks	30
Bavaria (1995)	good	3–10	none	10–20
Brandenburg (1993)	adequate	10	6 weeks	25
City of Bremen (1994)	good	10	3 months	25
Bremerhaven (1996)	inadequate	10	6 weeks	30
Hamburg (1998)	good	2–3	6 months	No quorum
Hesse (1993)	good	10	6 weeks	25

SURVEY 3
GLOBAL OVERVIEW OF DIRECT DEMOCRACY IN SELECTED REGIONS OF THE WORLD

STATE YEAR OF INTRODUCTION	EVALUATION OF PERMISSIBLE ISSUES RATINGS[1]	CITIZENS' INITIATIVE (BÜRGERBEGEHREN)		REFERENDUM (BÜRGERENTSCHEID)
		ENTRY QUORUM %	TIME ALLOWANCE FOR CORRECTIVE INITIATIVES	APPROVAL QUORUM %
Meckl.-W. Pommerania (1994)	inadequate	2.5–10[2]	6 weeks	25
Lower Saxony (1996)	adequate	10	3–6 months	25
N.Rhine-Westphalia (1994)	adequate	3–10	6 weeks–3 months	20
Rhineland-Palatinate (1994)	inadequate	6–15	2 months	30
Saarland (1997)	adequate	5–15	2 months	30
Saxony (1993)	good	15[3]	2 months	25
Saxony-Anhalt (1993)	deficient	6–15	6 weeks	30
Schleswig-Holstein (1990)	satisfactory	10	6 weeks	25
Thuringia (1993)	inadequate	13–17	4 weeks	20–25

Notes: where quorums are stated in actual numbers, they have been converted to percentages here.

[1] Using the referendum rating system produced by Mehr Demokratie e.V.
[2] The entry quorum only drops below 10% when the population size exceeds 50,000
[3] The quorum can be lowered to as little as 5% by statute

The table shows the range of variation in the procedural rules:
- In most states important policy areas (such as town planning) cannot be the subject of citizens' initiatives. Only in Hamburg, Bavaria, Hesse and Saxony are there virtually no restrictions on subject-matter.
- Many states have a high entry quorum, often around 10%. Hamburg has the most citizen-friendly quorum at 2–3%, followed by Bavaria and North-Rhine Westphalia at 3–10% (in both cases, the quorum sinks as the population number rises).
- If we consider the referendum approval quorums, Hamburg, Bavaria and North-Rhine Westphalia are once again out in front. Most German states have high approval quorums of 25% or 30%, which in practice have sometimes led to refusals to debate issues, or even to outright referendum boycotts.

SURVEY 3
Global overview of Direct Democracy in selected regions of the world

Practical experience

Federal level
The Federal Republic is one of the very few countries in Europe with no experience at all of national referendums. There were, however, two referendums during the Weimar Republic (1919–1933): one in 1926 on a proposal to expropriate the wealth of princely families, the other in 1929 aimed at rejecting the reparations proposals of the "Young Plan". Despite a majority "Yes" vote on both occasions, both referendums failed to reach the required turnout quorum: only 39.6% of voters took part in 1926; a mere 14.9% in 1929. The quorum made it possible for both referendums to be effectively and successfully defeated by boycotting tactics and a refusal to debate the issues. Otmar Jung's research has produced important data on the Weimar experience and on other aspects of direct democracy in Germany. There were many other attempts to secure popular referendums. Of the total of 33 initiatives considered, a submission was presented in 13 cases, three of which were taken forward into the initiative process, two of them resulting in a referendum. There were partial successes in some cases.

During the Nazi period (1933–1945), there were three manipulated plebiscites: in 1933, on withdrawal from the League of Nations; in 1934 on ratification of Hitler's assumed leadership; in 1938, on the annexation of Austria.

State level
Practical experience at the state level is quite different. Here there have been 204 processes: 14 referendums to *ratify the state constitution*; 10 referendums on *changes to state boundaries*. 18 *obligatory constitutional referendums* (nine in Bavaria, eight in Hesse and one in Bremen (in 1994, on a revision of the constitution).
In addition, there have been 162 citizens' initiatives and referendums (Volksbegehren and Volksentscheide) i.e. launched "from below", as well as 30 non-binding popular petitions. The table below gives an overview of the frequency and regional distribution of the citizens' initiatives and petitions.

Table 3: Citizens' petitions, citizens' initiatives (CI), citizens' referendum processes (CRP) and citizen-initiated referendums (CIR) (as of January 2005).

State	Provision since	Number of years (to 2005)	Number of CI and submissions	Number of CRP	Number of CIR	A CRP takes place on average every ... years	Additional popular petitions
Baden-Württemberg	1953	52	4	—	—	infinite	none
Bavaria	1946	59	35	14	5	4.2	none
Berlin*	1995	36	8	1	—	36.0	2

SURVEY 3
GLOBAL OVERVIEW OF DIRECT DEMOCRACY IN SELECTED REGIONS OF THE WORLD

STATE	PROVISION SINCE	NUMBER OF YEARS (TO 2005)	NUMBER OF CI AND SUBMISSIONS	NUMBER OF CRP	NUMBER OF CIR	A CRP TAKES PLACE ON AVERAGE EVERY ... YEARS	ADDITIONAL POPULAR PETITIONS
Brandenburg	1992	13	20	7	—	1.9	none
Bremen	1947	58	9	3	—	19.3	6
Hamburg	1996	9	18	7	4	1.3	2
Hesse	1946	59	4	1	—	59.0	none
Mecklenburg-W. Pommerania	1994	11	16	—	—	infinite	—
Lower Saxony	1993	12	6	2	—	6.0	11
NRW	1950	55	9	2	—	27.5	4
Rhineland-Pal.	1947	58	4	1	—	58.0	none
Saarland	1979	26	3	—	—	infinite	none
Saxony	1992	13	9	4	1	3.3	none
Saxony-Anhalt	1992	13	2	2	1	6.5	5
Schleswig-Holstein	1990	15	11	3	2	5.0	none
Thuringia	1994	11	4	3	—	3.7	—
Total			500	162	50	13	10.0	30

* Berlin: excl. 1949–1974

We can draw the following conclusions from the table:
- The citizens of Hamburg and Brandenburg make the most frequent use of direct democracy. But so far there has not been a single citizen-initiated referendum, because all the referendum processes have failed – due to the ban on the free collection of signatures.
- There have been no referendums at all in Baden-Württemberg, the Saarland and Mecklenburg-Western Pomerania; this comes as no surprise, given these states' very high, to prohibitive, procedural hurdles.
- "Bottom-up" i.e. citizen-initiated referendum votes have so far happened in only five states: most of them have been in Hamburg and Bavaria.
- In terms of absolute numbers, the most processes, initiatives and referendums have been in Bavaria, but Hamburg has been catching up quickly in recent years.

A more detailed analysis of the statistics reveals the following:
- 2004 saw the 50th citizens' initiative process. Of these, 62% failed; only one in four resulted in a referendum. The reason lies in the excessively high quorums in conjunction with the inadequate signature collection periods (e.g. in Bavaria) and/or the ban on the free collection of signatures.

SURVEY 3
GLOBAL OVERVIEW OF DIRECT DEMOCRACY IN SELECTED REGIONS OF THE WORLD

- "Education and culture" was the most frequently chosen subject area (30%), followed by "democracy and domestic politics" (22%). "Protection of the environment", "social issues" and "the economy" were the next most popular themes, each accounting for 10% of the processes.
- Observation shows that these instruments are predominantly used by citizens' initiative and campaign groups; organizations and political parties appear mainly as coalition partners and/or supporters.
- 25% of the processes were directly successful: the indirect positive effects (public awareness, spread of information etc.) cannot be quantified.

LOCAL AUTHORITY LEVEL

Table 4: Number of citizens' initiatives (Bürgerbegehren) and citizen-initiated referendums in Germany (to 31.12.2004)

FEDERAL STATE	PROVISION SINCE	NUMBER OF DISTRICTS/ COMMUNITIES	CITIZENS' AND COUNCIL INITIATIVES	NUMBER GOING TO REFERENDUM
Bavaria	1995	2,056	1,313	808
North Rhine-Westphalia	1994	396	354	103
Baden-Württemberg	1956	1111	341	152
Schleswig-Holstein	1990	1,132	222*	120*
Saxony	1993	779	215*	132*
Hesse	1993	426	218	76
Brandenburg	1993	1,489	160*	43*
Rhineland-Palatinate	1994	2,305	99	37
Lower Saxony	1996	1,032	87	28
Saxony-Anhalt	1993	1,295	72*	51*
M'burg-W.Pommerania	1994	1,069	72	23
Thuringia	1993	1,053	44*	15*
Hamburg (districts)	1998	7	46	4
Bremen	1994/1996	2	4	1
Saarland	1997	52	5	0
Total		14,204	3,252	1,593

* Estimates/extrapolations due to insufficient data.
Sources: database of the Research Centre for Citizen Participation and Direct Democracy at the University of Marburg, supplemented by the own research and estimates.

SURVEY 3
GLOBAL OVERVIEW OF DIRECT DEMOCRACY IN SELECTED REGIONS OF THE WORLD

Every year, there are around 200 citizens' initiatives in Germany, about half of them in Bavaria. The specific procedural rules also affect the practice at the local authority level: in states with citizen-friendly procedures (Bavaria, Saxony, North Rhine-Westphalia) the instruments are well used. Baden-Württemberg's high placing in the table and its relatively large number of initiatives and referendums is due solely to the fact that citizens' initiatives have been possible there for so much longer. In other states such as Thuringia, Mecklenburg-Western Pommerania, Saxony-Anhalt and Rhineland-Palatinate there are very few processes, due clearly to the high hurdles and the very restricted range of issues allowed.

CURRENT DEVELOPMENTS

REFORM ENDEAVOURS AT THE STATE AND LOCAL AUTHORITY LEVELS

The direct-democratic wave of reform in Germany can be divided into two phases: between 1989 and 1998 direct-democratic procedures were introduced, and in some cases also reformed, in virtually all the federal states. In the second phase – still ongoing – one can observe a trend towards smaller parliamentary reform debates and reforms of the existing provisions, mostly selective changes to quorums or time periods (though larger-scale reforms have been introduced in recent years in Thuringia, North Rhine-Westphalia and Rhineland-Palatinate). At the same time, however, there have also been negative developments: results of referendums have frequently been ignored by parliaments (Hamburg, Schleswig-Holstein) and during the '90s there were some court rulings which blocked the further growth of direct democracy.

THE FEDERAL LEVEL AND THE DEBATE ABOUT A REFERENDUM ON THE EU CONSTITUTION

To date, all attempts at introducing citizens' initiatives and referendums at the national level have been blocked by the Christian Democrats (CDU/CSU). Because introduction would mean a change to the Federal Constitution, a two-thirds majority in parliament is required, for which the support of these two parties is necessary. The first attempt and failure was at the beginning of the '90s (in the course of the revision of the constitution following on German re-unification); the second was in 2002, put forward by the ruling coalition of the Social Democrats and Greens. The proposal was approved by a majority in parliament – but by less than the required two-thirds. Recently the issue has once again been subject to lively debate: the Liberals (FDP) proposed a referendum on the EU Constitution. There was support for the proposal among some Conservatives (CDU/CSU), as well as in all the other political parties. But some leading politicians – especially the then Chancellor Gerhard Schröder, Foreign Minister Joschka Fischer and leader of the opposition Angela Merkel – strongly opposed the idea of a referendum. The former Red-Green coalition pursued a different plan and tried once again to get agreement for the general introduction of initiatives and referendums. This attempt was once again blocked by the opposition – a lost opportunity for more direct democracy in Germany.

FURTHER INFORMATION:
- Research Centre for Direct Democracy and Citizen Participation at the University of Marburg (www.forschungsstelle-direkte-demokratie.de)
- Mehr Demokratie e.V. (www.mehr-demokratie.de)
- Local authority level: Information Centre on Citizens' Initiatives (www.buergerbegehren.de)

SURVEY 3
Global overview of Direct Democracy in selected regions of the world

Austria

Austria is a very cautious country in terms of direct democracy. This alpine state does have elements of direct citizen participation, many years of experience of non-binding signature-collecting campaigns and has even had two referendums. But citizens cannot demand or initiate a binding "bottom-up" referendum process. This has led to louder calls by a variety of political actors in recent years for reform and the introduction of initiatives and referendums on the Swiss model. What follows is an outline of the existing rules and details of experience to date.

The rules

Federal level

Referendums are binding and were formally inscribed in the constitution in 1958. A total revision of the constitution triggers an obligatory referendum. A partial revision triggers a facultative referendum, if one third of one of the chambers of Parliament (National Council or Federal Council) requests it. In addition, the National Council can optionally decide to submit a simple law to the people for approval (plebiscite).

Since 1989, purely consultative (i.e. not legally binding) public opinion polls can be carried out at the initiative of the National Council, but this has never been done so far.

Most of Austria's experience of participative democracy relates to agenda initiatives (officially termed "Volksbegehren" – popular submission or initiative). Since its introduction in 1963, this procedure has been used on 32 occasions. It allows citizens to submit a proposal. If a prescribed number of signatures is collected, the proposal is presented to parliament: but parliament decides whether to implement the proposal or not – hence the correct term for this procedure is popular petition.

It works as follows: a minimum of around 8,000 signatures (0.1% of the registered electorate) is required to launch the "Volksbegehren". Up to 1999 this could also be done by eight members of the National Council or by twelve members of three different state parliaments (four from each). The "Volksbegehren" is successful if 100,000 signatures of registered voters (about 1.7% of the registered electorate) – or the signatures of 16.6% of the registered voters from each of three federal states – are collected within seven days. Signatures must be given in special centres. If the initiative secures the necessary signatures, the proposal must be debated in parliament and the initiative group is entitled to claim expenses up to a maximum of 11,000 Euro.

State and local authority levels

State level

Two of the federal states have obligatory referendums for specific subject areas: in the Vorarlberg, any draft law which aims to abolish the instruments of direct democracy automatically goes to referendum. In Salzburg, a referendum is obligatory in the event of a total revision of the state constitution.

SURVEY 3
**GLOBAL OVERVIEW OF DIRECT DEMOCRACY
IN SELECTED REGIONS OF THE WORLD**

All the states have facultative referendums, but citizens cannot secure a binding referendum through signature collection. Between 1984 and 2001, the Vorarlberg uniquely had such a provision (based on the Swiss model) – though with a prohibitive signature quorum of 20%. However, the courts then ruled the provision unconstitutional.

In most federal states there is what is known as a "popular veto": the possibility of challenging decisions made by the state parliament. The quorums vary and there is no obligation to hold a binding referendum. All federal states also have consultative popular opinion polls, which are initiated either by the state parliament, in some cases by the state government, or by popular signature collection (quorums of 2–11%).

Agenda initiatives: eight of the nine federal states (Salzburg is the exception) have non-binding popular petitions with a signature quorum of between 2% and 5% of the registered voters. In the Burgenland, Lower Austria, Upper Austria, Steiermark and Vorarlberg there is also a popular petition relating to local administration, mostly with higher quorums.

LOCAL AUTHORITY LEVEL

Austria differs considerably from Germany and Switzerland here. Only consultative popular opinion polls are allowed in all 2,360 local authority areas. These can be requested by the community councils or by citizens by means of signature collection. Only in rare cases – such as the amalgamation of communities – is the result binding.
Corrective initiative: in Steyermark and Burgenland citizens can try to prevent the implementation of a decision of the local council by means of a referendum. In both states such an initiative has to be supported by the astronomically high quorum of 25% of the registered voters, and there is a turnout quorum of 40% for the referendum itself.

EXPERIENCE

NATIONAL LEVEL
There have been two national *popular referendums*:

1978: nuclear power/Zwentendorf (facultative, binding referendum).
The first referendum took place on 5.11.1978 on the issue of nuclear power (commissioning of the Zwentendorf nuclear power station). The turnout was 64.11% and 50.5% voted against the use of nuclear power. Before the vote there had been intense debates and protests. The final veto on Zwentendorf and other nuclear power stations followed a few weeks later, when the National Council passed a law banning the building and operation of nuclear power stations (still in force).
1994: EU accession (obligatory, binding referendum).
On 12.06.1994 Austrians voted on accession to the EU. On a turnout of 82.35%, the "Yes" vote amounted to 66.58% of the votes cast and Austria duly joined the EU.

SURVEY 3
GLOBAL OVERVIEW OF DIRECT DEMOCRACY IN SELECTED REGIONS OF THE WORLD

At the end of this section there is a table listing all 31 Austrian popular petitions.
An analysis of these produces the following picture:
- There has been a total of 32 agenda initiatives, of which 30 reached the required signature quorum.
- Five of the 32 agenda initiatives (all three pre-1970 petitions) were implemented by parliament. In two other cases the petitions enjoyed partial success.
- It is striking that only just over half of the agenda initiatives (20 out of 32) were launched by citizens through signature collection. The remaining 12 were initiated by minorities in parliament – an option not available since 1999.
- The agenda initiative was often used as a tool of the parliamentary opposition. It is only recently that it has been used more frequently by citizens' movements and campaign groups.
- Successes/side-effects: in addition to three direct successes and two partial successes, there was also frustration when initiatives were in practice ignored. But in every case there are indirect successes in terms of greater levels of participation, knowledge, awareness and agenda-setting, with increased media attention.
- In addition to their function as a vehicle for the articulation of protest, agenda initiatives also served as a mirror of society.

STATE AND LOCAL AUTHORITY LEVELS
Direct democracy and citizen participation in decision-making are the exception at the state and local authority levels. Public consultations have taken place only rarely – for example, in Vienna (on the Park, the River Danube power station and the World Fair), in Vorarlberg, Salzburg (speed limit on roads), Steiermark (protection of the environment) and Upper Austria (new Opera House). Data gathering and presentation need to be improved.
One of the most recent public consultation took place at the beginning of 2005 in Salzburg on whether the city should apply to host the 2010 Winter Olympics. A majority voted in favour of applying. There are also sporadic examples of non-binding public consultations at the local authority level.

Three conclusions can be drawn from the experience at the state and local authority levels:
1) Direct-democratic procedures and citizen participation are exceptions at the state and local authority levels.
   There are only isolated examples of their use.
2) What use was made of them was dominated by the political parties: they were used by political parties, but also by parliamentary majorities and state governments. This is due primarily to the rules of procedure: there are "top-down" public consultations, but no genuine "bottom-up" direct-democratic procedures as in Switzerland or in the German federal states and local communities.
3) In a small number of cases it is possible to see the anticipatory effect of the "threat of a referendum" e.g. in the Vorarlberg in the Fussach or Rüthi cases; or in 1972/73 when a proposal relating to the conditions and pensions of politicians was withdrawn.

SURVEY 3
Global overview of Direct Democracy in selected regions of the world

Current developments

Efforts at introducing reforms
The first attempt at introducing "genuine" direct-democratic procedures with a linkage between initiatives and referendums was made in 2000 by the ruling ÖVP (Austrian People's Party) – FPÖ (Austrian Liberal Party) coalition. The proposal was for a signature quorum of 15%. But the parties were unable to agree on a common solution, and a two-thirds majority was required for a change to the constitution.
More recently, the "Initiative for More Direct Democracy" has been collecting signatures for a popular petition on the same subject, but no formal initiative (Volksbegehren) has been launched yet. Opinion polls show 60%–65% support for "genuine" direct-democratic procedures and support for a change to the constitution is also growing in the political parties.

Debate on a referendum on the EU Constitution
Despite demands from the trade unions, the Peace Movement and sections of the Opposition in parliament there will be no referendum in Austria on the first proposal for an EU Constitution – it was ratified by the Austrian Parliament in May 2005. But Austrian Chancellor Wolfgang Schüssel had earlier expressed support for a referendum in all countries of the EU. This idea now has greater contemporary relevance and importance after the rejection of the Constitution in France and Holland.

SURVEY 3
Global overview of Direct Democracy in selected regions of the world

Year / Signature collection period	Subject	Number of valid signatures	Turnout as % (rank)	Submission made by – Initiators/supporters – Result
1964 10.– 12.10.1964	Austrian Radio	832,353	17.27 (5)	34,841 supporting signatures; *demands implemented/politically successful*
1969 4.5.– 11.5.1969	Gradual introduction of a 40-hour week	889,659	17.74 (4)	Members of the National Council; *demands implemented/politically successful*
1969 12.5.– 19.5.1969	Abolition of Grade 13 in secondary schools	339,407	6.77 (14)	Members of the state parliament; *demands implemented/politically successful*
1975 24.11.– 1.12.1975	Protection of human life/against the 3-month legal period for abortions	895,665	17.93 (3)	762,664 supporting signatures; Supported by the Catholic ChurchDemands not implemented, existing ruling remains
1980 3.11.– 10.11.1980	Ban on nuclear power Pro-Zwentendorf Initiative	421,282	8.04 (11)	33,388 Supporting signatures; Demands not implemented
1980 3.11.– 10.11.1980	Ban on nuclear power Anti-Zwentendorf Initiative	147,016	2.80 (27)	13,516 Supporting signatures; Demands not implemented; but there was a referendum on Zwentendorf:
1982 10.5.– 17.5.1982	Conference centre – brake on public spending law (Building project in Vienna)	1,361,562	25.74 (1)	Members of state parliament (ÖVP – Austrian People's Party); Demands not implemented, but public opinion mobilised
1985 4.3.– 11.3.1985	"Konrad-Lorenz-Initiative" (against Hainburg power station, for Hainburg national park, other issues)	353,906	6.55 (15)	56,870 Supporting signatures; supported by environmental groups and the "Krone" newspaper. Demands not implemented

290

Survey 3
Global overview of Direct Democracy in selected regions of the world

Year / Signature collection period	Subject	Number of valid signatures	Turnout as % (rank)	Submission made by – Initiators/supporters – Result
1985 22.4.– 29.4.1985	Increase in length of civilian service (alternative to military service)	196,376	3.63 (23)	48,774 Supporting signatures; Demands not implemented
1985 4.11.– 11.11.1985	Initiative against interceptor jets – for a referendum	121,182	2.23 (30)	18,433 Supporting signatures; Demands not implemented
1986 3.3.– 10.3.1986	Anti-fighter jet initiative in Steiermark (Styria)	244,254	4.50 (18)	140,817 Supporting signatures; Demands not implemented
1987 22.6.– 29.6.1987	Anti-Privileges Initiative	250,697	4.57 (17)	Members of the National Council (FPÖ); Demands not implemented
1989 29.5.– 5.6.1989	Reducing class sizes	219,127	3.93 (22)	26,643 Supporting signatures; Demands not implemented
1989 27.11.– 4.12.1989	Safeguarding freedom of Austrian Radio	109,197	1.95 (31)	Members of the National Council Demands not implemented
1991 11.11.– 18.11.1991	For a referendum on joining the EU and the European Monetary Union	126,834	2.25 (29)	Members of National Council (Greens) Demands not implemented, *but subsequent EU accession was decided by referendum*
1993 25.1.– 1.2.1993	"Austria first" (problem of asylum seekers)	416,531	7.35 (13)	Members of the National Council; Demands not implemented
1995 12.6.– 19.6.1995	Initiative "Pro the motorcycle"	75,525	1.31 (32)	12,812 Supporting signatures; too few signatures
1996 18.3.– 25.3.1996	Protection of animals initiative	459,096	7.96 (12)	Members of the National Council and animal protection organisations; Demands not implemented
1996 18.3.– 25.3.1996	Neutrality initiative	358,156	6.21 (16)	31,166 Supporting signatures; Demands not implemented

SURVEY 3
GLOBAL OVERVIEW OF DIRECT DEMOCRACY IN SELECTED REGIONS OF THE WORLD

YEAR / SIGNATURE COLLECTION PERIOD	SUBJECT	NUMBER OF VALID SIGNATURES	TURNOUT AS % (RANK)	SUBMISSION MADE BY – INITIATORS/SUPPORTERS – RESULT
1997 7.4.– 14.4.1997	Genetic engineering initiative	1,225,790	21.23 (2)	Members of the National Council, supported by the "Krone" newspaper and others; Demands not implemented, *a few concessions granted*
1997 7.4.– 14.4.1997	Women's initiative www.uff.at	644,665	11.17 (8)	Members of the National Council (SPÖ, Greens), referred to committee; Demands not implemented
1997 24.11.– 1.12.1997	For a referendum on the Austrian Schilling	253,949	4.43 (19)	Members of the National Council (FPÖ); Demands not implemented
1997 24.11.– 1.12.1997	"Nuclear-free Austria" initiative	248,787	4.34 (21)	Members of the National Council (FPÖ); Demands already implemented before signature collection week
1999 9.9.– 16.9.1999	Family initiative	183,154	3.17 (25)	16,875 Supporting signatures; Initiators: Families League, Catholic Families Association and others; *Demands partially implemented*
2000 29.11.– 6.12.2000	Initiative for a new EU referendum	193,901	3.35 (24)	8,243 Supporting signatures; Demands not implemented
2001 6.11.– 13.11.2001	Education campaign and tuition fees initiative	173,594	2.98 (26)	48,626 Supporting signatures; Demands not implemented
2002 14.1.– 21.1.2002	Initiative for a veto on Temelin (nuclear power station)	914,973	15.53 (6)	16,562 Supporting signatures; Initiators: FPÖ, supported by the "Neue Krone" newspaper; Demands not implemented
2002 3.4.– 10.4.2002	Initiative "Social Welfare State Austria" www.sozialstaat.at	717,102	12.20 (7)	38,212 Supporting signatures; Cross-party campaign group; Demands not implemented

SURVEY 3
GLOBAL OVERVIEW OF DIRECT DEMOCRACY IN SELECTED REGIONS OF THE WORLD

Year / Signature collection period	Subject	Number of valid signatures	Turnout as % (rank)	Submission made by – Initiators/supporters – Result
2002 29.7.– 5.8.2002	Initiative against interceptor jets	624,807	10.65 (9)	18,325 Supporting signatures; Demands not implemented, as decision was made to buy the jets
2003 10.6.– 17.6.2003	Initiative "Nuclear-free Europe"	131,772	2.23 (28)	9,567 Supporting signatures; Initiators: Greenpeace and others; Demands not implemented
2004 22.3.– 29.3.2004	Pensions initiative	594,287	10.53 (10)	33,477 Supporting signatures; Initiators: SPÖ, trade unions; Demands not implemented to date
2006 6.3.– 13.3.2006	Initiative "Austria stay free"	258,281	4.28 (20)	

SOURCE:
Office of Statistics of the Austrian Interior Ministry: http://www.bmi.gv.at/wahlen (status as of 01.07.2006) plus data from private research.

FURTHER INFORMATION:
- www-bmi-gv.at/wahlen
- www.direktedemokratie.at
- www.volksgesetzgebung-jetzt.at

SURVEY 3
GLOBAL OVERVIEW OF DIRECT DEMOCRACY IN SELECTED REGIONS OF THE WORLD

ITALY: SOUTH TYROL (PROVINCE OF BOZEN)

Until 1945, there was no experience or tradition of direct democracy in South Tyrol; until then – except for a brief blossoming in the early 1920s – it had not even had the opportunity of familiarising itself with representative democracy. But the tradition of unchallenged representation was continued long after 1945. The modern history of South Tyrol began with the rejection by the Allies of a referendum on the province's political affiliation which had been demanded by 158,628 South Tyroleans. The effective need to assert themselves as a minority within the Italian state and to fight for administrative autonomy with separate representation in Rome long made it impossible for any democratic pluralism to emerge, resulting in an unchallenged acceptance of the ruling political representation (the South Tyrolean People's Party, continuously in power since 1945). The 1957 introduction at the regional level of the so-called "abrogative referendum" (provided for in Art. 75 of the Italian Constitution) – i.e. the possibility of holding a referendum on the validity of an existing law or parts of the same; and the 1972 introduction of the citizens' initiative (the citizens' right to propose new legislation – but with no opportunity to submit the initiative to referendum) were thus fairly meaningless. In almost 50 years, not a single referendum has been called, and only 6 citizens' initiatives, of which only three made it as far as the regional parliament. Neither instrument – despite enjoying lower hurdles of c. 2% for the referendum and 0.5% for the citizens' initiative – has any real potency which would make their use interesting: both of them end up in the regional parliament, which can fill the legislative vacuum with its own "sovereign" powers and decide for itself on any proposed draft legislation.

It was not until the beginning of the 1990s that there was any movement around these political rights. Interest awakened and grew with the prospect – opened up by a new national law and made available to local authorities by a regional law – of introducing real rights of co-decision making for citizens. Of course, the complete unfamiliarity of the local institutions with direct citizen participation has meant that the absence of procedural rules has so far largely prevented the application of the right – provided for in the statutes of every local authority – to hold public consultations to examine and reach decisions on local issues. It was only ten years later, in 2005, that a regional law made it compulsory for this right to be provided for and be made usable. The determination of the procedural rules continues to remain within the autonomous powers of the local authorities.

The mid-nineties also saw the emergence of an initiative supported by a broad coalition of organisations active in the social, cultural and environmental fields and aimed at securing extended, binding and easily used rights of political co-decision making. The first move was to launch two citizens' initiatives: one to introduce the binding legislative initiative at the regional level, another to introduce the bye-laws initiative at the local authority level. A striking early victory for draft legislation in the regional parliament was knocked back by the Italian government, leaving the first phase of the initiative with no concrete results. A new basis for action was provided in 2001 with the reform of the Italian constitution and of the statute of autonomy for South Tyrol. Since then, the regional parliament is under the obligation to make provision for the whole area of direct democracy, especially the decision-making legislative and administrative initiative. As a result of a further push using a citizens' initiative, the regional parliament was urged in 2003 to enact appropriate procedural rules. However, neither the instruments themselves nor their rules of application – neither at regional nor local level – are likely to turn out to be so citizen-friendly that there will be no need in the coming years to continue working hard at improving them – using the existing provisions themselves to "ratchet up" the quality of direct democracy.

SURVEY 3
GLOBAL OVERVIEW OF DIRECT DEMOCRACY IN SELECTED REGIONS OF THE WORLD

LIECHTENSTEIN

HISTORY
Binding direct-democratic rights were established in Liechtenstein with the 1921 constitution. Even before the new constitution came into force, there had been two referendums and one public consultation in the period 1919–1921. The provisions in the 1921 constitution were modelled on those of neighbouring Switzerland. They represented a radical departure from the predominantly monarchical principles which had obtained until the fall of the Austro-Hungarian Empire - the primary reference point for the Liechtenstein royal family. They also marked a reorientation of foreign policy in the direction of Switzerland, the Principality of Liechtenstein having previously cooperated closely with Austria. The consequences of this change of direction were postal, customs and currency treaties with Switzerland concluded during the 1920s. This laid the foundation for the sustained economic upturn in Liechtenstein, especially after WWII, which freed the country from centuries of persistent poverty.

DIRECT-DEMOCRATIC RIGHTS
Direct-democratic rights are established in Liechtenstein at both political levels – those of the state and of the local authorities. At the local level, regular use is made of referendums, especially in connection with expensive public building projects. But other local issues can also be decided by referendum. In recent times, these have included issues of local authority legislation and the relationship between local authorities (political) and community councils (civilian), for example.

For a long time, community councils had the sole right to decide (by referendum) on granting naturalisation rights to foreign nationals. Recent developments in citizens' rights have meant that a claim to citizenship falls to the applicant by right after a certain number of years of residency, leading to a sharp fall in the number of referendums on naturalisation.

At the national level, to which the remainder of the section is devoted, there is a broad repertoire of direct-democratic rights which go further than the corresponding provisions in Switzerland in certain respects. These are:

- the *referendum* against non-urgent decisions of the Landtag (Parliament) – a referendum launched by the collection of signatures;
- the *initiative* (citizens' initiative), a referendum initiated by signature collection on the subject of a draft law and based on a specific initiative text, which may be submitted either as a "formulated initiative" (formally worded draft legislation), or as a "simple initiative" (basic proposal);
- the *authorities' referendum*, a referendum launched by a decision in Parliament on a law previously adopted by Parliament;
- the *popular consultation*, a referendum launched by parliament concerning the principles of a law which is to be passed;
- the *petition*, which can also be submitted by people who do not have the right to vote.

In the course of the 20th century, and at the beginning of the 21st, the popular direct-democratic rights were amended, extended or adapted to meet new situations on several occasions. The main changes were:

SURVEY 3
Global overview of Direct Democracy
in selected regions of the world

- *Voting rights* for elections and referendums were changed several times during the 20th century. Firstly, the voting age was progressively lowered to 18. Secondly, *voting rights for women* were eventually introduced by referendum in 1984, after several earlier failed attempts. Finally, *postal voting* became a general option in 2004.
- The *number of signatures required* was adjusted upwards several times in line with the increase in the size of the electorate. Currently, with around 17,000 registered voters, the number of signatures required to launch a referendum is 1,000 for legal and financial decrees, and 1,500 for constitutional changes and state treaties.
- The *international treaties referendum* was introduced in 1992. Prior to this, there was no provision for direct-democratic participation in decision-making in respect of international treaties.
- In 2003, the possibility of a legal *abolition of the monarchy* was introduced. In the event of a conflict between the Prince and the people, a "vote of no confidence" can first be submitted by means of a signature collection. The Prince decides whether to accept or reject the criticism. If he rejects it, the people can launch an initiative to abolish the monarchy with a signature quorum of 1,500 signatures. If the initiative is successful, parliament has to draft a republican constitution which is then put to referendum. The Prince may present his own draft constitution (as a counter-proposal) at the same time. If the republican constitution is accepted in the referendum, the monarchy is abolished. The Prince has no right of veto.

Matters subject to referendum
Referendums may be held on laws (new laws, amendments to laws, the constitution, alterations to the constitution), financial decrees, international treaties and directives relating to policy or legislation.

Further citizens' rights relevant to direct democracy concern specific voting rights outwith normal elections.

- with a minimum of 1,000 signatures, the people can order parliament to be convened; 1,500 signatures are required to dissolve parliament
- since the revision of the constitution in 2003, in the event of a disagreement between the Prince and Parliament, the people may decide on the appointment of judges.

Obligatory referendum
Obligatory referendums were only introduced with the revision of the constitution in 2003. They apply to the process of abolition of the monarchy mentioned above. A successful referendum can introduce a republican constitution. A referendum is also obligatory in the case of the appointment of judges, when there is no agreement between the Prince and the Parliament.

SURVEY 3
GLOBAL OVERVIEW OF DIRECT DEMOCRACY IN SELECTED REGIONS OF THE WORLD

PROCEDURES

INITIATIVE
In the case of citizens' initiatives, a checking process is employed in order to ensure that unconstitutional proposals, or proposals which contradict exist international treaties, do not make it to a referendum. The time periods allowed are significantly tighter than in Switzerland. The stages of the process from the initial notification of an initiative to the final referendum are as follows:

- notification of an initiative to the government
- checking of the text of the initiative by the government (conformity with the constitution and with international treaties) and reporting back to parliament
- at its next sitting, parliament either authorizes the initiative or declares it null and void
- if authorization is granted, the initiative is formally announced by the government
- signature collection begins; the demand/proposal (Begehren) is submitted within six weeks of the formal announcement
- parliament debates the proposal at its next sitting. It can either accept or reject the proposal. If it rejects the proposal, there must be a referendum, and Parliament has the right to submit a counter-proposal. If it accepts the proposal, there is the option of a referendum
- the government must set the date for the referendum within 14 days of the decision in parliament. The referendum is held within three months of the parliamentary sitting at which the decision was made

REFERENDUM
Parliamentary decisions which may be subject to referendum (all laws stated to be non-urgent, constitutional amendments, financial decrees, international treaties) are always announced and advertised as being available for referendum. In order for a referendum to be called on any of these subjects, the required number of signatures must be collected and handed in within 30 days. The government must set a date for the referendum within the next three months.

BINDING/NON-BINDING?

THE PEOPLE AND PARLIAMENT
The binding or non-binding character of direct-democratic rights varies with the specific right and its relationship to the parliament. Referendum demands (Referendumsbegehren) and formulated initiative demands, which are approved by a majority of the votes cast, are binding on parliament. But in the case of non-formulated initiatives, parliament can either reject them or reach a decision which meets the initiators' demands. In both cases, the formal demand process is terminated. But parliament can decide to put the initiative to a referendum, in which case the outcome is binding. There is further room for manoeuvre in the possible transformation of a non-formulated initiative into formally-worded draft legislation. Petitions are non-binding. They are only dealt with in parliament if they are formally presented by a member of parliament. But there is no obligation on parliament to act upon them.

SURVEY 3
GLOBAL OVERVIEW OF DIRECT DEMOCRACY IN SELECTED REGIONS OF THE WORLD

THE PEOPLE AND THE PRINCE

As a result of the dual construction of the Liechtenstein constitution as a mixed monarchical-democratic constitution, considerable powers are bestowed on the head of state, who performs various official duties. The Prince – or his representative – have the right of sanction. In just the same way that no law can be ratified without the approval of parliament or the people, ratification must also be approved by the head of state. This applies to financial decress and international treaties, as well as to ordinary laws. This means that citizens' initiatives are also subject to the right of sanction. An initiative which has been approved by a majority of citizens in a referendum can only be implemented if the head of state sanctions it.

USAGE

Since 1919 there have been 92 referendums in Liechtenstein at the national level, if counter-proposals and simultaneous alternative proposals on the same subject are counted separately. In terms of subject-matter, the list of referendums is headed by proposals to change voting rights (22), followed by referendums on taxes and other payments to the state (11), socio-political issues (9), energy and transport (8) and political rights (8). The temporal sequence of the issues reflects the level of socio-economic development and the public's change of attitudes. Whereas in the first half of the 20th century the focus was on questions of infrastructure, commerce and finance – plus voting rights – in more recent decades referendums have revealed increased emphasis on questions of culture, education, the environment, civic issues, citizens' rights and international issues.

Forty-one of the 92 referendums were launched by the authorities; twenty-nine resulted from an initiative; twenty were facultative referendums Of the 92 referendums, the proposal was accepted in 41 cases, rejected in the other 51. There are no significant differences between the earlier and later periods in this respect. Neither are there any major differences between accepted and rejected proposals in terms of who triggered the referendum. Authorities' referendums, citizens' initiatives and facultative referendums were all rejected more often than accepted. The initiatives had the least likelihood of being successful.

The Prince has used his right of sanction to reject the result of a referendum on only one occasion. This was in 1961 and concerned a proposal for a new law on hunting, which Prince Franz-Josef II did not accept. After renewed debates in parliament, a new hunting law was passed which secured the approval of both the people and the Prince. In 2002, a constitutional initiative caused quite a stir. After years of fierce debate about a change to the constitution which had involved the royal house, the government, the parliament and ultimately also the wider public, Prince Hans-Adam II and heir to the throne Prince Alois launched a citizens' initiative in August 2002. They used this unconventional means to try to gain support directly from the people for their own constitutional proposals after it had become clear that the required qualified majority in parliament would not be found. The referendum was held on 16th March 2003, after concerns relating to constitutional and international treaty law had been brushed aside by the government, the constitutional court and the parliament during the preliminary phase of checking the initiative. The Princes' initiative received a clear endorsement, securing just under two-thirds of the votes. In the run-up to the referendum, a counter-proposal was contested by the royal house and the Prince announced that he would his

SURVEY 3
Global overview of Direct Democracy
in selected regions of the world

right of veto if this proposal were to be accepted by the people. Debate around the referendum was heavily influenced by the threat announced by the royal family that in the event of the referendum going against them, they would leave the country and cease to provide it with its head of state. These unusual features of the March 2003 constitutional referendum raised far-reaching questions about the separation of powers in the Liechtenstein political system, the extent to which referendums could be manipulated and non-relevant issues come to dominate the process. The threat of the use of the veto by the head of state also pointed up the formal limits to direct democracy in Liechtenstein.

Further information:
- Official portal; English version (www.liechtenstein.li/en/eliechtenstein_main_sites/)
- Government portal; German only (www.gesetze.li)
- Website of the independent Liechtenstein Institute founded in 1986; German only (www.liechtenstein-institut.li)
- Government website detailing all referendums since 2002; German only (www.abstimmung.li)
- Geneva University-based "Research and Documentation Centre on Direct Democracy"; German, French and English (www.c2d.unige.ch)

Belgium

Ever since the Kingdom of Belgium was created, somewhat surprisingly, in 1830, its future has been uncertain. The last referendum, held in 1950 to determine what constitutional rights the monarch should be granted, shattered its foundations by revealing a strong regional polarisation. Belgians had been called to approve or reject the return of King Leopold III, whose behaviour towards the German Nazi regime had divided public opinion. Overall, 57.7 percent voted in favour of allowing the King to return to the throne - thanks to overwhelming approval in Flanders (72 percent), but despite a clear "no" in Brussels and Wallonia. The King's return triggered strikes and demonstrations in Walloon industrial towns and Leopold III eventually resigned in favour of his son, Baudouin. This crisis convinced Belgium that any public consultation would create tensions between the Flemish and Walloon populations. "We would have talked more about the future of our country than the future of our continent," argued former Flemish minister Herman Van Rompuy in a recent parliamentary speech on the possibility of a referendum on the EU Constitution.

In the eyes of Belgian politicians more than anywhere else, the perceived political risk involved with referendums is considerable. Only the Parliament and the King can decide which law, rule or international treaty may be approved under the current Constitution, which states: "All power emanates from the Nation. This power is exerted in the manner established by the Constitution"; i.e. elected representatives cannot be bound by any form of mandate, even from the people. Belgium today lives under a strictly representative regime which rules out popular votes.

And yet, referendums remain an open political issue. On June 1, 2004, Liberal prime minister Guy Verhofstadt announced his intention of holding a non-binding referendum on the EU Constitution. His proposal illustrates Belgium's desire to strengthen mechanisms of direct democracy, even though the Council of State rejected the proposal on legal grounds; it considered that Mr Verhofstadt had promised to "follow the advice" of the result and despite the U-turn of his social-liberal coalition partner, the Spirit Party, which had decided to drop its previous support for a referendum,

SURVEY 3
GLOBAL OVERVIEW OF DIRECT DEMOCRACY IN SELECTED REGIONS OF THE WORLD

arguing that it could be hijacked by the far-right Vlaams Belang party campaigning against Turkish membership of the EU. In fact, soon after winning the election in 1999, Mr Verhofstadt's coalition appointed a commission on "the renewal of politics" in the two federal parliamentary assemblies to propose ways of amending the Constitution to allow federal referendums. A draft law was even submitted to Parliament in February 2002 allowing at least 3 per cent of citizens over 16 to initiate an advisory legislative referendum. This effort also failed, as well as a general advisory consultation on the EU Constitutional Treaty suggested in October 2003.

Changes have been more substantive at the sub-national level. Strictly non-binding "popular consultations" were officially allowed in 1995 for communes and in 1997 at the regional level. Their restrictive scope and procedures ensure that they "do not provoke another region or community." In practice they are seldom used, and if so, they are merely "comparable to an opinion poll," according to Belgian constitutional experts. Yet the rationale behind popular consultations is the encouragement of direct dialogue with citizens and is part of a wider trend. Amendments have been submitted to parliament on several occasions aimed at extending their scope and it is anticipated that such efforts could succeed in the future.

Direct democracy also remains an important political issue at the national level. There have been creative attempts to circumvent the ban on direct popular consultations, especially for the ratification of the EU Constitutional Treaty. A few Members of Parliament suggested at the end of 2004 that if a referendum was not possible, citizens should be asked to voluntarily share with Parliament their "questions, criticisms, doubts and various opinions which the EU constitutional treaty generates." The main francophone parties, in particular the Liberal party, regularly discuss the possibility of popular consultations. Such interest is motivated in part by the need to improve the legitimacy of a discredited political class. Issues of proximity with the people and popular participation have also been on the political agenda in the run-up to the October 2006 municipal elections.

However, many remain deeply sceptical of direct democracy in Belgium. For Jean-Luc Dehaene, former Primer Minister, "everywhere there is a referendum, the debate always ends up covering other issues than what the referendum is about." Belgium's fear of fragmentation and the strength of the prevailing majoritarian model leave little room for further direct democracy in Belgium, especially at the federal level, though future efforts may prove more successful.

SURVEY 3
Global overview of Direct Democracy in selected regions of the world

Quebec

On 30 October 1995, after a long and bitter campaign, a razor-thin margin of 26,000 votes denied Quebec the right to become a sovereign state. Some 93 per cent of voters took part. There were allegations of vote rigging. The media and politicians vehemently criticised the campaign and the very idea of direct democracy, considering that the "near-death experience" had proved "useless, inappropriate, costly, predictable, illegal, and a source of division." In the rest of Canada, "something snapped" as secession suddenly became a realistic threat.

The 1995 referendum was the sixth in a series of provincial and federal referendums, several of which had been used strategically by sovereigntists since modern Canada was created in 1867. The Quebecois had taken part in two federal direct consultations (1898 and 1942) and four provincial referendums. After an initial vote in 1919 on the prohibition of alcohol, Quebec's first referendum on "sovereignty-association" with Canada was in 1980. The separatists were crushed by a 60–40 margin. Many political leaders perceived the ensuing 1992 vote on a special status for Quebec (the Charlottetown agreements) as a "huge mistake". Referendums have become an object of confrontation between separatists and those who believe that the spectre of another consultation scares away investment. According to the polls, between 55 and 60 percent of Quebecois today are tired of the "neverendum referendum" - the debate over whether Quebec should become a separate country - which has dominated Quebec politics for three decades. Even the Bloc Québécois, the sovereigntist party, no longer mentions referendums in its manifesto.

Quebec has nevertheless developed legislation allowing provincial (legislative) and municipal referendums. The former are fairly uncommon, the latter more frequent. In practice, courts have always ensured that referendums remain exceptional. Attempts to introduce a citizens' initiative in western provinces, and binding referendums, were declared unconstitutional by the "Manitoba law" in 1919. It was argued that they usurped the power of the lieutenant governor, as a representative of the crown, and that they interfered with the powers to veto legislation of the federal government, which appoints the lieutenant governors and has the power to instruct them. Any referendum in Canada can therefore only be advisory. There is little hope in this context of a constitutional amendment making direct democracy possible. The political elite, mistrustful of popular consultations and scorched by the 1995 experience, is thus reinforced by legal constraints.

Yet Quebec, and more generally Canada, has tried since the 1970s to experiment – more or less successfully – with participatory democracy and more recently with "cybergovernment" as a means to "communicate directly with the people." The use of commissions on the future of Quebec and commissions involving citizens chosen at random, known as "estates-general", is growing. In Canada, as elsewhere, the weight of history may give way in the future to more direct forms of dialogue with citizens. It could even lead to more, and better, referendums. But for the foreseeable future, the referendum that would never end has come to a halt.

SURVEY 3
Global overview of Direct Democracy in selected regions of the world

France

Although, according to article 3 of the current French Constitution, referendums are one of the two means by which French citizens exercise their sovereignty – alongside parliamentary legislation – their practice is limited. Referendums are not binding, but merely advisory. There is no minimum turnout quorum: in the 1988 consultation on the self-determination of New Caledonia, the abstention rate reached 63 per cent. In essence, French national referendums are not seen as a popular right but as a prerogative of the President designed to ensure his institutional supremacy. Locally, referendums can be used on issues for which sub-national authorities are responsible, but strictly representative democracy remains the norm. There is no right of recall of parliament and no citizens' right of initiative in France, although citizens have a limited right of petition at the local level.

Yet the idea of direct democracy is making progress in France. Although constrained by a plebiscitarian tradition that goes back to the early days of French democracy, French citizens are massively in favour of more and better direct democracy, and there are signs that policy makers may be slowly catching up.

National referendums: a tool for consolidating the President's supremacy

Apart from approving territorial changes, referendums today can be used in France mainly to revise the Constitution and amend legislation. Under article 89, constitutional referendums are mandatory if the proposed revision comes from Parliament. If it comes from the Government, the President can choose to have it approved by Parliament or by the people. In principle, the referendum should be the norm and parliamentary approval the exception. In reality, only one referendum has been used to date, in 2000, to finalise the revision of the Constitution which introduced the five-year presidential term.

The key provision in the Constitution, however, is article 11, which gives the people direct legislative power. The President may "submit to a referendum any government bill which deals with the organisation of the public authorities, or with reforms relating to the economic or social policy of the Nation and to the public services contributing thereto, or which provides for authorisation to ratify a treaty that, although not contrary to the Constitution, would affect the functioning of the institutions" (i.e. essentially EU treaties). The range of issues thus covered is wide, even unclear, giving the Government, Parliament, and, ultimately, the President, huge latitude to determine what is relevant. Laws approved by referendum are equal to laws approved by the Parliament; both may therefore be revised either way at any time.

The rules governing referendum campaigns are not precisely defined either. Problems encountered over the years have been tackled by transposing solutions developed for parliamentary elections. The Constitutional Council oversees the legality of the overall process and the results and the Council of State advises the government on the procedure. The audiovisual authority monitors the campaign strictly to ensure a "fair" allocation of airtime in the media for political parties of a certain size. Unlike in elections, political parties receive no official funding for referendum campaigns. Public authorities must provide citizens with balanced information.

SURVEY 3
Global overview of Direct Democracy in selected regions of the world

Overall, referendums are a tool in the hands of the President. In theory, Parliament and the government can propose legislative referendums (not the people). In reality, no referendum has ever been initiated by Parliament so far in France, despite an attempt by the Senate in July 1984 to organise a popular vote on the reform of private schools. Proposals therefore normally come from the Government, and must be approved by the President. If he (or perhaps one day, she) belongs to the same political majority, he in effect controls the Government. When the President and the government represent different political families – "la cohabitation" – the President can veto the government's proposal even if, politically, it is unlikely that a President would refuse to allow citizens to express their opinion. This situation has never occurred. Overall, there would really be no possible obstacle to a President who was determined to organise a referendum.

The recent but promising advent of local popular consultations
Since 1992, "territorial units of the Republic" – communes, departments, regions, special-status areas and overseas territories – can organise local referendums on issues for which they are competent. Although strictly limited in time, local "petitions" were introduced in 1995. A fifth of voters registered in the commune can request a consultation from the municipal council on a construction project for which the council is responsible. Local popular votes have been binding since 2003, with a quorum of 50% of registered voters. They have been used increasingly regularly since 1990 – overall on average about two per month – and are slowly but surely becoming a normal feature of local democracy.

A damaged reputation
French public opinion and decision makers' perception of direct democracy is deeply influenced by a history of authoritarian use. "Referendum-plebiscites," as they are sometimes called, were indeed used from 1799 (by Napoleon Bonaparte) to 1969 (by General de Gaulle) as a pretext for asking the people to demonstrate its allegiance to its political leaders. In total, 24 referendums have been organised in France since the 1789 French Revolution (Table 1).

Referendums played a marginal role during the revolutionary period, although direct democracy was the object of much intellectual attention and later inspired other countries. The 1789 French Declaration of the Rights of Man and the Citizen made referendums possible: "The law is the expression of the general will; all citizens have the right to contribute personally, or through their representatives, to the making of laws." Condorcet wrote about the possibility of organising popular initiatives. He proposed complex direct democracy mechanisms in 1793 for a new democratic national constitution (the "Montagnard" Constitution). Although his proposals were never implemented, the Revolution conceptualised fundamental principles of modern democracy, including the constitutional initiative and legislative referendums. The two consultations of 1793 and 1795 on ambitious draft constitutions were unfortunately followed by the "Terror" and Napoleon used the 1799 referendum to seize power. The following seven referendums organised during the 19th century – four by Napoleon, three by his nephew, Louis-Napoleon – were largely used to bolster the Bonapartist regimes, sometimes very explicitly, as when the people was asked to make "Bonaparte Consul for life", or give his family hereditary control over power.

SURVEY 3
GLOBAL OVERVIEW OF DIRECT DEMOCRACY IN SELECTED REGIONS OF THE WORLD

Unsurprisingly, French democrats became very wary of direct popular consultation. The long battle against anti-democratic forces during the second half of the 19th century and the first half of the 20th century generated a dogmatic culture of representative democracy based on the notion of popular sovereignty. Only elected representatives could promote the general interest and the people's role was limited to choosing elected officials. Local referendums were quite popular at the end of the 19th and the beginning of the 20th century, but were forbidden because of attempts by anti-republican forces to use them to destabilise democracy. Like Interior Minister Ernest Constans, many believed at the end of the 19th century that "the consultation of electors on an administrative municipal question goes without doubt against the representative regime (…)". Local referendums were eventually outlawed in 1905.

In the 1920s, however, two political thinkers, Carré de Malberg and Tardieu, recommended greater use of referendums to counter the dominance of parliament. Their thinking deeply influenced General de Gaulle who in 1945 imposed a referendum – against the reluctance of the main political parties – to give legitimacy to the Constitution of the Fourth Republic. On October 21, 1945 the French approved the creation of a constitutional assembly and thus expressed their opinion directly on a legislative issue for the first time since 1870. In May 1946, French citizens rejected the Constitution proposed by the assembly in France's first ever negative referendum. These two referendums demonstrated that popular votes could be used democratically and did not automatically favour the country's leaders.

In the following ten years, referendums appeared as a possible tool for strengthening the President's supremacy against an all-powerful parliament. In 1958, the Constitution of the (current) Fifth Republic allowed referendums on other than constitutional matters for the first time in France's history. Yet referendums did not become a regular feature of French political life. Only eight legislative referendums have been organised since 1958, approximately one every five years. Three were used to modify France's territory, two to amend the Constitution, and three to ratify EU treaties. There were no referendums at all between 1972 and 1988, i.e. two full presidential mandates, revealing how popular consultations are not essential to the French political system, but only an option left at the discretion of the Head of State.

Referendums were also associated with plebiscites until 1969, when De Gaulle resigned after his proposals were rejected. Although all subsequent Presidents have systematically stated that they would not resign if a majority rejected their proposal, Jacques Chirac needed to do so repeatedly in the May 2005 referendum on the EU Constitution. And yet the campaign was still dubbed the "Raffarindum", as the people's vote was believed to determine the future career of France's unpopular Prime Minister, Jean-Pierre Raffarin. President Chirac only agreed with great reluctance to organise the 2000 and 2005 consultations and future presidents will most probably be just as cautious after the nerve-wracking 2005 campaign which led to a massive rejection of the EU Constitutional Treaty. This was already apparent when French authorities preferred the parliamentary procedure to popular approval for the Amsterdam (1999) and Nice (2001) treaties, after the 1992 Maastricht Treaty was approved by only a very narrow margin.

SURVEY 3
GLOBAL OVERVIEW OF DIRECT DEMOCRACY IN SELECTED REGIONS OF THE WORLD

At the local level, popular consultations were reintroduced in 1971, but only for consulting people on the opportunity of merging two municipalities. After failed attempts in the late 1970s to widen the scope of local referendums, reforms were introduced in 1992, 1995 – with, for the first time in France's history, a citizens' right of initiative – and 2003. Relatively few "local initiative referendums" have been organised, however, and the overall impact on local democracy has been limited.

Table 1: French National Referendums

DATE	ISSUE	ABSTENTION RATE	RESULTS (% OF VOTES)	
			YES	NO
4 AUGUST 1793	Constitution of 24 June 1793	73.3	99.32	0.68
22 AUG. 1795	Constitution of 5 Fructidar Year III (1799)	86.3	95.62	4.38
13 DEC. 1799	Constitution of Year VIII (1799)	96.2	63.75	36.25
2 AUGUST 1800	Bonaparte 1st Consul	56.9	99.9	0.1
10 MAY 1802	Consulate for life	48.8	99.8	0.2
6 NOV. 1804	Napoleon is given imperial status	66.7	99.7	0.3
22 APRIL 1815	Amendment to the constitutions of the Empire	81.2	99.65	0.35
20-21 DEC. 1851	Louis-Napoleon is given greater powers and a ten-year presidency	20.3	92.1	1.9
21-22 NOV. 1852	A hereditary empire is reinstated for Louis-Napoleon	20.3	96.9	3.1
8 MAY 1870	Parliamentary empire	16.9	82.4	7.6
21 OCT. 1945	Assembly is granted constitutional powers	20.1	96.4	3.6
21 OCT. 1945	Transitional regime	20.1	66.27	33.63
5 MAY 1946	Constitution project	19.3	47	53
13 OCT. 1946	Approval of the Constitution of the Fourth Republic	31.4	53.57	46.33
28 SEPT. 1958	Approval of the Constitution of the Fifth Republic	17.37	82.6	17.4
8 JANUARY 1961	Self-determination for Algeria	26.24	74.99	25.01
8 APRIL 1962	Evian Agreements on the independence of Algeria; De Gaulle proposes the direct election of the President by the people	24.66	90.81	9.19

SURVEY 3
Global overview of Direct Democracy in selected regions of the world

Date	Issue	Abstention Rate	Results (% of votes) Yes	No
28 Oct. 1962	Revision of the Constitution: direct election of the President	23.03	62.25	37.75
27 April 1969	Creation of the Regions and changes in the Senate	19.87	47.59	52.41
23 April 1972	Ratification of the EEC enlargement treaty	39.76	68.32	31.68
6 Nov. 1988	Self-determination for New Caledonia	63.10	79.99	20.00
20 Sept. 1992	Ratification of the Maastricht Treaty	30.31	51.04	48.95
24 Sept. 2000	Length of Presidential mandate reduced to 5 years	69.68	73.21	26.79
29 May 2005	Ratification of the EU Constitutional Treaty	30.26	45.13	54.87

Plus ça change... from representative to participatory and direct democracy

French politics has changed significantly since Montesquieu once wrote that people are remarkably competent to choose to whom they should entrust their authority, but not to manage themselves. While French politicians have traditionally been hostile to referendums, France has organised referendums slightly more frequently over the past twenty years than before: nine since 1958 (a small figure, admittedly, compared to the hundred plus laws approved each year by the Parliament). Opinion polls show that a majority of the French favour using referendums more often. They wish their votes to be separated from the person who asks the question. Most people would also welcome a citizens' right of initiative. But are French political leaders ready to catch up with the general public mood?

For French political officials, referendums are not an everyday means to "democratise democracy." Popular consultations have rarely been an electoral issue. They were briefly on the political agenda in the early 1990s when local referendums were introduced and President François Mitterrand suggested extending the range of topics to which referendums could be applied. In 1993, a reform allowing one-fifth of voters in each French department to initiate a referendum was considered but rejected. Once elected in 1995, President Jacques Chirac extended the scope of referendums to "social and economic policy and public services," covering a potentially huge range of issues. Since then, however, referendums and direct democracy have largely been a non-issue. An attempt in 1999 to introduce a draft law allowing local, regional and national popular initiatives failed and a similar proposal, introduced in June 2002, has made little progress. Direct democracy is not a political priority in France. Because laws approved by referendum are considered to be the "direct expression of the people's will" and as such are not controlled by the Constitutional Council, French officials fear that they could damage fundamental public liberties. Most also think that "the introduction of a citizen's right of initiative could have multiple and unpredictable consequences."

SURVEY 3
GLOBAL OVERVIEW OF DIRECT DEMOCRACY
IN SELECTED REGIONS OF THE WORLD

At the local level, democracy is still dominated by a parliamentary conception of representation and the general interest that goes against a more extensive use of popular consultation. Most of all, the key difficulty remains the tendency for referendums to be used as a general vote of confidence in the Executive rather than as a decision on a specific issue. In the 2005 consultation, the primary explanation given by voters for their rejection of the EU Treaty was "bad economic and social conditions in France", a reason related more to the management abilities of the Government than the merits of the Treaty.

On the other hand, the keenly fought 2005 campaign may profoundly reshape French perceptions of referendums. The intense debate on French and EU matters contrasted sharply not only with debates in other countries, but also with the image of referendums as a tool to enable the President to register people's stamp of approval directly on crucial political issues at strategic moments, or as a last resort solution in situations of institutional deadlock. Many noted voters' eagerness to get involved in public debates and decision-making and their mistrust of the advice of political representatives. Indeed, the campaign triggered huge interest, as demonstrated by the very high turnout (nearly 70%). Copies of books commenting on the EU Treaty topped library sales for weeks ahead of the vote. For the first time in years, French citizens had the opportunity to conduct a rich, multi-level, multi-entry debate about the future of French and EU society and they seized it fully. According to polls, voters felt that party political arguments over the heads of citizens did not provide the clear, unbiased information they expected in order to make their own, informed choice. Tentative signs that French politicians may be rising to the challenge can perhaps be found in the slow development in previous years of participatory democracy in France.

The "top-down" division between the governing and the governed that has reigned in France for two hundred years is thus being challenged. Many French citizens and policy makers are realising that the legitimacy of a public decision does not depend solely on who made it, but also on how it was made. How fast French political elites will provide new means to deliberate and decide with citizens is unclear though. Perhaps the 2007 presidential election will allow such discussions. To date, however, no party or any possible presidential candidate has yet mentioned direct democracy in its manifesto.

SURVEY 4
Glossary of direct-democracy terms

A

Abrogative referendum Popular (referendum) vote by means of which voters may retain or repeal a law or decree that has been agreed and promulgated by the legislature and already implemented.

Accumulation The capacity to cast more than one vote for a favoured candidate. In Switzerland electoral constituencies that are allocated more than one seat on the National Council and where the election is therefore conducted according to the system of proportional representation, the name of any candidate may be entered twice on any ballot paper.

Acquisition of citizenship The administrative acquisition of (Swiss) citizenship as the result of an official decision by the authorities.

Administrative referendum The right granted to eligible voters to hold a referendum on an administrative or governmental decision made by parliament. The Finance Referendum is one kind of administrative referendum.

Agenda initiative A direct democracy procedure which enables a number of citizens to submit a proposal which must be considered by the legislature but is not put to a vote of the electorate.

Alternative proposal A synonym for counter-proposal.

Approval quorum A requirement for passing a (referendum) vote which takes the form of a minimum number or percentage of the entire electorate whose support is necessary for a proposal to be passed.

Assembly democracy Democratic system where eligible voters exercise their political rights in an assembly. Assembly democracy – the original form of democracy – is widespread in Switzerland. There are citizens' assemblies in the majority of communes. In two cantons (Glarus and Appenzell Inner-Rhodes), popular assemblies are held at the cantonal level.

Authorities' initiative Relates to the issuing of a single act which is within the area of competence of parliament and which would be subject to referendum if it were issued by parliament. Decisions or acts within the parliament's area of competence are not subject to the authorities' initiative, nor are decisions or decrees within the area of competence of the government and the administration – though the rules governing competence can be changed through the avenue of the popular initiative. In Switzerland a number of cantons provide for the authorities' initiative (also known as the "parliamentary decision initiative").

B

Ballot paper (for elections) The official form which eligible voters must use for elections. For the elections to the Swiss National Council, voters can fill out a special, non pre-printed form themselves, and may change the form or make additions to it.

Ballot paper; voting slip The official ballot paper, on which voters mark or indicate their choice, e.g. indicate with a Yes or No whether they accept or reject the referendum proposal.

Ballot text Text which appears on the ballot paper, typically in the form of a question or a series of options. For a referendum it may be a specified question text, or a question seeking agreement or rejection of a text; for an initiative, a question asking for agreement or rejection of a proposal identified by the title of the popular initiative; for a recall, a question asking for agreement or rejection of the early termination of office of a specified office holder.

Binding Description of a (referendum) vote where, if a proposal passes, the government or appropriate authority is legally compelled to implement it.

SURVEY 4
Glossary of direct-democracy terms

C

Candidate Person who can be elected. In Switzerland a candidate's name is entered on a list for the election to the National Council. In electoral constituencies that have been allocated only one seat and where the majority system therefore applies, any citizen of voting age may be elected.

Canton A member state of the Swiss Confederation. The cantons – also frequently referred to in Switzerland as the "states" – are the original states which joined together in a federation in 1848 and ceded a part of their sovereignty to it. Switzerland has 26 cantons.

Cantonal initiative Non-binding right of submission of a proposal by a canton. Any canton may submit a draft decree for approval by the Federal Assembly or suggest that a proposal be worked up into a formal bill. In a number of cantons, the cantonal initiative can be demanded via a popular initiative.

Cantonal majority In the case of a mandatory referendum, a majority of the cantons is required in addition to a popular majority in order for the proposal that has been submitted to the People to be accepted. It is accepted when the popular vote has been in favour of the proposal in a majority of the cantons. In calculating the majority, the results in the cantons of Obwalden, Nidwalden, Basel City, Basel Country, Appenzell Outer-Rhodes and Appenzell Inner-Rhodes each count as half a cantonal vote.

Capable of carrying through a (facultative) referendum process Not a legal term. Groups are referred to as "fit for referendum" if they are considered capable of gathering the required number of signatures to formally launch a facultative referendum.

Chambers (of the bi-cameral parliament) In Switzerland the Council of States and the National Council each form one chamber of the parliament.

Citizen-friendly In the context of initiatives and referendums, the degree to which the rules on thresholds, hurdles, quorums, voting methods etc. make the process as free and fair as possible for the eligible voter.

Citizen-initiated referendum A referendum which is called by a formal demand made by a given number of citizens.

Citizens' Initiative A synonym for popular initiative.

Compulsory voting Duty of the eligible voters to participate in the election or referendum vote. The voter may cast a blank vote, i.e. not choose any of the given options. In Switzerland, forms of compulsory voting are known in 11 cantons.

Consensus democracy A form of democracy which aims to involve as large a number of players (political parties, trade unions, minorities, social groups) in the political process as possible and to reach decisions by consensus. Because it is relatively easy to overturn a parliamentary decision in a referendum, both parliament and – even before the matter is debated in parliament – also the government must look for compromise solutions which will satisfy all the important political groups capable of launching a referendum. It was the referendum which led historically to the formation of consensus democracy.

Constitutionality The quality of being in accordance with and not contradictory to the constitution of a country.

Constructive referendum A popular proposal which is linked to a referendum. The constructive referendum gives a certain number of eligible voters the right to present a counter-proposal to a decree which is subject to the optional referendum. The counter-proposal is presented together with the decree. In Switzerland this possibility currently exists in the cantons of Bern and Nidwalden.

SURVEY 4
Glossary of direct-democracy terms

Consultation The consultation is an important stage in the Swiss legislative process. Draft laws and constitutional amendments which have far-reaching political, economic or cultural effects, are circulated amongst all interested parties, who can submit their comments.

Consultative referendum A politically significant but legally non-binding ballot decision – which may have included citizens who are not registered voters. The consultative referendum can in principle have as subject-matter anything with which the state concerns itself or wishes to concern itself. A consultative referendum is a contradiction in terms, it refers to a decision of the electorate, which is legally not a decision but an advice. Very often what is called a "consultative referendum" is in fact, in the terminology that is used here, a plebiscite.

Council of States The smaller chamber of the Federal Parliament (Federal Assembly) in Switzerland, comprising 46 members. The Council of States is the chamber representing the cantons because its members act as delegates of their respective cantons. Nowadays, the members of the Council of States are elected in their cantons by the citizens there who are eligible to vote, in the same way as the members of the National Council, but according to regulations laid down under cantonal law.

Counter-proposal A proposal to be presented to a (referendum) vote as an alternative to the proposal contained in a popular initiative or referendum. The counterproposal may originate in the legislature or in a given number of citizens. In Switzerland the Federal Assembly may submit a counter-proposal both to a general popular initiative and to a formulated popular initiative in the event that it wishes to address the concern raised in the popular initiative but wants to deal with the matter in a different way from that proposed by the authors of the initiative. In such a case, a vote is held in accordance with the rules on the double yes vote.

D

Deciding question Where an original initiative and a counter-proposal are to be voted on in the same referendum, there is the possibility of a Double Yes result, as voters may vote in favour of both proposals. In such cases, the deciding question is used to determine which version should be implemented should both proposals be approved.

Direct counter-proposal A proposal (e.g. a draft law) which enters the decision-making process at the same stage as the initiative and is voted on in the referendum together with the original proposal and as a specific alternative to it.

Direct democracy A form of state in which the sovereign power is held by the People i.e. national sovereignty belongs directly to the People. The People also exercise their sovereignty directly, for example by means of popular legislation (the People propose and approve the laws). This is the essential distinction between "direct" and "indirect" democracy.

Direct democracy procedure Procedures which a) include the right of citizens to participate directly in the political decision-making process on issues and b) at the same time are designed and work as instruments of power-sharing which empower citizens. The following types of procedures can be distinguished: referendums, initiatives and counter-proposals. Each type of procedure exists in different forms, and each form can be institutionalized in various ways. Forms of referendums are: citizen-initiated referendums (popular referendums), referendums initiated by a representative authority, referendums initiated by a minority of a representative authority, mandatory (obligatory) referendums. Forms of initiatives are: popular initiative (citizens' initiative), agenda initiative. Forms of counter-proposals are: counter-proposals made by an authority (for example by parliament), counter-proposal made by citizens.

SURVEY 4
Glossary of direct-democracy terms

Direct initiative procedure Procedure where the initiative proposal bypasses the legislature and is placed directly on the ballot once the petition signatures are verified.

Double "Yes" If a counter-proposal in response to a popular initiative is submitted, the voters may approve both the counter-proposal and the initiative and at the same time indicate which of the two they would prefer if both were approved. The proposal (initiative or counter-proposal) that is ultimately accepted is that which receives the most "Yes" votes.

Double majority Requirement for a proposal to pass which includes both a majority of the overall total votes cast and a majority of the votes in at least a specified proportion of defined electoral areas. In Switzerland a double majority of People and States (cantons) is required for obligatory referendums. In other words, in order to be accepted, a majority of cantons must have voted in favour, in addition to an overall majority of all those who voted. This means that all the votes cast are counted twice: once for the overall number, and then for each separate canton. At least 50%+1 of those who voted (the "People"), plus a majority of the cantons, must approve the proposal. In calculating the cantonal majority, it must be remembered that the cantons of Obwalden, Nidwalden, Basel City, Basel Country, Appenzell Outer-Rhodes and Appenzell Inner-Rhodes each have half a cantonal vote. In the case of referendums held to approve or reject laws, a simple majority of the votes cast is sufficient.

E
Elected Chosen to a public office through an election.

Election Procedure by which the members of certain authorities or other public bodies are appointed through being voted for by those eligible to vote or by the members of an electoral body (in Switzerland e.g. Federal Assembly, Federal Council).

Election by simple majority Electoral system in which the seats to be allocated go to those obtaining a majority of the votes, while those obtaining a minority, even when it is only slightly less, receive no seats. In Switzerland the rules of the majority system apply, for example, to the elections to the Federal Council and to the Federal Supreme Court. The elections to the National Council, on the other hand, are governed by the system of proportional representation, with the exception of elections in electoral constituencies that have been allocated only one seat.

Elector Used here as a synonym for "voter". Other authors use "elector" for a person who has the right to vote in an election and "voter" for a person who has the right to vote in a referendum.

Electoral constituency The election to the National Council is held throughout the confederation at the same time. The cantons form the electoral constituencies.

Electorate The total number of eligible voters.

Eligible voter/s Person/s who has/have the right to vote.

E-voting / electronic voting Form of voting where the voters are able to vote with the aid of a special electronic voting system by completing an "electronic ballot paper", which is then sent via a data network to the office responsible for the vote. In Switzerland the cantons of Geneva, Zurich and Neuchâtel are currently conducting electronic voting pilot schemes under the auspices of the Federal Chancellery, whereby the primary concern is to ensure the security of the procedure (preservation of voting secrecy, prevention of voting fraud).

Explanation from the Federal Council cf. Referendum booklet.

SURVEY 4
Glossary of direct-democracy terms

F

Facultative/optional referendum A procedure that leads to a (referendum) vote which is called by a formal demand, which may emanate from a given number of citizens or, but not exclusively, from a state representative body (government, parliament, president or some other defined agent). If the right to call a popular vote procedure belongs exclusively to a state representative body, the procedure in question is, in the terminology used here, not a referendum but a plebiscite. In Switzerland a popular (referendum) vote is held if 50,000 eligible voters or eight cantons have requested a referendum (referendum requested by the cantons) on, for example, a new or amended federal act or on an international treaty. The relevant decree of the Federal Assembly is approved if the People vote in favour of it (popular majority).

(Swiss) Federal administration The Swiss Federal Administration includes the central federal administration with its seven Departments (ministries), the Federal Chancellery, the general secretariats and Federal Offices, together with the decentralised federal administration with its government commissions and other units under administrative control, as well as independent institutions and businesses. Among the main tasks of the Federal Administration are the implementation of decrees issued by the Federal Assembly, and in particular of federal acts, as well as the duties assigned by the Federal Council, including the preparation of Federal Council business and legislation. Each department is headed by a member of the Federal Council, and the Federal Chancellery by the Federal Chancellor. The autonomous federal public law undertakings such as the Swiss National Accident Insurance Organisation (SUVA) and the Swiss National Bank do not form part of the Federal Administration.

(Swiss) Federal Assembly (Federal Parliament) The highest authority of the legislature in the Swiss Confederation (legislative power), consisting of two chambers, the National Council and the Council of States. The two chambers normally deal with their business (federal legislation, budgetary decisions, international treaties, etc.) separately, and a decree is valid only when it has been approved by both chambers. For elections (of members of the Federal Council, judges of the Federal Supreme Court, the Federal Chancellor) as well as for the receipt of declarations made by the Federal Council on significant issues, the National Council and Council of States meet together as the United Chambers of the Federal Assembly.

(Swiss) Federal Chancellery As the general administrative office of the Swiss Federal Council, the Federal Chancellery coordinates Federal Council business and is also the office of the President of the Confederation. In addition, it has special responsibility for political rights, is in charge of official publications (Federal Gazette, compilations of federal legislation) and coordinates the release of information to the public and the translation services for the Federal Administration. The Federal Chancellery is headed by the Federal Chancellor.

(Swiss) Federal Constitution The Federal Constitution is the supreme legislative act of the Swiss Confederation and forms the legal foundation for all other legislation and for the federal structure of the state. It regulates the fundamental rights and duties of citizens and of the entire population as well as the structure and powers of the federal authorities. Any total revision or amendment (partial revision) of the Federal Constitution must be submitted to the People and the cantons for approval (mandatory referendum).

(Swiss) Federal Council (Government) The national government, i.e. the highest authority of the executive in the Swiss Confederation (executive power). The Federal Council has seven members, who are elected by the United Chambers of the Federal Assembly, and has the task of managing and supervising the Federal Administration. The Federal Chancellor is head

Survey 4
Glossary of direct-democracy terms

of the general administrative office of the government, the Federal Chancellery. The Federal President chairs the meetings of the Federal Council.

(Swiss) Federal Court The highest authority of the judicial power in the Swiss Confederation. The Federal Supreme Court, as the supreme court of appeal, is responsible for ensuring that court decisions conform to the Constitution, and is the only court with jurisdiction in federal law cases that cannot be dealt with by cantonal courts, e.g. those relating to certain criminal offences against the state. The various chambers of the Federal Supreme Court are specialised courts in a variety of legal fields such as those of bankruptcy, civil, criminal and administrative law. The Federal Insurance Court in Lucerne has jurisdiction in cases relating to social insurance law.

Federal decree A ruling by the Swiss Federal Assembly on constitutional provisions, important single acts and general decisions. A Federal decree that is not subject to approval by referendum is called a "simple Federal decree".

Federal law/Federal Act Decree of the Swiss Federal Assembly that is of general application and of unlimited duration and which directly creates rights or obligations in relation to those persons affected by it, i.e. that creates law. This form of federal decree must be promulgated as a federal law and is subject to an optional referendum; in the case of urgent federal laws that have no basis in the constitution, a vote of the People and the cantons must be held (mandatory referendum).

Federal popular (referendum) vote. In general, any vote at the Swiss federal level is designated a "popular vote", as the result of the vote of the cantons is determined by the voting of the eligible voters in each canton. A popular vote in the true sense, i.e. a ballot in which the eligible voters alone vote and not the cantons, is for example held in the case of an optional referendum.

Federation In Switzerland, the institutions of the central, "national" level of politics – the federal government, parliament and authorities.

Finance referendum Also referred to as the "referendum on public expenditure". Such referendums relate to parliamentary decisions on public expenditure, and therefore differ from referendums on new or amended legislation. Any parliamentary decision which involves the expenditure of public money can be the subject of a finance referendum. Although this form of referendum does not exist at the Swiss national (federal) level, it is widely used at both cantonal and local levels.

Formulated popular initiative proposal (for partial revision of the federal constitution). In Switzerland a popular initiative by means of which 100,000 eligible voters can demand the partial revision of the Federal Constitution. The initiative proposal is presented as a properly formulated draft bill.

Fundamental right Fundamental human right. Fundamental rights do not only guarantee the legally enforceable claims of individuals; as objective principles, fundamental rights permeate the entire system of law and order. They are binding on all organs of the state, especially the legislature.

G

General popular initiative In Switzerland a popular initiative by which a minimum of 100,000 eligible voters may, in the form of a general proposal, request the adoption, amendment or repeal of a constitutional or legislative provision. The general popular initiative is an innovation that was accepted by the People in a popular vote on 9 February 2003.

SURVEY 4
GLOSSARY OF DIRECT-DEMOCRACY TERMS

H

HARMONISATION In Switzerland the so-called "harmonisation" (of differences) takes place when both chambers of the Federal Assembly have debated a proposal in detail and have approved it by a majority in each case, but where the precise wording of the decrees or acts from the two chambers differs. The subsequent debates concern only the differences.

HUMAN RIGHTS These are rights which belong to everyone by virtue of being human. They are inalienable: they cannot be denied by law. Examples of human rights are the right to life, to freedom of religion and to freedom of speech.

I

INDIRECT COUNTER-PROPOSAL A proposal which is not presented as a formal alternative to an original initiative proposal. In Switzerland the indirect counter-proposal may come from parliament or the government and enters the decision-making process at the same level as the original initiative proposal.

INDIVIDUAL INITIATIVE (IN ZURICH) In the canton Zurich an initiative can be launched by a single individual. The initiative will go to (referendum) ballot if it is supported by the Cantonal Council.

INDIRECT INITIATIVE PROCEDURE Procedure where the initiative does involve the legislature and the initiative proposal must be considered by the government and parliament before it is placed on the ballot.

INITIAL PROPOSAL The first text deposited by the proponents of a referendum, initiative or recall.

INITIAL SIGNATURE QUORUM Minimum number of signatures required to launch an initiative.

INITIATIVE A procedure which allows a certain number of citizens to submit a proposal to be dealt with by the legislature. One form (popular initiative) leads to a (referendum) vote, a second (agenda initiative) to the consideration of the proposal by the legislature.

INITIATIVE COMMITTEE The proponents of the initiative. In Switzerland an initiative must be submitted by a minimum of 7 and a maximum of 27 sponsors. An absolute majority of the sponsors has the right to withdraw the initiative.

L

LEGALITY The quality of being in accordance and not in conflict with the laws of a country or with international law.

LEGALITY CHECK The scrutiny by a public authority of the constitutionality and legality of a proposal.

LEGISLATIVE INITIATIVE A legislative initiative can demand that a law be enacted, amended, supplemented or repealed. All Swiss cantons make use of the device of the legislative initiative.

LEGISLATIVE REFERENDUM Referendum vote on laws. All laws passed by parliament in all Swiss cantons are subject to popular referendum. In some cantons this is obligatory, in others optional.

LEGISLATURE The constitutional organ that is empowered to make law through the formal enactment of legislation.

LIST (OF CANDIDATES FOR ELECTIONS) List with names of eligible candidates. In Switzerland lists of candidates for elections are examined and, if required, corrected by the relevant canton and by the Federal Chancellery. They are numbered and given a title for easier identification.

M

MINIMUM PARTICIPATION/TURN-OUT QUORUM IN A (REFERENDUM) VOTE. It is possible to make the validity of the ballot dependent on a minimum number of eligible voters having taken part.

SURVEY 4
Glossary of direct-democracy terms

Minimum participation quorums used to be required in some places. The subject is once again a matter for debate in certain areas. The demand for minimum quorums is problematic, however, as they can falsify the result of a referendum if, for example, both No-votes and Non-votes are counted together.

Multiple option vote The voter is able to choose between a number of different versions of the same basic proposal presented on the same occasion. Multiple option votes occur when an initiative proposal and a counter-proposal by the parliament, two or more initiative proposals, or a referendum proposal by parliament and a counter-proposal initiated by eligible voters are put to the vote at the same time.

N

(Swiss) National Council The larger chamber of the Swiss Federal Parliament (Federal Assembly), the National Council has 200 members. It is also known as the People's Chamber, because its members are elected in a general election by the People, the citizens who are eligible to vote.

(Swiss) National languages There are four national languages in Switzerland. The most widely used language is German, followed by French, Italian and Rhaeto-Romanic, an ancient variety of Latin still spoken in Alpine regions, but currently struggling to survive.

O

Obligatory/mandatory referendum A (referendum) vote which is called automatically under circumstances defined in the constitution or in legislation. In Switzerland a popular (referendum) vote must be held if the Federal Assembly decides to carry out a total or partial revision of the Federal Constitution, to join an organisation for collective security (e.g. the UN) or a supranational community (e.g. the EU), or to introduce urgent federal legislation without the required constitutional basis. Such a decision requires the approval of both the popular majority and the majority of the cantons. A referendum is also mandatory for popular initiatives aimed at a total revision of the federal constitution; for popular initiatives aimed at a partial revision of the federal constitution which were presented as a general proposal and which have been rejected in the Federal Assembly; and to reach a decision where the two Councils have disagreed as to whether a total revision of the federal constitution should take place or not. In all three cases, the referendum is decided by a simple majority of the voters.

P

Partial revision (of the constitution). Parts of the constitution are revised.

Participation/turnout The number of eligible voters (expressed as the actual number or as a percentage of the electorate) who turned out to vote in a referendum ballot or election. The turnout figure is the total of all the ballot papers, whether valid, invalid or blank.

Pass A popular (referendum) vote passes when it is valid and the prescribed majority requirements for approval of the proposal within it are met.

Penalty (for failing to vote where there is compulsory voting). The term "voting sanction" is used in cases where there is a penalty for failing to comply with the compulsory voting rule. In Switzerland such sanctions exist only in the canton Schaffhausen and in a number of communes in the canton Graubünden

Petition Written submission with no particular form that any person may send to an authority. A petition may contain a proposal, a criticism or a request, and the subject matter may be any state activity. In Switzerland the federal authorities must acknowledge a petition, but need not respond to it.

Plebiscite A public consultation controlled "from above". In the case of a plebiscite, it is

Survey 4
Glossary of direct-democracy terms

the "powers that be" – usually the President or Prime Minister – which decide when and on what subject the people will be asked to give their opinion. Such polls are frequently only consultative i.e. their results are not formally binding on parliament or government. In reality, plebiscites are instruments of power which those in power use in an attempt to reinforce or salvage that power with the help of the people. Their aim is not to implement democracy, but to provide a kind of legitimacy for decisions those in power have already taken. In the terminology used here, plebiscites are not classified as direct democracy procedures, because they do not fulfil the criteria of power-sharing.

Political rights Political rights are the fundamental rights of the People under direct democracy. They enable citizens of voting age to participate in the shaping of law and politics in the state. Political rights include the right to vote and the right to participate in elections, as well as the right to submit a popular initiative or referendum request, and the right to sign such a request.

Popular assembly Assembly of eligible voters. One of the oldest (pre-modern) forms of democracy, still practised today in Appenzell Inner-Rhodes and Glarus. The eligible voters of a canton or a commune gather in the open air on a certain day in order to elect the government and reach decisions about laws and public expenditure. Everyone has the right to speak on any issue. Voting is by show of hands. By its very nature, the popular assembly is unable to respect the principle of secrecy of voting demanded in modern forms of democracy.

Popular initiative A direct democracy procedure and a political right that allows a given number of citizens to put their own proposal on the political agenda and initiate a (referendum) vote on it. The proposal may be, for example, to amend the constitution, adopt a new law, or repeal or amend an already existing law. Whether the proposal is put to a vote of the electorate or not is not at the discretion of the authorities. The initiative procedure may include a withdrawal clause, which gives the registered committee (sponsors) the possibility to withdraw their initiative, for example in the event that the legislature has taken action to fulfil the demands of the initiative or part of them.

Popular initiative for a complete revision of the federal constitution. In Switzerland, a popular initiative by which a minimum of 100,000 eligible voters may propose the total revision of the Federal Constitution.

Popular majority A popular majority is equivalent to a majority of the valid votes cast. In Switzerland the adoption of a new Constitution or of amendments to the Constitution (mandatory referendum) require both a popular majority and a majority of the cantons. For new acts and amendments to acts (optional referendum), only a popular majority is required.

Popular referendum A synonym for citizen-initiated referendum. In Switzerland, popular referendum is also used as a synonym for optional referendum.

Popular referendum vote cf. (Federal) popular (referendum) vote

Popular submission (Solothurn) In the canton Solothurn, 100 registered voters have the right to present a written submission to the parliament. The parliament treats the submission in the same way as a submission from one of its members.

Postal voting Method of voting in which voters send their ballot papers to the office responsible for the vote by post and are not required to go to the polling station in order to vote.

Proponents The persons who first sign and deposit an initiative proposal, and are registered as such. In Switzerland a synonym is "initiative committee".

SURVEY 4
Glossary of direct-democracy terms

Proposal The complete text of a referendum or initiative.

Publication The act of making a proposal for an initiative public by the appropriate authority after it has been registered and checked for compliance with the substantive and formal requirements of registration.

Qualification for the ballot The act of declaration by the appropriate authority that verification of a citizen-initiated referendum or a popular initiative has been completed and additionally, in the case of a popular initiative, that the legislature has taken all steps to submit any desired counter-proposal.

Q

Qualified majority A majority requirement demanding that for a proposal to be passed, it must receive a proportion of the vote in excess of 50% plus 1 – for example 2/3 or 3/4.

Quorum The minimum level of support required for a vote to pass a proposal.

R

Recall A procedure that allows a specified number of citizens to demand a vote on whether an elected holder of public office should be removed from that office before the end of his/her term of office. The Swiss parliament, unlike parliaments in other countries, cannot bring the government down, nor can the government dissolve parliament. In a few cantons, citizens have the right to recall parliament or the government by means of a popular initiative.

Recall of an initiative A procedure that allows the proponents of an initiative to withdraw their proposal. In Switzerland a popular initiative can be recalled or withdrawn by the initiative committee. At the federal level, recall is permitted only up to the time when the government announces the date for the referendum. An initiative presented as a general proposal can no longer be withdrawn once the Federal Assembly has approved it.

Referendum A direct democracy procedure which includes a popular (referendum) vote on e.g. a constitutional amendment or a bill; the right of the electorate to either accept or reject the issue, which may originate from a decision or proposal of the authorities or from a popular initiative. Note: a popular vote procedure, which is controlled exclusively by the authorities, is not a referendum but a plebiscite. In Switzerland voters can decide on – accept or reject – new or amended constitutional provisions, federal acts, and certain other decrees of the Federal Assembly (federal decrees).

Referendum booklet (explanatory booklet or pamphlet) Also known as the "Explanation from the Federal Council". In Switzerland, a pamphlet or booklet in which the proposal(s) being submitted to the voters are explained and which includes the arguments of the committee responsible for the initiative or referendum together with the opinion of the Federal Council, is published by the Federal Chancellery in the four official national languages and sent to all eligible voters via the communes along with the other voting documents three to four weeks before the voting day.

Referendum initiated by authorities Some Swiss cantonal constitutions provide for the cantonal parliament to submit to referendum a decree which is not subject to an obligatory referendum.

Referendum on international treaties At the Swiss national level, all international treaties which are of unlimited duration and which may not be terminated, provide for accession to international organisations or introduce a multilateral harmonisation of law are subject to the optional referendum. Accession to organisations for collective security or to supranational communities is subject to mandatory referendum. Most cantons also have a special referen-

SURVEY 4
GLOSSARY OF DIRECT-DEMOCRACY TERMS

dum dealing with sovereign treaties with other cantons or foreign states. In both the federal and cantonal cases, it is not the treaty as such which is subject to referendum, but parliament's agreement to the treaty.

REFERENDUM ON PUBLIC EXPENDITURE cf. Finance referendum

REFERENDUM PROPOSAL (Text of the) proposal that is submitted to the People in a (referendum) vote. In Switzerland it may be either a popular initiative requesting a partial revision of the Federal Constitution with or without a counter-proposal from the Federal Assembly, or a referendum.

REFERENDUM QUESTION A synonym for ballot text: the question put on the ballot paper in a popular (referendum) vote under a direct democracy procedure.

REFERENDUM REQUESTED BY THE CANTONS In Switzerland, an optional referendum that is held when a minimum of eight cantons decide to request the same.

REFERENDUM SLOGAN A recommendation, catchphrase or slogan issued by a political party, its parliamentary section or some other group with reference to a forthcoming referendum vote.

REFERENDUM VOTE OR BALLOT Procedure by which eligible voters may accept or reject a proposal by casting a ballot. In Switzerland voting may take place at the polling station using a ballot paper (voting at the polling station), or by post (postal voting).

REGISTERED COMMITTEE The proponents of a referendum, initiative or recall when they are officially registered in the form of a committee. In Switzerland only the initiative committee has to be registered.

REGISTRATION OF A POPULAR INITIATIVE The act of depositing an initiative for publication and collection of signatures, whereby the legal process of the initiative is officially started. In Switzerland registration is made at the Federal Chancellery.

REJECTIVE REFERENDUM A procedure leading to a popular (referendum) vote which may either retain or repeal a law or decree that has been agreed by the legislature but has not yet come into force.

RIGHT TO BE ELECTED/TO STAND AS A CANDIDATE. The right of a citizen of voting age to stand as a candidate. In Switzerland citizens of voting age may stand as a candidate for the National Council, the Federal Council or the Federal Supreme Court. The right to be elected in elections to the Council of States is regulated on a cantonal basis.

RIGHT TO ELECT Right of citizens of voting age to elect. In Switzerland citizens of voting age have the right to elect the 200 members of the National Council and the 46 members of the Council of States. The election of the National Council is governed by federal law and that of the Council of States by cantonal law.

RIGHT TO PARTICIPATE IN ELECTIONS Right to elect and to be elected. In Switzerland any citizen of voting age has the right to participate in the election to the National Council as a voter (right to elect) or to stand as a candidate for election (right to be elected). Anyone who has the right to participate in elections also has the right to vote.

RIGHT TO VOTE Right to participate in a (referendum) vote. At the Swiss national level, the right of citizens of voting age to participate in popular votes at the federal level. Exceptionally, foreigners holding residence permits are also permitted to vote at the cantonal or communal level. Anyone who has the right to vote also has the right to participate in elections.

SURVEY 4
GLOSSARY OF DIRECT-DEMOCRACY TERMS

S

SIGNATURE The signature by a citizen in formal support of a proposal for a referendum, initiative or recall.

SIMPLE FEDERAL DECREE Cf. Federal decree

SIMPLE MAJORITY A majority requirement of more than half of the total number of valid votes cast. Proposals put to the People in a referendum vote are accepted if a majority of those who vote is in favour; conversely, they are rejected if a majority votes against them.

SUBMISSION The act of depositing collected signatures with the proper authority in a popular initiative or citizen-initiated referendum process. On the Swiss national level the authority is the Federal Chancellery.

THE SWISS "STATES" I.E. THE CANTONS The cantons are also known as the "States"

THE SWISS CONFEDERATION The Swiss Confederation is the official name for Switzerland. In day-to-day Swiss usage, the full name is often abbreviated to "Confederation" (Eidgenossenschaft): it stands for the country as a whole – People, government and authorities. When the reference is specifically to the government, parliament and authorities alone, the term "Federation" (Bund) is employed.

T

TITLE The formal name given to the proposal in a popular initiative or citizen-initiated referendum. In Switzerland the proponents of an initiative can choose the title of the initiative as long as it respects certain legal requirements.

TURNOUT QUORUM A specified minimum turnout required for a (referendum) vote to pass a proposal.

U

UNITARY INITIATIVE In the case of the unitary initiative, it is not the initiative group, but parliament, which decides whether the proposal is to be treated as a constitutional or a legislative initiative. In Switzerland the unitary initiative is used in a number of cantons. At the federal level, unitary initiatives are covered by the General Popular Initiative.

UNITY OF SUBJECT MATTER When voting in referendums, Swiss voters have only two options (other than deciding not to vote at all): they can vote either "Yes" or "No". In order to ensure that voters' voting intentions are completely freely expressed and unequivocal, there is a requirement for the referendum issue/proposal to be reduced to a single political question. The principle of unity of subject matter applies to all referendums, regardless of whether they result from a popular initiative or are mandatory referendums.

V

VALIDITY 1. Of a (referendum) vote, that any necessary quorum is achieved 2. Of a signature or vote, that it is correctly in accordance with procedures and regulations

VALIDITY CHECK The scrutiny of a submission by a public authority for conformity with procedures and regulations.

(DECLARATION OF) VERIFICATION The declaration of acceptance by the proper authority that the submission contains at least the required number of valid signatures and complies with the law, regulations and procedural rules.

VOTE An electoral event concerning an issue in which the electorate expresses choice through casting a ballot.

VOTE FOR A CANDIDATE Vote that a candidate receives when his or her name is written on the ballot paper.

VOTER An eligible voter who casts a ballot at an election or a vote under a direct democracy procedure or plebiscite.

SURVEY 4
Glossary of direct-democracy terms

Voting at the polling station Voting in which the voter places his ballot paper in the ballot box at the polling station. In Switzerland the ballot paper may be filled out either outside or inside the polling station. Voting at the polling station is nowadays being increasingly superseded by postal voting and already in some places by electronic voting (e-voting).

Voting rights for foreigners Right to vote for foreigners. At the Swiss federal level and in most cantons, only Swiss citizens have the right to vote. Exceptionally, foreigners holding residence permits are also permitted to vote – for example in the cantons of Jura and Neuchâtel.

Sources:
- Swiss Federal Chancellery: Get to grips with political rights (Bern 2004) (www.admin.ch/ch/e/bk/order/politik/index.html)
- International Institute for Democracy and Electoral Assistance (IDEA): expert group "direct democracy glossary" (Stockholm 2004/05)

Towards the First
World Conference on Direct Democracy
Lucerne/Switzerland 22-24 May, 2008

At the same time as modern representative democracy has become a global norm – based on a set of principles including fundamental freedoms, basic political rights, the separation of powers, the rule of law and acceptance of international law – procedural forms of direct-democratic decision making have been extended to many countries across the world at the local, regional or national level.

Initiatives, referendums and recall votes – as a complement to elections – are thus playing an increasingly important role in involving citizens in the political process. However, discussions on the appropriate use of DD instruments, on the interactions and relationships between DD instruments and the forms of representative democracy, and on the ramifications of the process of the design, adoption and implementation of DD instruments are often not as well informed and inclusive as they could be.

In 2004, International IDEA, an intergovernmental organization founded in 1995 with member states from all continents, launched a global project to gather data, assess developments and raise awareness about the appropriateness, design and implementation of direct-democratic processes worldwide. International IDEA has developed an *analytical structure for DD procedures*, a *global direct democracy glossary* and a *questionnaire on DD procedures worldwide*. Using these new tools, a *global database on DD procedures* is under construction and a Global Handbook on Direct Democracy will be prepared.

The new tools for developing and assessing direct democracy will be the subject of a worldwide consultation process in 2007 and 2008, including regional workshops planned in Asia, Europe, Latin America and Africa, as well as the first World Conference on Direct Democracy, scheduled to take place in Lucerne/Switzerland on May 22-24, 2008. The process aims to contribute towards the creation of:

- A WORLD MAP OF DIRECT DEMOCRACY, including a database on the global existence and practice of initiatives, referendums and recalls, bringing together existing research and compiling new data.
- GLOBAL CRITERIA FOR DIRECT DEMOCRACY related to the design, the use and the evaluation of DD activities, including guidelines, recommendations and practice case studies worldwide.
- A DIRECT DEMOCRACY TOOLKIT for practitioners and researchers across the world offering, among other tools, training and capacity-building materials.
- A NETWORK OF PRACTITIONERS AND EXPERTS in the field of direct democracy which will further knowledge and the exchange of ideas both within the network and between the network and other interested actors.

For updates and information on the DD World Conference process visit
www.iri-europe.org or www.idea.int

THE INITIATIVE & REFERENDUM INSTITUTE EUROPE
Europe's Direct Democracy Think Tank

IRI Europe was founded in 2001. The Institute's main mission is to develop insights into the theory and practice of direct democracy among politicians, the media, NGOs, academics and the public throughout Europe. IRI Europe is an independent non-partisan and non profit-making organization with headquarters in Marburg (Germany), offices in Brussels (Belgium) and Bülach (Switzerland) as well as representations in Falun (Sweden), Helsinki (Finland), Edinburgh (Scotland) and St.Ursanne (Switzerland).

Since the early days of this millennium IRI has assisted and advised the EU constitution drafters – first in the Convention and subsequently in the EU institutions and member states and finally within the electorates across Europe – in seizing the opportunity of developing democratic tools which are both issue-based and pan-European. IRI Europe has quickly become the premier research and educational institute on the Initiative and Referendum process across Europe.

With a comprehensive network of experts and correspondents throughout the region, the Institute is uniquely equipped to provide the know-how and the tools Europe now needs. IRI Europe's informational and educational materials include Handbooks and Guidebooks, Toolkits for Free and Fair Referendums, as well as dedicated materials for schools. In all its projects IRI Europe cooperates closely with partners from civil society, governmental institutions and international players.

The Institute is led by academics, journalists and politicians from different political parties, backgrounds and countries. A small team of staff coordinates IRI Europe, which has an open approach to cooperation and which has developed a far-reaching reputation as Europe's Direct Democracy Think Tank.

The Initiative & Referendum Institute Europe has recently:

- launched several COUNTRY PROGRAMMES in cooperation with governmental and non-governmental partner organizations across Europe. The countries involved include Hungary, Poland, Spain, France, Russia and the Balkan Region.
- drafted a comprehensive TEACHING TOOLKIT concept for secondary schools across Europe with dedicated materials for teachers.
- strengthened its comprehensive INITIATIVE FOR EUROPE programme featuring a transnational development project for a more structured dialogue between authorities and initiative committees.
- published new editions of the renowned IRI GUIDEBOOK TO DIRECT DEMOCRACY in English, French, German, Spanish and Italian.

- established Europe's first DIRECT DEMOCRACY RESEARCH CENTER at Marburg University including the launch of a comprehensive I&R Database, the publication of scientific literature and the holding of annual Research Conferences.
- developed a GLOBAL NETWORK of Direct Democracy Think-Tanks and Research Institutes in the Americas and Asia in order to support International IDEA's preparations for the 1st World Conference on Direct Democracy in 2008.

CONTACT

For more information check out our Web services at www.iri-europe.org and/or contact one of our offices and experts by E-Mail or Phone:

IRI Europe
Box 200540
DE-35017 Marburg, Germany

Phone (Infoline) +32 26 48 59 71
Fax +49 6421 28 28 991
info@iri-europe.org
www.iri-europe.org

Brussels Office: +32 26 48 59 71, brussels@iri-europe.org
Office Switzerland: +41 44 863 71 71, bulach@iri-europe.org

ABOUT THE AUTHORS AND EDITORS

Bruno Kaufmann works as a broadcast and newspaper correspondent and is co-founder and president of the Initiative & Referendum Institute Europe. He coordinates the preparations for the 1st World Conference on Direct Democracy in 2008 (by International IDEA) and has a Master's degree in Social Sciences from the University of Gothenburg.
kaufmann@iri-europe.org

Rolf Büchi has a PhD from ETH Zurich and a Master's degree in Social Sciences from the University of Helsinki. He works with the educational programmes of the Initiative & Referendum Institute Europe and is the author of many books and publications on Direct Democracy.
buchi@iri-europe.org

Nadja Braun has a PhD in Law at Bern University and works at the political rights section of the Swiss Federal Chancellery (the opinions expressed in the Guidebook do not represent any official statement).
nadjabraun@gmx.ch

Paul Carline has a degree in modern languages from Manchester University and works as a freelance translator. He is responsible for English translations and proof-reading at the Initiative & Referendum Institute Europe.
carline@iri-europe.org

ACKNOWLEDGEMENTS

Many people contribute to IRI's Guidebook to Direct Democracy development and regular updates. We would like to thank all the contributors, translators and reviewers for their dedication and interest

Martina Caroni (German Edition), Virgina Beramendi-Heine (Survey 3, Latin America Section), Victor Hugo (Spanish Translation), Domitila Barbolla (Spanish Edition), Victor Cuesta (Spanish Edition), Ariane Gigon Bormann (French Translation), Michel Chevallier (French Edition), Stephen Boucher (Survey 3, Francophone Section), Frank Remeth (Survey 3, German & Austrian Section), Stephan Lausch (Survey 3, South Tirolean Section), Wilfried Marxer (Survey 3, Liechtenstein Section), Brian Beedham (English Edition), Anna Capretti (Italian Translation), Amy Clark, Denise Hegnauer, Lukas Jaggi, Ruth Widmer.

It would not have been possible to develop and produce this Guidebook without the assistance of supporters and experts of democracy development. Our special thanks go to:

Andreas Gross, Hans-Urs Wili, Adrian Schmid, Theo Schiller, Martina Caroni, Roger de Weck, Diana Wallis, Heidi Hautala, Brian Beedham, Andrew Ellis, Nigel Smith, Matthias Godmann, Trudi Dinkelmann, Agnetha Bodström, Malin Stawe, M. Dane Waters, Jüri Ruus, Gita Feldhune, Palle Svensson, Heiko Dittmer, Carsten Berg, Werner Bussman, Volker Mittendorf, Justus Schönlau, Susana del Río, Boris Voyer, Daniel Zovatto, Elisabeth Erlandsson, Roland Erne, Marta Darulova, Lars Feld, Gebhard Kirchgässner, Tito Tettamanti, Michel Chevallier, Giuliano Amato, Jürgen Schulz, Michael Efler, Roman Huber, Hans Göttel, Elisabet Cidre, Jürgen Meyer, Víctor Cuesta, Josef Leinen, Lars Knuchel, Alain Lamassoure, Fabrice Filliez, Otmar Jung, Alexandre Trechsel, Rudolf Staub, Andreas Auer, Olof Pettersson, Thorsten Almquist, George Kokkas, Mads Qvortrup, Annemarie Huber-Hotz, Bruno Frey, Alkuin Kölliker, Algis Krupavicius, Esther Kaufmann, Gret Haller, Ruth Metzler, Leopoldo Salgui, Jiri Polak, Ralph Kampwirth, Martijn Laman, Martin Bühler, Thomas Hug, Sonja Jansen, Even Lynne, Claude Lonchamp, Adrian Taylor, Staffan Eriksson, Gerard Légris, Gijs de Jong, Per Bolund, Daniel Haener, Karin Gilland Lutz, Dotcho Mihailov, Henrik Dahlsson, Lutz Hager, Ellie Greenwood, Nicolas Berger, Frank Rehmet, Urs Bucher, Micheline Calmy-Rey, Judith Winter, Vladimir Rott, Onno Seroo, Juan Carlos García, Bianca Rousselot, Margot Wallström, Hansjochen Vogel, Liliane Kueffer, Pär Sköld, Eric Lastic, David Altman, Andrzej Kaczmarczyk, Fredi Krebs, Joseph Deiss, Lukas Schmutz, Stewart Arnold, Nicolas Fischer, Deborah Newton Cook, Birgitta Swedenborg, Bruno Vanoni, Virginia Beramendi-Heine, Arjen Nijeboer, Eisse Kalk, Niesco Dubbelboer, Daniel Schily, Miguel Ferro Sousa, Bernhard Marfurt, Robert Reich, Markus Börlin, Ivo Sieber, Pierre Mairesse, Simon O´Connor, Jos Verhulst, Percy Vogel, Konrad Schily, Lars Bosselmann, Annika Philips, Bernard Nezmah, Hajrulla Ceku, Markus Dürst, Walter Fust, Chantal Nicod, Lisa Schilling, Gabriela Dömötör, Ursula Marti, Cecilia Malmström, Marie Utter, Björn Jerkert, Alar Kilp, Larry LeDuc, Johannes Voggenhuber, Aimée Lind Adaniak, Juan Font, BoPer Larsson, Anna Unger, Miklos Rosta, Daniel Oross, Gabor Györi, Peter Kolossa, Joanna Kowalska, Christoph Frei, Viktor Szabadai, Christoph Wicki, Hans Widmer, Lisa Paus, Gerd Langguth, Wara Wende, Gerald Häfner, Detlev Plückhahn, Marcus Veith, Suzann-Viola Renninger, Johannes Winkel, Henri Monceau, Stefania Kapronczay, Vera Koltai, Csaba Gali, Ivan Krastev, Nadeja Popova, Uwe Serdült, Anna Lindström, Åsa Ehinger Berling, Lena Langlet, Urs Bucher, Nicolas Brühl, Adrian Sollberger, Marion Carrel, Frederic Allemand, Christoph Premat, Ariell Rouby, Robert Tesh, Lucia Kubosova, Christoph Brändli, Ruedi Lais, Magdalena Musial-Karg, Rafal Kramza, Yi-Cheng You, Mike Marsh, Werner Joos, Victor Hugo, Urs Geiser, Tor Bjørklund, Erika Beckman, Stina Larserud, Ted Becker, Sigvard Wohlwend, Zoltan Tibor Pallinger, Stefan Hostettler, Lukas Schmutz, Johan Aeschlimann, Georg Kreis, Ron Bailey, Roger Macnair, Raban Daniel Fuhrmann, Peter Nizak, Ann-Cathrine Jungar, Lilia Zaharieva, Kristina Lemon, Jan Diederen, Eric Lastic, Isidoro Rando, Odette Kalman

INDEX

Symbols
1st August Initiative 150
20th century 51, 58, 80, 107, 147, 295

A
Aargau 81, 88, 119, 127, 133, 139, 154, 164, 166
Abrogative referendum 249, 294, 308
Absinthe *See* Ban on absinthe
Accelerator ("political") 25
Accessibility 30
Accumulation 308
Acquisition of citizenship 168, 308
Active voting right 161, 186
Adamiak, Aimée Lind 255
Administrative referendum 29, 308
Africa 106, 321
Agenda initiative 110, 239, 254, 308, 310, 314
Agenda setter 77
Albania 109
Alternative proposal 308
America 38, 83, 106
Ancient Greek 74
Anières 100, 130
Annan, Kofi 102
Appenzell 81, 138
Appenzell Inner-Rhodes 21, 44, 99, 122, 127, 133, 143, 164, 308, 311, 316
Appenzell Outer-Rhodes 21, 44, 98, 122, 127, 143, 164, 309, 311
Apprenticeship Initiative 118
Approval quorum 184, 308
Argentina 265, 267
Aristocracy 120
Army 12, 158, 270
Army XXI 27
Asia 106, 321
Assembly democracy 120, 308
Asylum policy 173
Ataturk, Kemal 264
Attacks 60, 154
Australia 107
Austria 109, 181, 236, 239, 286
Authorities' counter-proposal 235

Authorities' initiative 308
Authorities' minority referendum 234, 249

B
"Bürgerbegehren" 277
Ballot(s) 28, 50, 125, 147
Ballot paper 20, 308
Ballot paper (for elections) 308
Ballot paper; voting slip 308
Ballot text 243, 308, 318
Baltic republic 242, 252
Ban on absinthe 149, 193
Barroso, José Manuel 257
Basel-City 21, 46, 119, 122, 127, 133, 164, 166, 309
Basel-Country 119, 122, 127, 133, 155, 164, 166, 309
Basler Nachrichten 60
Bavaria 88, 93, 107, 277
Béguelin, Roland 61
Belarus 106
Belgium 109, 236, 239, 299
Benz, Matthias 70
Berberat 154
Berlin 278
Bern 28, 46, 58, 77, 119, 126, 133, 152, 164, 309
Bern, University of 74
Biedermann, Horst 102
Biel/Bienne 156
Binding 89, 100, 108, 132, 140, 239, 308
Björklund, Tor 255
Blocher, Christoph 22
Bolivia 267
Brake(s) 7, 14, 25, 31, 74, 79
Braun, Nadja 324
Brazil 267
Bretton Woods 42, 217
Brian Beedham 324
Büchi, Rolf 264, 324
Bülach 39
Bulgaria 109, 236, 240
Bund, Der 34
Bürkli, Karl 37
Business Federation 83

INDEX

Bützer, Michael 81

C

C2D (Research and Documentation Centre on direct democracy) 119, 237
California 83, 183
Calmy-Rey, Micheline 6
Canada 301
Candidate 308, 314, 319
Canton(s) 13, 20, 27, 36, 42, 58, 80, 88, 98, 139, 143, 160, 309, 318
Cantonal government 6, 21, 46, 154, 178
Cantonal initiative 309
Cantonal majority 309, 311
Cantonal parliament 21, 61, 317
Capable of carrying through a (facultative) referendum process 309
Car-free days 19
Carline, Paul 324
Carouge 100, 130
Casinos 194, 197, 203
Catholic 7, 53, 61
Ceaucescu, Nikolai 258
Chambers (of the bi-cameral parliament) 309
Châtillon 155
Chavez, Hugo 89
Chile 268
Chirac, Jacques 306
(Swiss) Christian Democratic Party (CVP) 22, 163
Christian Democrats (CDU/CSU) 285
Cidre, Elisabete 257
Citizen-friendly 245, 279, 285, 309
Citizen-initiated referendum 309, 310, 316, 317
Citizen law-making 176
Citizens' initiative 110, 160, 170
Citizens role 151
City government 21
Civil right(s) 14, 20, 99, 167, 189
Civil society 8
Claude: 125
Co-determination 14, 46, 161
Code of conduct 75
Collection of signatures 81, 88, 99, 283, 295, 318

Collection of signatures (time allowance) *See* Time allowed for collection of signatures
Collective learning processes 47
Cologny 100
Colombia 268
Comité de Moutier 154
Commune(s) 29, 49, 186, 308
Communities 80, 263, 277
Compromise 45, 54, 71, 93, 123, 182, 309
Compulsory voting 309, 315
Confederation *See* Swiss Confederation
Conflict 154, 314
Connecticut 106
Consensus democracy 13, 53, 309
Constitutionality 309
Constitutional referendum 34, 42, 106, 133, 144, 151, 242, 248, 250, 252, 254, 258
Constitution of 1869 35
Constructive referendum 98, 145, 225, 309
Consultation 123, 155, 310
Consultative 91, 110, 239
Consultative referendum 240, 243, 253, 260, 310
Content and formal legal requirements 182
Control of government 90
Conversation 73
Corban 155
Cortébert 155
Costs of direct democracy 82
Couchepin, Pascal 50
Coughlan, Anthony 249
Council of States 21, 43, 100, 123, 309, 310, 312, 318
Counter-proposal 50, 92, 98, 147, 235, 264, 310, 314
Courchapoix 155
Courrendlin 155
Courtelary 152, 155
Credit Suisse 80
Cross-party committee 75
CVP *See* (Swiss) Christian Democratic Party (CVP)
Cyprus 109, 236, 240
Czech Republic 109, 241

INDEX

D
Death penalty 67, 190
Deciding question 144, 235, 264, 310
Decision-maker 69, 151
Decision-making 10, 13, 122, 129, 144, 178, 184, 209, 211, 234, 310, 314
De Gaulle, Charles 60, 108
Deiss, Joseph 5, 8, 50
Delémont 152
Democratic movement 34, 176
Democratic revolution 33, 37, 106, 176
Denmark 108, 236, 241
Design 87, 180, 232, 252
Development of democracy 77, 180
Dialogue 6, 14, 60, 90, 156, 183, 300
Direct democracy procedure 308, 310, 316
Direct initiative procedure 311
Disabled people 26, 50, 159
Distance-related heavy vehicle duty 82
Distribution of power 10, 151
Dominican Republic 269
Double majority 45, 264, 311
"Double yes" 98, 144, 183, 310
Dubs, Jakob 66

E
E-vote 100 *See also* Electronic voting
Eastern Europe 106, 259
Economic effect (of direct democracy) 178
Economic performance 81, 178
Economiesuisse 80
Economy 14, 80, 108
Ecuador 107, 269
Education 268
EEC 6, 80, 83
Election 164, 177, 187, 308, 311
Elector 311
Electoral commission 245, 272
Electorate 6, 26, 51, 80, 89, 107, 310, 311
Electronic voting 30, 130, 185, 311, 320 *See also* E-vote
Eligible voter 26, 124, 152, 185, 311, 319
Elite 34, 68

Employment law 80
EMU accession/membership 246
Energy 50, 224
Equality 37, 50, 67, 120, 185
Equal rights for the disabled 19, 26, 159
Erdogan, Reçep Tayyip 264
Escher, Alfred 66
Estonia 109, 236, 242
EU Commission 110
EU constitution 15, 105, 285, 299, 304
EU law 102
EU membership 243, 255
Europe 93, 106, 177, 232, 237, 277, 282, 321, 322
European Citizens' Initiative 15, 110
European federation 108
European integration 144
European Journal of Political Economy 179
European Parliament 9, 102, 110
European Union 9, 38, 42, 144, 229, 273
Europe des patries 60
Exclusion of issues 184, 278
Exclusion of women 99
Expulsion of foreigners 167

F
Face-to-face debate 74
Fair rents 19, 227
Fair representation of women 146, 224
Farmer(s) 36, 53
FDP *See* Radical Democratic Party (FDP)
Federal administration 123, 312
Federal Assembly 22, 26, 35, 53, 140, 205, 263, 310, 312
Federal Chancellery 28, 99, 124, 312, 317
Federal Constitution 26, 34, 42, 122, 132, 138, 144, 159, 173
Federal Council 6, 22, 28, 101, 123, 129, 147, 311, 312
Federal Court 99, 313
Federal decree 313
Federalism 13, 42, 62, 71, 122
Federal law/Federal act 313
Federal states 88, 277, 280, 285
Federation 13, 35, 42, 108, 309, 313

328

INDEX

Feld, Lars 81, 179
Feldhune, Gita 251
Feldmann, Markus 154
Fifth Republic 304
Finance referendum 28, 35, 80, 100, 144, 308, 313
Financing and transparency 185
Financing of referendum campaigns 83
Finland 109, 236, 243
Font, Joan 261
Foreigners 52, 98, 167, 186, 318
Founding fathers 107
France 7, 38, 75, 107, 236, 244, 289, 302
Franches-Montagnes 152
Freedom 37, 66, 151, 314, 321
Free trade treaty 108
Freienbach 29
French-speaking 30, 58, 156
French Revolution 38
Frey, Bruno 81, 179
Fribourg 29, 34, 98, 119, 133, 164
Fribourg, University of 80
Fundamental right(s) 82, 99, 141, 312, 313, 316

G

Gas pedal 28, 165
General initiative 20, 100, 173
General popular initiative 26, 99, 144
Genesis of a (new) law 122, 123
Geneva 100, 119, 125, 128, 133, 164
Gengel, Florian 34
Gerber, Elisabeth R. 83
German-speaking 30, 58
German Federal Republic 88
German states ("Länder") 278
Germany 75, 81, 88, 109, 236, 244, 277
GfS research institute 186
Glarus 38, 46, 126, 134, 164, 308, 316
Glattal railway 20, 115
Goldmann, Mattias 262
Gothenburg, University of 324
Governance 66, 166
Government's Explanations 75
Grandval 155

Graubünden 29, 46, 54, 88, 119, 127, 134, 164, 315
Great Britain 108, 236, 245
Greece 20, 109, 236, 246
Grimsson, Olafur 248
Groff, Alfred 253
Gross, Andreas 90, 165
Grosser Rat 61
Grütlianer (der) 176
Guatemala 270

H

Haenni, Dominique 156
Hahnzog, Klaus 107
Harmonisation 314, 317
Health insurance 19, 191
Health law 116
Helsinki, University of 324
Helvetic constitution of 12th April 1798 137
Helvetic Republic 34, 137
Hesse (German state) 278
Hilty, Carl 137
Hitler 282
Hospital costs 117, 225
How the popular initiative is worded 181
How the referendum question is worded 182
How the signatures are collected 92, 181
Human rights 9, 15, 90, 174, 180, 266, 314
Hungary 109, 236, 246, 322
Hydro-electric power 42

I

Iceland 236, 248
IDEA (International Institute for Democracy and Electoral Assistance) 321
IEA (International Association for the Evaluation of Educational Achievement) 102
IMF (International Monetary Fund) 42, 217
Immature citizens (politically immature people) 66, 151
Implementation 91, 99, 130, 177, 272, 287, 312, 321
Indirect counter-proposal 43, 50, 171, 314
Information for citizen 93
Initiative & Referendum Monitor 2004/2005 177

INDEX

Initiative(s) 6, 9, 19, 26, 34, 43, 50, 52, 59, 81, 88, 98, 109, 144, 159, 165, 173, 178, 180, 232, 308, 314, 321
Initiative committee 43, 88, 173, 183, 314
Innovation 7, 14, 80, 91, 313
Institutional legitimacy 91
Integration 15, 58, 90, 98, 106, 266
Integration policies 166
Inter-Jura Assembly 156
Interaction with government and parliament 182
international law 173
Introduction of direct democracy 35, 54, 106, 265
Invalidation 249
Ireland 108, 185, 236, 245, 248
IRI (Initiative & Referendum Institute Europe) 322
IRI Europe Country Index on Citizen lawmaking 176
Irish Republic 108
ISKB (Association of owners of small power stations) 45
Italian-speaking 30
Italy 9, 89, 107, 236, 249, 294

J

Jung, Otmar 245
Jura 14, 46, 57, 98, 119, 128, 134, 152, 154, 164, 320
Jura Liberation Front 60, 154

K

Karamanlis, Kostas 246
Kaufmann, Bruno 264, 324
Kirchgässner, Gebhard 81
Kitchen table 77
Kjaerulff-Schmidt, Steffen 242
Kriesi, Hanspeter 76
Krupavicius, Algis 253

L

"Länder" 277

(Swiss) National Languages 315
Lajoux 155
Lake Zurich 29
Landbote, Der 66, 176
Landschaftsrappen 44
Landsgemeinde 37, 38
Lange, Friedrich Albert 37
Latin America 265, 272, 321
Latvia 109, 236, 250
Laufen 152
Laufental 60, 75
Law 66, 92, 110, 122, 123, 147, 313, 314
Law on citizens' initiatives 89
Left/Green 21
Legislative initiative 26, 35, 144, 314
Legislative referendum 7, 28, 45, 144, 303, 314
Legislature 237, 277, 314
Legitimacy 7
Legitimacy, dual 46
Les Genevez 155
Les Rangiers 60, 155
Liberal 34, 66, 80, 100, 176, 285
Liechtenstein (Principality of) 109, 236, 251, 295
Lifelong detention (for perpetrators of sexual or violent crimes) 148
Lithuania 109, 236, 252
Longchamp, Claude 77, 83, 125
Lucerne 119, 126, 134, 164, 166, 313, 321
Luxembourg 109, 236, 253

M

Magic formula 22, 53
Malheiros, Manuel 257
Malta 109, 236, 254
Marburg 110, 284, 322
Marburg University 81
Massachusetts 107
Media 6, 14, 51, 59, 74, 109, 177, 180
Media bill 248
Merkel, Angela 285
Mervelier 155
Metzler, Ruth 22, 50
Mexico 270
Meyrin 100

330

INDEX

Micotti, Sébastien 81
Middle Age(s) 38
Military service 42
Minorities 47, 58, 71, 288, 309
Mittendorf, Volker 90
Modern direct democracy 10, 35, 68, 76, 120, 232
Moeckli, Georges 59, 154
Monarchy 120, 251, 254
Money 19, 81, 101, 177, 185, 313
Monnet system 108
Montagnard constitution 107
Moratorium on nuclear power station construction 150
Motorway card 83
Moutier 61, 152, 154, 155
Moutier, Comité de 59
Mouvement séparatiste jurassien 59, 154
Mühlemann, Lukas 80
Multicultural state 8, 33
Multilingual communities 77

N

Nation 18, 34, 60
National Council 21, 123, 145, 161, 185, 193 *See also* Swiss National Council
Nationalism 57
NATO 246, 259
Naturalization 167
Natural right 39, 120
Nea Dimokratia 246
Netherland(s), The 109, 236, 254
Neuchâtel 98, 100, 119, 128, 134, 164
Neuenstadt 152
Neue Zürcher Zeitung 59, 98, 157
Neutrality 248, 291
New Hampshire 107
New social movements 165
Newspapers 76
New Zealand 105
Nidwalden 21, 38, 44, 122, 126, 134, 164, 309, 311
Nijeboer, Arjen 254
Non-nuclear electric power 19
Noriega, Manuel 270
North-Rhine Westphalia 279

North America 38, 277
North Dakota 89
North East 245
Northern Ireland 245
Norway 105, 109, 236, 255
Nuclear power station(s) 50, 101, 145, 150, 217, 239, 287
Number of signatures 88, 173, 180, 185, 272, 309

O

Obwalden 21, 44, 122, 134, 164, 309, 311
Oceania 106
Ochs, Peter 137
Offe, Claus 71
Oligarchy 90
Ombudsman 101
Openness 15, 30, 186
Opinion 6, 19, 41, 61, 76, 123, 147, 151, 183, 316
Opinion poll(s) 51, 67, 82, 269, 286
Oser, Fritz 102

P

Panama 270
Papandreou, George A. 246
Parliament 7, 9, 26, 42, 51, 68, 82, 90, 108, 122, 147, 173, 234, 309, 312
Parliamentarian democracy 39
Parliamentary stage 123
Partial Revision 142
Partial revision 173, 312, 313, 315
Partial revision (of the constitution) 315
Participation 30, 35, 63, 67, 80, 90, 98, 121, 177, 178, 233, 314, 315
Participatory procedures 151
PASOK (Panhellenic Socialist Movement) 246
Pass 315
Pass a proposal 311, 317, 319
Passive voting right 161, 186
Passport 98
Peace 21, 166
Peace Movement 289
Penalty (for failing to vote where there is compulsory voting) 315

INDEX

Perrefitte 155
Peru 271
Petition 162, 311, 315
Pinochet, Augusto 268
Plebiscite 11, 91, 108, 177, 233, 266, 310, 315
Poland 109, 236, 256, 322
Political agenda 9, 26, 181, 316
Political education 97, 102, 262
Political parties 9, 20, 51, 74, 94, 123, 142, 165, 265, 309, 322
Political rights 28, 65, 129, 151, 161, 173, 186, 308, 316, 321
Political rights for women 67
Pommerehne, Werner W. 178
Pompidou, Georges 108
Popular assembly 38, 120, 316
Popular consultation 300, 304
Popular counter-proposal 235
Popular demand 88, 165, 278
Popular initiative 7, 9, 26, 30, 42, 52, 88, 99, 109, 142, 145, 159, 165, 172, 182, 278, 303, 308, 310, 313, 316
Popular proposal 235, 309
Popular referendum 124, 145, 147, 151, 155, 180, 316
Popular referendum proposal 234, 238
Popular referendum vote 124, 147, 238, 316
Popular sovereignty 10, 35, 120
Popular vote(s) 11, 18, 26, 34, 52, 66, 87, 106, 124, 147, 177, 189, 232, 234, 312, 318
(Neo-)Populist 265
Porrentruy 152
Portugal 109, 236, 257
Postal voting 30, 76, 125, 129, 296, 316
Power sharing 233
Pre-modern democracy 12, 39
Prevention of false pricing 149, 213
Price of land 88
Prince Alois (of Liechtenstein) 296, 298
Private media 75
Private school(s) 303
Privilege 36, 39, 101, 120
Prohibition of alcohol 243, 301
Prohibition of ritual slaughter without prior anaesthetisation 149, 191
Prohibition on the setting up of casinos 149, 194

Pro Infirmis 27
Proportional election of the National Council 193, 194
Proportional representation 71, 308, 311
Proportional system 35
Proposal 11, 18, 20, 72, 92, 114, 115, 117, 123, 129, 142, 144, 147, 152, 154, 156, 158, 159, 161, 168, 171, 173, 181, 183, 186, 190, 195, 197, 199, 201, 206, 208, 233, 242, 247, 250, 252, 258, 263, 308, 310, 314, 317, 319
Protect the Alpine region from transit traffic 150, 220
Protestant 155
Province of Bozen 294
Publication 161, 218, 237, 312, 317, 318
Public debates 109
Public debt 14, 81, 178
Public radio 75
Public service 81, 178
Public spending 80, 290

Q

Qualification for the ballot 317
Qualified majority 184, 317
Quebec 301
Quorum 92, 109, 145, 180, 184, 242, 245, 246, 249, 252, 308, 309, 314, 315, 317, 319

R

Radical Democratic Party (FDP) 21, 53, 100, 163, 285
Railway 20, 115, 190, 191, 192, 195, 199
Rassemblement Jurassien 152, 154
Rebévelier 155
Recall 232, 308, 314, 317, 319
Recall of an initiative 317
recall votes 321
Referendum 6, 9, 18, 31, 49, 54, 73, 95, 103, 111, 114, 119, 124, 126, 129, 133, 142, 146, 147, 152, 154, 158, 160, 161, 165, 169, 173, 177, 178, 180, 186, 189, 195, 198, 210, 215, 225, 232, 237, 239, 242, 252, 256, 262, 308, 309, 312, 313, 315, 316, 317, 320, 321
Referendum booklet (explanatory booklet or pamphlet) 317

332

INDEX

Referendum democracy 35, 67
Referendum dinner 74
Referendum initiated by authorities 317
Referendum on international treaties 20, 144, 145, 149, 195, 210, 317
Referendum on public expenditure 313, 318
Referendum proposal 257, 315, 318
Referendum Question 115, 182, 318
Referendum requested by the cantons 312, 318
Referendum slogan 318
Referendum vote or ballot 318
Refuse disposal 81
Registered committee 316, 318
Registration of a popular initiative 318
Rejective referendum 318
Relationship between church and state 22, 116
René 252
Representative 9, 104, 123, 129, 137, 151, 161, 176, 178, 184, 232, 310
Resolution of differences 123
Restaurants 73
Restoration 34, 170
Restriction of subject-matter 93
Restrictions on the constitutional initiative 173
Return to direct democracy 149, 200
Rhaeto-Romanic 198, 315
Rhineland-Palatinate 279
Rhinow, René 252
Rico, Guillem 261
Right of initiative 9, 88, 102, 110, 161, 306
Right of petition 162
Right of veto 36, 46, 296
Right to be elected/to stand as a candidate 318
Right to elect 318
Right to participate in elections 316, 318
Right to referendum 161, 215
Right to vote 311, 316, 318, 320
Riigikogu 243
Ritschard, Willy 62
Road 115, 148, 197, 203, 216, 217, 224
Roggenburg 155
Roman-catholic Church 248
Romania 109, 236, 258
Rossemaison 155

Roten, Iris von 69
Rothenthurm initiative for the protection of moorland 150, 216
Rothenturm 52
Rousseau, Jean Jacques 106
Ruppen, Paul 264

S

Saarland 88, 278, 283
San Diego, University of 83
Sartori, Giovanni 67
Savioz, Marcel R. 178
Saxony 279
Schadenfreude 50
Schaffhausen 46, 119, 127, 135, 164, 166, 315
Schaffter, Roger 61
Schaller, Christian 239
Schelten 155
Schiller, Theo 90
Schindler, Dietrich 102
Schmid, Adrian 50
School(s) 102, 115, 193, 214, 322
Schwyz 29, 38, 52, 119, 126, 135, 138, 164, 166
Scotland 245, 322
Second home 88
Second World War 58, 107
Secret elections 126
Seibt, Constantin 18
Separatism 58, 60
Signature 9, 13, 26, 43, 46, 80, 88, 129, 133, 157, 159, 161, 180, 186, 319
Signature quorum 145, 180, 314
Signature threshold 92
Simple Federal decree 313, 319
Simple majority 145, 177, 184, 248, 253, 259, 260, 263
Slovakia 109, 236, 259
Slovenia 236, 259
Smoking 84
Social Democratic Party (SP) 21, 22, 53, 100
Social movement(s) 39, 165
Social welfare 165, 166
Society 7, 12, 21, 22, 36, 49, 51, 71, 159, 180, 232

INDEX

Soldier(s) 27, 53
Solothurn 46, 119, 127, 135, 164, 166, 316
Soto, Juan Pablo de 261
South Africa 107
SP *See* Social Democratic Party (SP)
Spain 109, 236, 260
Sport 206
St. Ursanne 322
St. Gallen 46, 119, 127, 135, 164, 166, 187
Stutzer, Alois 70, 81, 179
Submission 309, 315, 316, 319
Subsidiarity 42
Supreme Court 182, 311, 313
SVP *See* Swiss People's Party (SVP)
Sweden 109, 236, 262
Swiss "States" (cantons) 309, 319
Swiss Army 155, 192, 204, 216 *See also* Army
Swiss citizenship 98, 101
Swiss Confederation 22, 309, 319
Swiss Confederation, the 139, 309, 312, 313, 319
Swiss Constitution 174, 264
Swiss federal constitution of 1848 138
Swiss federal constitution of 1874 140
Swiss federal constitution of 1999 141
Swiss franc 46
swissinfo/Swiss Radio International 186
Swiss National Council 315 *See also* National Council
Swiss People's Party (SVP) 21, 22, 53, 99, 163, 187
Swiss Verkehrsclub (VCS) 50
Swiss voters abroad 76
Switzerland 6, 74, 80, 88, 93, 98, 101, 108, 122, 125, 161, 173, 180, 191, 236, 251, 262, 278
Switzerland's membership of the United Nations (UN) 150, 226

T

Taaffe, Dolores 249
Tagwacht 60
Taiwan 105, 110
Taxpayer 81
Tax rise 82
Tell, William 39, 120

Terpe, Horia Paul 258
Territory 63, 139, 157, 245, 250
Thurgau 119, 127, 135, 164, 166
Ticino 119, 128, 135, 164, 166
Time allowances 92, 181
Time allowed for collection of signatures 92, 181
Title 308, 314, 319
Tobacco 197, 201, 206, 212
Total revision 142, 144, 173, 189, 239, 261, 263, 312, 315, 316
Transnational 94, 105, 110, 273, 322
Transport 165, 166
Trechsel, Alexander 148
Treichler, Johann Jakob 66
Turkey 109, 240, 264
Turku 67
Turnout 246, 249, 250, 256, 257, 258, 260
Turnout quorum 92, 184, 249, 252, 319
TV 18, 75
Tyranny 39, 120
Tyrol 294

U

Unitary initiative 319
United Nations (UN) 102, 106, 144, 150, 174
United Nations Development Programme (UNDP) 106
United States of America (USA) 75, 80, 89, 107, 181, 278
Unity of subject matter 142, 173, 175, 319
Upper Engadine 88
Uri 119, 126, 135, 164, 166
Uribe, Alvaro 268
Uruguay 271
Uster 39
Utopia 105

V

Verification (Declaration of) 319
Valach, Milan 241
Valach, Veronika 241
Valais 46, 119, 128, 135, 139, 164, 166
Validating the referendum ballot 184
Validity 182
Validity check 319
Vanoni, Bruno 264
VAT 82
Vatter, Adrian 101, 134, 166, 180
Vaud 46, 98, 119, 128, 136, 164, 166
VCS *See* Swiss Verkehrsclub (VCS)
Vellerat 156, 221
Venezuela 265, 271
Verhofstadt, Guy 239, 299
Verhulst, Jos 240
Villiers, Michel de 244
Violation of mandatory rules of international law 173, 175
Violation of the principle of unity of form 173
Violation of the principle of unity of subject matter 173
Volksbefragung 61
Volksblatt 66
Vote(s) 67, 74, 81, 88, 98, 106, 114, 119, 121, 123, 125, 129, 147, 161, 173, 319
Vote for a candidate 319
Voter(s) 70, 88, 98, 123, 132, 147, 177, 272, 311, 319
Voter turnout 6
Voting at the polling station 318, 320
Voting rights for foreigners 320
Voting slip 158, 160, 169, 172, 308
VOX-Analyses 125

W

"Willensnation Schweiz" 60
Wales 245
Wallis *See* Valais
Water Resources 169
Water resources 209
Waters, M. Dane 238
Weimar Republic 277
Wili, Hans-Urs 232, 264

Winterthur 21, 39
Wochenzeitung (WoZ) 18
Wohlwend, Sigward 252
World Bank 42, 217
World Conference on Direct Democracy 321
World War(s) 51, 250 *See also* Second World War
Wyoming 89

Y

Young people 7, 19, 102
Youth 154, 222

Z

Zauberformel *See* Magic formula
Zug 119, 126, 136, 164, 166
Zumbühl, Mark 27
Zurich 29, 35, 39, 114, 115, 119, 126, 129, 130, 136, 164, 166, 176, 314
Zurich, City of 19, 114
Zurich, University of 81, 102